BRUCE DICKINSON

MAIDEN VOYAGE

THE BIOGRAPHY JOE SHOOMAN

MUSIC
PRESS

Published by Music Press Books
an imprint of John Blake Publishing Ltd
3 Bramber Court, 2 Bramber Road,
London W14 9PB, England

www.johnblakebooks.co.uk

www.facebook.com/johnblakebooks ◼
twitter.com/jblakebooks ◼

First published in paperback in 2007
This edition published in 2016

ISBN: 978 1 78606 031 0

British Library Cataloguing-in-Publication Data:

A catalogue record for this book is available from the British Library.

Design by www.envydesign.co.uk

Printed in Great Britain by CPI Group (UK) Ltd

1 3 5 7 9 10 8 6 4 2

Papers used by John Blake Publishing are natural, recyclable products made from
wood grown in sustainable forests. The manufacturing processes conform to the
environmental regulations of the country of origin.

Every attempt has been made to contact the relevant copyright-holders, but some
were unobtainable. We would be grateful if the appropriate people could contact us.

CONTENTS

FOREWORD

BY IAN GILLAN

Bruce Dickinson. What a guy.

The first time I met Bruce Dickinson was on the cusp of the eighties when he turned up at my studio, Kingsway Recorders, during the nascent period of what was to become known as the New Wave of British Heavy Metal. Here was a singer with a smile and an easy-going manner, but when he opened up those pipes it was clear there was something special going on. He sucked all the air out of the room with his talent and I thought, hey, this kid has something to say.

It was no surprise to me that after Bruce joined Iron Maiden they knocked down audiences all over the world, putting out album after album that explored metal and rock and inspired bands in their turn. Music is a rallying point for like-minded people and to be responsible for the continuation of that creative energy is a privilege and a thrill. Since he came back into Iron Maiden in the late nineties, they've managed to draw on those NWOBHM roots and branch out in loads of interesting directions. It's not a surprise to me that they are still delighting their millions of devoted fans all over the planet. Bruce's familiar stance as he plants his foot on a wedge and gets the crowds screaming is now iconic and four decades in the business speaks for itself. You don't spend that long at the top of your game if you stand still: you need to always move things forward whilst always being true to the fans and yourselves.

Being up front with a band means you are often the focal point and you get caught out pretty damned quick if you're not giving everything to that moment onstage, or in the studio. There ain't no place to hide. Despite what those ropey TV talent shows might say, there are no shortcuts to the top. Fame is a secondary effect of following your talent and your dreams and getting out there on the road to tour and develop as a band, as musicians and as people. Bruce is a living example of where a musical gift allied to an extraordinary work ethic can get you.

These days he flies planes and fronts Iron Maiden in the same way he came through my door. He is unnervingly confident, professional and delivers all with an effortless panache. That's not a noun I care to associate with aviators; thank the heavens he possesses a mellifluous announcing voice – imagine finding out he's your captain for the day with one of those familiar screams. Pretty ironic that one of his nicknames is 'The Air Raid Siren', isn't it? You just know when some people are going places, but they are rarely intelligent. Mostly it's bluster and rhino shit, but Bruce is above all that. He has no time for bullshitting when there's a job to get done.

He's bounced back from that shocking illness with all the vigour and determination of a man who has always taken life by the scruff of the neck and wrung every drop of fun, creativity and adventure out of it.

I am very proud to know him and have watched his career with great interest.

Rock on.

ig

AUTHOR'S PREFACE

A decade is a long time in rock 'n' roll – and when you talk about a phenomenon like Bruce Dickinson, it becomes an aeon. Since I wrote a book with the rather long-winded title *Bruce Dickinson: Flashing Metal with Iron Maiden and Flying Solo* back in early 2007, there have been more ground-breaking, ambitious, symphonic studio albums; phenomenal worldwide tours; a movie (and book); live DVDs; radio and TV shows; the setting-up of airlines... In short, the usual whirlwind of activity we've come to expect from a man who is a true polymath as well as simply one of the greatest singers metal and rock has ever produced. There has also been a shocking illness that, thankfully, the subject of this book faced down and conquered like a true warrior of the road.

Maiden Voyage catches up with the years since 2007 and enhances that original biography with new information and significant new interviews. As with *Flashing Metal*, the book you now hold in your hand is a journalist and fan's look at the career and music of a man and a band that have inspired me over the years. I am very grateful indeed to all those who have contacted my publishers over the years with insights and thoughts on both.

Huge thanks are due to all who have contributed to the original editions as well as the new interviewees. Special thanks to the brilliant Maria Ericksen for her great ancestry research. Thanks also to those brilliant people that have helped with organising said interviews, opened doors, provided transcripts, made sources available or otherwise aided with their own awesome research, ideas, inspiration, tip-offs, photos and information:

Blaze Bayley; Jon Beeston; Chris Dale; Neil Daniels; Paul Di'Anno; Alex Elena; Maria Ericksen; Jack Endino; Rob Grain and the estate of Paul Samson; Robin Guy; Jennie Halsall; Mike Hanson; Rob Hodgson; Henrik Johansson; Steve Jones; Dean Karr; Neal Kay; Spencer Leigh; Dave Ling; Erwin Lucas; Bill Liesegang; John McCoy; Joel McIver; Tony Miles; Tony Newton; Keith Olsen; Tom Parker; Tony Platt; Dave Pybus; Raziq Rauf; Matthias Reinholdsson; Doug Sampson; Michelle Ferreira Sanches; Brigitte Schön; Stuart Smith; Starchild Anita; Thunderstick; Karen Toftera; Bernie Tormé; Chris Tsangarides; John Tucker; Joakim Stabel.

We have made every effort to credit all sources where available and welcome corrections for future editions.

Thanks to Martin Roach and Dave Hanley for all at IMP over the years plus James Hodgkinson and all at John Blake for letting me loose on this one again. As always, enormous thanks to Suzy for her patience beyond the call of duty. Many thanks, too, to the translators of all the overseas editions over the years, including Ricardo Lira, Helen Ljungmark, Matthias Mader and all the Maiden and Bruce fans who have got in touch over the years with corrections and suggestions. This book is for you.

Special thanks to the incredible Ian Gillan of the mighty Deep Purple for the foreword, and to Phil Banfield for helping it happen.

Up The Irons!

CHAPTER ONE

HISTORY

There are times to get married that are auspicious, and there are times that are unlucky. For Austin Hartley and Lily May Booker, Monday, 7 August 1939 was their big day. The pair got hitched at St John's Church in the Nottinghamshire town of Worksop, situated at the northern edge of the world-famous Sherwood Forest.

According to a contemporary report by the *Worksop Guardian*, Austin was the youngest son of Mr and Mrs J Hartley of 70, Manton Crescent and Lily May was the eldest daughter of Mr and Mrs J Booker of 4, Gateford Road. The vicar, Rev. C R G Haye, was on hand to perform the rites. The paper drew a lovely word picture of the occasion. 'Given away by her father,' wrote the reporter, 'The bride was daintily gowned in white figured crème and carried a bouquet of pink carnations.' One Thomas Priest was listed as best man, and the party – complete with page boys dressed in blue and the bride's attendants wearing 'pink net with plate head-dresses' – went on for a party at the bride's parents' house. For those sartorially inclined readers, the paper also revealed that Mrs Booker wore a pale green dress 'with a black edge-to-edge coat', while Mrs Hartley matched the coat but paired it with a cool little stripy number. History also records that Austin presented a cheque to his new wife, while she in return gave him 'a trouser presser'. Other presents included linen and a bedroom set from the bride's parents and from the groom, some blankets and another cheque. And so it was done.

By a quirk of bad timing, less than a month later the newly wedded bliss was shattered by the declaration of war by Great Britain and France on Hitler's Germany. Hitler's refusal to withdraw from an invasion of Poland set in motion a brutal and sustained battle that swept the world and decimated Europe. By the end of World War II, in 1945, at least 60 million people had died, international infrastructure was damaged and the consequent rebuilding of the world foisted penury upon all participants. Rationing of goods in the UK was to last fourteen years, with the final restrictions on sale of scarce goods not coming until 4 July 1954. Despite the privations caused by the war, Lily May and Austin produced two kids themselves – most important to our story being Sonja Hartley, born in October 1941.

Meanwhile, Maurice Dickinson of Sheffield, Yorkshire (born 11 November 1904) was busy getting romantic with his own squeeze, Ethel May Chandler of North Witchford. The Dickinsons have been traced back to one Joseph Dickinson, whose christening in Hoyland, Yorkshire, is registered as 5 January 1794. Maurice and Ethel May made good use of their time, producing six surviving progeny. Bruce Dickinson was born on 22 November 1936, also in North Witchford. The post-rationing period was to bring him and Sonja together. They married in January 1958 and just a few months later the then sixteen-year-old Sonja gave birth to a son: Paul Bruce Dickinson. Sonja was a talented dancer who had won a scholarship to the Royal College of Ballet prior to falling pregnant with Paul Bruce, which effectively ended her career. Bruce Dickinson Sr was a mechanic in the army, while his wife worked part-time in a shoe shop.

It wasn't easy street, by any means. It was only through immense hard work that a reasonable level of stability was possible for young couples starting out in life. Therefore, when Paul Bruce Dickinson gave his first public performance ('Scream For Me, Midwife!') on 7 August 1958, it was a tricky situation to reconcile for his young parents. Finances pretty much dictated that the young boy was left with Maurice and Ethel May, a coal-face worker and a housewife/hairdresser respectively. Thus, the first six years of Bruce's life were spent in the loving and happy care of his grandparents, before his parents moved to the larger city of Sheffield to find better-paid work.

The young Bruce was lucky enough to be growing up during one of the most exciting times for British pop music. Rock 'n' roll exploded in 1956, but two years later the rebel Elvis Presley went into the army, only to come out again in 1960 as the archetypal all-American boy and subsequently embark on a series of terrible movies. Despite his own career descending into mediocrity during the early 1960s, Presley and his compatriots had already lit unquenchable fires of self-belief and rebellion among a generation that were truly finding their own way through life.

The rock 'n' rollers had introduced black rhythm 'n' blues artists to the world – and none more so than to ported cities such as Liverpool, where the influx of American soldiers and workers brought with it vinyl gems recorded by artists with exotic monikers such as Muddy Waters, Howlin' Wolf and Chuck Berry. For any teenager remotely interested in music, a new record was a new event, something to be shared and played over and over again in wide-eyed wonder. Skiffle groups began to spring up all over the place, bound together by the twelve-bar blues and the harmonica, playing covers of these exciting new sounds, and wearing slick bikers' jackets inspired by Marlon Brando's 1953 film *The Wild One*.

One of these skiffle groups was even named after the gang in that film (albeit with one differing vowel) – Scouse mop tops The Beatles. Dickinson was later to remark that his first musical memories were dancing to 'The Twist' – Chubby Checker's version – and badgering his grandfather (then still only in his forties) to buy him The Beatles' 1963 smash 'She Loves You'. In an interview with Beatles expert, author and broadcaster Spencer Leigh, Dickinson would later reveal that his, 'Favourite Beatles track by a million miles is "Let It Be". I find it so amazingly uplifting; it's like a hymn, and I like some hymns.' It would be impossible for anyone excited by music to have ignored the growing impact of the early Beatles, whose nascent career wrapped up the lip-curling, raw, sexual aggression of the rockers – honed to perfection in Beatleland by their gruelling stints as house band in dodgy clubs in Hamburg's Reeperbahn – with a stunning natural pop sensibility and a growing edge of innovation encouraged and developed by legendary producer George Martin. The fact that the technology on which to play their records was becoming more affordable, allied to the emergence of pirate radio stations including Radio Luxembourg, meant that the musical life of kids growing up in the 1960s was to be richer than ever before.

For Bruce – newly landed in Sheffield to move back in with his parents, and his sister Helena (born in Worksop on 31 December 1963), this musical education was bolstered by regularly watching TV show *Jukebox Jury* and bashing away on an elderly, nigh-unplayable acoustic guitar he'd discovered. As it turned out, it had belonged to Pops Dickinson, who in a previous incarnation – according to Bruce – had appeared with his wife as a duo in a 'performing dog act'. Still, the music bug had struck. It proved a very useful diversion on which to draw during the relative instability of changing schools from the notoriously rough Manor Top Primary – where the new kid was, as often happens, the subject of ridicule and occasional physical digs here and there – to the posher private school, Sharrow Vale. Bruce's grandfather had, however, taught him to stand up for himself, to be proud of who he was and not to take stick from anybody – lessons that were to prove useful (and occasionally problematic) not only through his school life, but also in the crazy years to follow.

At an early age, Paul Bruce (whom we shall henceforth refer to as Bruce) started to become interested in all things mechanical. Bruce Sr had a car showroom. One day, dad rocked up helmetless on the classic Norton 750 Commando motorbike that he'd traded in for a car, as Bruce later explained to *Motorcycle News*. By this point, Bruce Sr was accumulating quite the collection of vehicles. 'It sat in the showroom, next to a brand new Meriden Bonnie, a Honda CB400-4, a Sunbeam S8 and an Ariel Square Four,' recalled the future singer. 'It was a nice collection of rare and cool-looking bikes, and they just sat there – people would walk in and ask if they were for sale, but Dad would say "Naah, sorry," and then manage to sell them a car!'

During 1971, by which time Bruce had turned thirteen, his folks had, with much industry and knuckle-whitening work, begun to put themselves on a stable financial keel. The Dickinsons bought a series of wrecked houses cheaply, refurbished them and then sold them on at a profit (they were so successful that they'd probably warrant their own *Property Ladder*-style TV reality show today). As there was enough cash to be able to offer their lad what used to be called a 'classical education', they packed number-one son off to Oundle, the exclusive Northamptonshire private boarding school.

Oundle had by then become as firmly an establishment experience as Eton, having been founded in 1556 by then Lord Mayor of London, Sir William Laxton. H G Wells even wrote a biography of one of the school's headmasters, Fredrick William Sanderson, which was published in 1924. Sanderson was something of a free-thinker in his time, his openness to individual development and firm belief in intellectual freedom being both unique and somewhat anti-establishment during his tenure – which spanned the cusp of the nineteenth and twentieth centuries.

Built on tradition, discipline and traditional methods of learning, the English private-school system was based on the learning of Latin, Greek and classical history – along with a large and regular slice of often harsh physical exercise. And though Oundle School had a left-field approach and a history of comparative innovation – and while the teenage Bruce welcomed the chance to be independent from his parents – he was later to admit that, within the forbidding walls of the beautiful school complex near Peterborough, bullying was rife. Once more, he didn't quite fit in – his rather itinerant school life and consequent self-reliant nature up until then saw to that. What's more, his sharp tongue and refusal to knuckle under to the established and entirely irrational pecking order of schoolboys often meant that he was involved in several incidents when older boys from Bruce's school house, Sidney House, would use their greater physical strength against him. However, even during the worst beatings, Bruce's self-sufficient spirit remained unsullied. As he told *Metal Hammer Special Editions,* his attackers could 'beat the shit out of me, but [they were] not superior'.

Later, Bruce was to comment that he believed parents sent their children to Oundle so they could take advantage of opportunities denied to themselves. Although he enjoyed the amateur dramatics, debating and fizz of activity of the school, he felt the place itself was harsh and reactionary. There are many ways in life to plot revenge strategies, and it is not always the reflex kick-back against one's antagonists that is the most advisable, or even the most practical, option. So, even when he was picking raw egg from his bedsheets, or drying out clothes that had been sodden with water while he was elsewhere, the cogs and gears of the young buck's sharp brain would work overtime in designing suitably wicked comebacks, fuelled somewhat by his growing interest in the military. Dickinson was active in the establishment of Oundle's first war-games society, and also rose to a high rank in his school's cadet force. He would get his own back on the tormentors in many ways, such as setting off smoke bombs on a night-time camping trip rampage through the schoolmasters' tents, or arranging for a significant amount of horse manure to be delivered to his housemaster. Most of the time, he got away with his pranks.

Musically, by now Dickinson had discovered acts such as Deep Purple, whose track 'Child in Time' he had first heard blasting out from the study of a fellow pupil. Purple became his main fixation, particularly their stunning 1970 LP *In Rock*, which was the first album he ever bought. As activities outside the confines of Oundle were restricted, and therefore access to the local record shops was intermittent at best, music became a powerful and magical force within the student community. Live bands made occasional appearances at Oundle, with Van der Graaf Generator, Wild Turkey and The Crazy World of Arthur Brown all causing a stir among the school's population. Arthur Brown, along with Purple's Ian Gillan, would become a massive influence on the young Bruce. The more music he heard, the more he felt an affinity with these heroes who stood outside the establishment, touring the world, living on their instruments and their wits.

By 1973, Bruce had taken his first tentative steps onto the stage himself, joining Oundle's amateur dramatic society and immediately feeling at home deciphering and delivering the works of Shakespeare. The sense of theatricality, allied to his growing, burning love for music, would inevitably mean that Bruce would be drawn to performing as a musician. Originally, it was the drums to which he was attracted – mostly because of his Purple fixation. He would later muse that his ambition was to be Ian Paice's left foot. But as he couldn't afford a drum kit, the young pretender had to be content with watching the rehearsals of school bands with richer (they owned a kit) but less talented (they couldn't play – and punk was still a good three years away) members. Liberating a set of bongos from

Oundle's music department, Bruce began to sit in on the sessions of one particular set-up that also featured guitarist Nick Bertram and vocalist Mike Jordan. During a particularly horrendous run-through of The Beatles' 'Let It Be', Bruce heard Jordan struggle on the high notes and joined in to bolster his bass-register bandmate's vocals. It was a moment of revelation: the soaring sound of Dickinson's vocal cords rapidly saw him abandon the bongos in favour of fronting his first 'band' – in the loosest sense.

'So, in the back of my head I thought, "Maybe I can do this?"' Bruce subsequently told *Hard Radio*, 'I've done a lot of amateur dramatics as a kid, both in and out of the classroom, and I loved being onstage, although I can never be an actor because it took everything far too seriously. The problem with acting is they always have to make such a big thing out of it… I could never hang out with these people! So the ideal thing of being a rock 'n' roll singer is combining the two elements.'

In subsequent rehearsals, the nascent musicians soon found themselves rolling along nicely, covering B B King songs and other blues classics, as well as the mighty 'Smoke On The Water'. Then, one of Bruce's most famous pranks was discovered – with rather serious consequences. 'I wee-d in the headmaster's dinner,' he shrugged in an interview with Spencer Leigh. 'We did it without him knowing; two of us. They were having a dinner party to celebrate that they had built the extension to this house that we used to live in, and they'd run out of cooking [oil]. The school prefects were all scoffing away in there, so it was our statement.'

Remembering his biology lessons, he would have known that a small amount of boiled urine was harmless to ingest (the pair had 'topped up' the cooking oil they had lent to the prefects responsible for cooking the meal), but this time the joke was a step too far. Enjoying a drink in the sixth-form bar, the two reprobates couldn't help but let their compadres in on the reason for their paroxysms of mirth as they watched everyone tucking into their added-value meal. Within the confines of a boarding school it was inevitable that the tale would spread like wildfire. And before long, the culprits were identified. 'We got grassed up,' continued the singer in the same interview, 'and I got thrown out. The kid that did it with me didn't, because he was a candidate for Oxford or Cambridge. They thought they'd suspend him for three months and then bring him back so that he could add to the school's statistics. It's the way they work.'

The resentment at being singled out was obvious, the rustication of his academically gifted co-conspirator inevitable. But in many ways, being expelled from Oundle was the best thing that could have happened to the unconventional pupil.

Bruce was to reminisce to *Motorcycle News* about the first time he'd heard Ritchie Blackmore's Rainbow, who then had the inimitable Ronnie James Dio up front. Bruce was in a garage, watching a mate mess about with a Triton motorbike: 'I remember asking who that amazing voice on the radio was – I was about sixteen, full of spots. He finished what he was doing and asked if I wanted to hop on the back. So I did, and we ended up doing a ton down the dual carriageway on it. I thought, "Oh, shit, that was fun!" – but then I went to university and never had time for bikes.' On the subject of motorcycles, Bruce began on a Velocette LE200 that his dad had hoiked from a skip, before moving on to a Mobylette scooter – which he didn't take to, likening the brake block-featuring vehicle to a pushbike, although he did manage to get 60 mph out of it going downhill and further souped it up by taking the exhaust off to make more noise. His final bike was a Honda SS50, which he described as 'just terrible'.

Fast forward to 1976, and Bruce began to complete his 'A' levels at a Catholic school back in the relative normality of Sheffield. This was a mixed-gender comprehensive school rather than the traditional single-sex public school that had been a major part of his formative years. During his first week at the new school, Bruce ran into four guys with whom he would hook up on a musical level. Suddenly, getting caught short seemed to have opened up a whole new world of possibilities.

CHAPTER 2

SHOTS
AND SPEED

The year 1976 was a key one for British music. Not only did Brotherhood of Man win the Eurovision Song Contest with their gory deathcore classic 'Save Your Kisses For Me', but around the UK musicians were galvanising themselves into groups following whispers emanating from London about a four-piece band who were all about passion, anti-grown-up sneer and celebration of youth: the Sex Pistols. While punk was close to exploding into the nation's consciousness and shattering the music industry's smug ivory towers, rock bands had been playing in pubs wherever a stage could be raised. Pub rock was in many ways a forerunner to both punk and the galvanisation of the UK's heavy metal acts, in terms of its energy and relatively liberal attitude to any musician who had the nous to form a band.

For Bruce Dickinson, 1976 was the year of a pivotal meeting. Sitting in class in his new school, he eavesdropped on a conversation between two of his fellow pupils, Phil Beaumont and Robert Hodgson. The pair (later joined by bassist Paul Widdicombe) were somewhat vexed that the vocalist in their nascent group had quit, and were wondering aloud whether to go ahead with a rehearsal that they'd had planned for the same evening. Ears pricking up, and with the 'triumph' of his pre-pissy-beans blues-rock knockabouts at Oundle still fresh in his mind, Bruce decided to pipe up that he had the ability to fill the vacancy. The pair invited him to rehearsals – where Bruce was surprised to discover that the drummer, Paul Bray, had gone to his old school. They played a set mostly comprising covers – including Wishbone Ash's entire *Argus* album – but the band were hardly professionals. Usually the rehearsals would take place in guitarist Hodgson's bedroom on his acoustic guitar, with Widdicome's bass barely ever plugged in. Still, it was a step up from what had come before, and Dickinson even went to the lengths of heading into Sheffield City Centre to purchase his very own microphone and amplifier – necessary, because his group was actually going to play live.

'They didn't even have a proper microphone,' recalled Bruce to *Hard Radio*. 'They had this cassette player mic that was taped to a jack plug – it was useless – nothing came out of it at all except this awful feedback! But they said to me, "Wow, you're the best singer we ever had – you're in the band." And I said, "Great! When do we start gigging?" And they said, "Gigging? We don't do gigs, we just rehearse in the garage once a week." And I said, "You mean you don't write your own material?" And they said, "God, no!" So, I ended up being the driving force of the band, and we actually did do some gigs.' 'The band actually wrote quite a few songs together,' remembered Hodgson for this book. 'Bruce mostly stuck to lyrics [but subsequently] I guess he might claim to be marginally the more successful in the songwriting area!'

The city itself was something of a mixed bag of individuals at the time. 'Saturday night out was Northern Soul night,' Hodgson recalled. 'There were clubs where you went and bought a pint and they gave you a knife with it.' Getting the band up to performance speed in Hodgson's dad's garage, the group put in many hours trying to knock off some of the rough edges. All very fine so far, aside from the name: Paradox. Bruce hated it, and drew – possibly for the first time in his musical career, but certainly not the last – on an element of his classical education to suggest a replacement moniker: Styx. In Greek mythology, Styx is the river that forms the boundary between Earth and Hades; to drink from the river Styx was also to attain immortality.

Styx finally played a gig at Sheffield's Broad Fall Tavern in the summer of 1976, but created such a racket that they actually woke up a sleeping steelworker, who had been on the night shift. The chap invaded the Broad Fall Tavern's stage, such as it was, and in his ire proceeded to bottle Hodgson and smash up Paul Bray's kit. Some reports have it that Bruce responded, wielding a chair. The incident even made the local paper, giving Styx a profile that belied the ramshackle nature of the group, who, in the best traditions of the punk-rock attitude, promptly split up. The experience of performing live, however, had left a big imprint on the seventeen-year-old singer – who now, of course, owned the essential bits of equipment too.

Bruce successfully completed his 'A' levels in June 1976, but was undecided as to what to do next. Finally leaving school is a daunting prospect: even the patchy educational career that Dickinson had had always offered another term to look forward to, new explosives to invent in physics and chemistry classes, new pranks to pull. Now all that had gone, and in common with many eighteen-year-olds, the would-be sticksman and newbie ex-Styxman was at something of a loose end. His interest in the military, combined with suggestions from his father, meant that there was really only one place for him: the army. Or, to be more specific, the Territorial Army (TA). The TA is essentially a part-time reserve force for the UK's regular army, often referred to rather disparagingly as the 'Weekend Warriors' – a reference to the fact that during the week the TA members might be working in banks, as postmen, bakers or candlestick makers, but come Saturday they don their uniforms to go out on manoeuvres and train in various army skills. If Dickinson was hoping for a safe haven away from the less savoury individuals of the city centre, he was sadly mistaken. Although he enjoyed the camaraderie of the set-up, the reality was far removed from what he had expected on joining. There was a serious culture of booze 'n' pulling in the TA, the likes of which the would-be singer had never previously encountered. Not that the youngster was averse to the odd bout of drinking himself, but he very quickly discovered that some of his compatriots took the carousing to another level entirely. On another note, in 2005, Bruce told *Metro* that he 'saw quite a few loose women while I was there, but they were never loose enough to do anything with me'.

He was making a reasonable success of the army, which had high expectations of him, he told *Enfer*: 'Considering my education, I was supposed to take the exam to become an officer. But I strongly disliked officers and army men in general.' Convinced that army life was not for him, he promptly decided to apply for university, and was accepted to read history at a London college, Queen Mary's – a decision that somewhat bemused his parents, not least because their son had never previously visited the capital in his life.

Queen Mary College provided many opportunities to develop and grow, and a relatively safe springboard between adolescence and adulthood. If you were an aspiring rock singer, you could take advantage of the fact that you were in England's capital city and further your musical education alongside your book smarts. So Bruce set about getting involved with the Entertainments Department, who were responsible for booking groups to play at the college. And there was nowhere better to be than London during that vibrant period at the dawn of the punk era. The Sex Pistols played some secret shows at the facility, and Dickinson soon found himself helping to set up the stage for the likes of Ian Dury and The Blockheads, mod-punks The Jam and even space-rockers Hawkwind. It was here also that Dickinson met one Paul 'Noddy' White, a multi-instrumentalist who went one step further than just owning an amp and a microphone: he was also in proud possession of a full PA system.

Needless to say, Bruce immediately enthused with his new compadre about the possibilities of forming a band. Rehearsing on a regular basis, the pair decided to name their project Speed – a reference, apparently, not to the amphetamine-based drug that was prevalent during the punk era, but rather to the accelerated pace of the tracks they were playing. Eventually, Speed became a five-piece outfit, with Bruce on vocals and rhythm guitar, pounding out the chords that White had taught him, one Martin Freshwater on lead guitar, Paul White playing either keyboards or guitar, Adam Hayand as bassist and the half-Welsh Steve Jones on drums. The latter was, in many ways, one of the most experienced among them. 'Prior to joining Speed,' Jones told me, '[which was] through an advert seen by a friend at Queen Mary College, I was in a band called Lucifer – which changed its name to Angel Witch after my departure.' More of those chaps a little later.

At the time, Jones was gainfully employed by the Post Office as an engineering apprentice, and he first met Bruce 'along with Noddy, Martin and Adam at an audition at their halls of residence. Firstly,' continues the erstwhile drummer, who went on to become elected member of the National Executive of the Communication Workers Union, 'none of the lads really fitted the image of a rock band. In some ways, at the time, Bruce less so than the others. In fact, his full beard made him appear more [like the] Goodie, Bill Oddie, than a rocker. It has to be said that [I joined the band] despite my disappointment with the apparent lack of image, a little short-sighted I know. It was Bruce's truly outstanding vocal range and control that grabbed me. It was also the original songs with a rock and [punk edge] that made me join.'

Speed's sound was a blend of breakneck hard rock/hefty Judas Priest-style metal and swirling, with added neo-classical keyboard action, much in the vein of The Stranglers, another bunch of pub rockers caught up within the growing punk scene by accident or design. 'Paul wrote most of the music,' recalls Jones. 'While I believe Bruce was the lyricist. There was usually a twist or message to the lyrics which I always liked, a far cry from Iron Maiden. Songs about "Snoopy" – a hermaphrodite who never sinned; or a degenerate "Tax Payer". Another was called "FBI", which also referred to the CIA and the KGB. There was also a song called "Dental Decay", which was every bit [reminiscent of the band] Status Quo. We always threatened to dump this [song] but the audience seemed to love it. I recall a gig at Queen Mary where the audience shouted their appreciation, to which Bruce's response was to say, "Strange!" – we never liked it that much, [it was] more something to fill the set with. We also had a song called "In the Moonlight" which started off with Noddy on the Hammond organ with – you've guessed it – [Beethoven's] "Moonlight Sonata". Probably the only song not played at breakneck speed.'

Hence the band's moniker, perhaps. But although the world elsewhere was being turned upside down by snotty lads and lasses with ripped clothes and attitude, not everybody was on the punk vibe at the time, as Jones points out. 'As far as other bands [around in that period were concerned, it was] all a bit odd really as the music scene at the time was a bit strange, particularly for people like me who were brought up on Zeppelin and Purple but were perhaps more comfortable playing Lizzy and the Stones. Punk threw a real spanner in the works for me.'

In retrospect, Jones considers that he saw something in the vocalist that would mark him out as a future go-getter. 'I believe Bruce was the President of the Students Union when Speed was on the go. I always sensed he was quite headstrong and focused even in the early days. Frankly, I think Bruce could have succeeded at anything he set his mind to.'

Being involved with the Entertainments Department had other perks. Speed played live on a regular basis and many concerts took place at the Green Man pub in nearby Plumstead. In order to get the band's equipment there, Bruce and the boys would borrow the college minibus, making room for the gear by unbolting most of the seats. The vocalist was really beginning to cut his teeth in the live arena, and during the latter months of 1977 through to June 1978, Speed began to pick up a mini-following among gig-goers in the East End of London. 'The main venues we played were Queen Mary College in Mile End,' notes Jones, 'as well as the halls of residence, the Green Man and a boozer in Basildon. I don't think we played with anyone of any "fame". [The audience reaction was] pretty good but I don't think we were really together long enough to have tested it properly. Bruce was always a fairly confident frontman. Took him a while to sort his image, but he got there in the end – I think!'

As for the now--bearded Bruce, he was throwing himself into the student lifestyle. So much so that he'd put on almost two stone by the end of his first year in college. Not that it was just ale that was on offer at the time. 'I tried out all sorts,' he told *Enfer*. '[Many things] coming my way [were] interesting to me, and I'd get into it!' However, Bruce realized he needed to calm himself down a little, and subsequently went on the wagon for several months, not even touching a drop of beer.

'I recall playing Bruce a tape of Lucifer,' says Jones. 'And he "jokingly" said they were in need of a good vocalist. There was a much heavier edge to Lucifer, which clearly appealed to Bruce. I was conscious that if Bruce went anywhere near [Lucifer's future incarnation] Angel Witch he could have been lost to Speed. Should that have happened, who knows how things would have turned out. In the early days it was touch and go as to which of these bands was going to hit the big time. I seriously think that Bruce was the defining factor. It was evident that whilst Speed worked, it wasn't what Bruce wanted; perhaps in the same way the Angel Witch sound wasn't for me.' As is often the case in college-based bands, a combination of workload, searching for a satisfying personal sound and other assorted use-your-imagination-type interests was bound to throw up a stumbling block, and Speed duly disbanded in the summer of 1978.

Later, some recordings that Noddy White and Bruce had put together for an unrelated college project subsequently surfaced on the single 'Man on the Street'/'On the Road', a seven–inch single that was released independently in 1980. 'Man on the Street' is a punk-influenced piece of fairly basic garage-band British rock, sounding a little like the Pink Fairies, with an enduring keyboard solo courtesy of one Gary Edwards, guitars courtesy of another mate, Steve Adams, and Jeff Moody providing the backbeat along with Noddy White himself on bass. 'On the Road', meanwhile, is a basic knockabout twelve-bar blues offering with a grotty-sounding Motörhead-esque guitar solo as the track winds up in pace and density, playing fast and loose with tempo throughout, before fading out in some bemusement. A curio, of course, by virtue of its singer, who offers some rather accomplished rock screams and whoops – which is probably why the single is so very sought-after among collectors and regularly fetches upwards of £300 in online auctions. It's mostly worth it, one feels, for the moustachioed photo of an otherwise exceedingly fresh-faced Bruce that adorns its black-and-white cover. It's important to note that although it was released under the Speed moniker, the actual line-up on vinyl is significantly different to the gigging unit – Speed had, to all intents and purposes, broken up prior to the recording sessions. It should be taken for what it was: a chunk of White's compositions recorded for the fun of it.

Bruce, however, had had a taste of fronting a band, and he wasn't done with rock 'n' roll quite yet. Twiddling his thumbs one day leafing through *Melody Maker* magazine, his gaze fell on a rather intriguing advertisement calling for a vocalist to put the finishing touches to a recording session. Intrigued, Dickinson proceeded to compile an audition tape – one that said much about his sense of humour. Rather than sending in a cassette of the usual sing-over-classic-track type, he set the tape recorder running in the corner of his room and made as many rock-style whoops and noises as he possibly could for half an hour. On the other side of the tape was a classic comedy set from John Cleese. Bruce wrote a note to the effect that if his would-be bandmates weren't enamoured by his vocals, perhaps they would care for the jokes on the B-side. Of course, even in such a rough-and-ready format, Dickinson's developing voice was still arresting enough to warrant a call-back from the chaps who had placed the advertisement, Phil and Doug Siviter. During the subsequent recording session – which spawned a track called 'Dracula' – the brothers Siviter were astonished at the singer's prowess.

Despite his relative lack of real experience, Bruce took on, and mastered, complex multi-tracked harmony lines with aplomb. Even at nearly four decades' distance, the track retains an atmospheric edge, its swirling backing and jerky guitar lines sweeping into a rock-ska verse and rather silly lyrics about waiting for the midnight hour on top. Still, it's clear that musically and vocally Dickinson had progressed considerably even in the course of the few months between Speed and this new band, called Shots. The line-up for the live gigs was Bruce on vocals, backed by guitarist Tony Lee, Arthur Young on bass and drummer Phil Adolphia.

Bruce's involvement with the Entertainments Department

came in handy once more: he was able to book his new band for support slots with a series of groups visiting Queen Mary's – including, notably, Manfred Mann's Earth Band. The Shots were firmly a gigging band, and played in many of the venues that were beginning to buzz with excitement at the new rock revolution as 1978 went by. One of the key venues in the rising tide of hard rock was The Prince of Wales in Gravesend, as Rob Grain – later to become road manager for the band Samson – recalls. 'The Prince of Wales pub was a mile from my house,' he told me. 'At the time, it was a few beers and a band but you didn't pay that much attention because there was a group on every night. I was working there as a stagehand, taking the money on the door. I wasn't employed at the time, so if the guv'nor had a band on of an evening, I used to go down and help him put the P.A. up and all that, which is where I learnt my job! It sorta crept up, it wasn't the case that all of a sudden there was this "thing" going on. Because you were there all the time, it crept up on you without you knowing and you suddenly noticed bands coming in from out of the area.' The venue wasn't exactly situated in the most salubrious of areas, however. 'It was on the edge of quite a big rough council estate,' recalls Grain. 'The guys from the estate, I used to go to school with – they were fine with me and used to buy me beers. Quite a lot of people used to say, "I'm not going to The Prince of Wales, it's full of pikeys" – but as soon as the bands would start, they'd go round to the other bar anyway. But there was never any trouble. What you used to find was, then and now, all through life, wherever you find a pub with live music you don't find trouble, fights, stabbings and people getting glasses shoved in their faces – because people are there for the music. The sort of people who are going to cause trouble and to start fights don't go to those pubs 'cause they can't stand the music.'

The bands, however, loved it. During 1977 and 1978, some of the major groups on the scene descended on the venue, which was getting quite a name for itself among the blossoming rock and metal movement. 'Paul Samson started playing there,' continues Grain. 'Right at the start when it was Paul, Chris Aylmer and Clive Burr. Another band on the scene was Hotline, [whose members included] bass player Jerry Scherwin who later joined Sledgehammer, Pete Jupp, who later joined Samson, and the guitarist was Bucket, who's now in Bad Company. It was a breeding ground, really. There was a band from Hastings called Die Laughing. The Nicky Moore Band played – and every night of the week there was a band playing in these pubs.'

Typically, there was some jostling for position among the owners of the venues in the vicinity, as they attempted to corner the rather lucrative market in rock fans. 'The Red Lion in Northfleet and The Prince of Wales were about three or four miles from each other so you used to get a bit of rivalry going. I used to use both pubs and knew the guv'nors, and so they would ask me, "See you tomorrow?" "Nah I'm going to The Red Lion to see so-and-so." "Well, you tell them from me that if they go and play there, don't bother trying to come back in here again!"'

The crowds, however, were often slightly demanding. Although they appreciated groups that made the effort, they still wanted to be entertained. Not that the bands exactly had a great set-up with which to work. 'The Prince of Wales had no stage, it was just a flat pub,' says Grain with a laugh. 'There was a corner where the bands would play, and in the corner was the entrance to the toilets. So anyone wanting to go to the toilet while the band were playing had to walk through the band, or down the side of the band.'

The Shots, however, had a chap up at the front for whom this basic facility was an opportunity to be grasped rather than a limitation to be endured. 'Bruce used to catch people. Between songs if someone went to or from the toilet he'd hassle them, start talking to them and stick a mic in their face,' laughs Grain. 'Just general larking about. I can always remember one instance with this big local biker, nobody messed with him. I knew one of his family in school and they were one of these families that nobody messes with, you know. He came out of the toilet as The Shots finished a song, so Bruce said something to him, and stuck the mic in his face. And the bloke just looked at him and went, "Bollocks!" And so Bruce said something else to him and he went, "Up Your Kilt!" And then Bruce said something else to him and he just went, "Don't push it" and walked off! And Bruce just went, "There you go, if you've got bollocks up your kilt, don't push it." And that's the sort of thing he did.'

Bruce's sense of humour and theatre was clearly developing. Musically, however, The Shots had a lot to offer too. 'As a band they were great,' continues Grain. 'The guitar player was really good. The songs were hard rock, as were most of the bands at that sort of time on the circuit. Song-wise there was "Snoopy", one called "Middle Class Song", and the covers were "Bad Motorscooter" by Montrose, "Under My Wheels" by Alice Cooper and – I may be wrong – but also "Halo of Flies" [by Alice Cooper]. All the bands would do their own material – but they would never get out of the pubs alive if they didn't do a few covers! No matter who they were. Hotline used to do "I'm Eighteen" and Jeff Beck's "Lead Boots".'

SHOTS AND SPEED

The Shots fitted into the scene nicely, although there was something rather different about their vocalist. 'He was a screamer,' say Grain with a laugh. 'What you did notice was that in actual fact you'd probably look forward to the song in the set that didn't have a scream in it. All the other bands who were on the circuit at the time, you'd find that the singer was good for one scream in the whole set, with him it was three screams a song! He was great with crowds. He could really get them going.' Bill Liesegang was later to join The Shots as a guitarist. He recalls the time well, not least for Dickinson's rather unique sartorial sense in those days. 'When I knew Bruce he was at college,' Liesegang told me in an interview for this book. 'His main thing was that he was into extreme theatrical people, like Arthur Brown. With The Shots, he was trying to steer the band into that kind of thing with masks and weirdness – Bruce used to wear these really sort of long boxing sort of lace-up boots and this sort of pudding-basin haircut and he looked quite extreme, really.

'At the time it wasn't really the thing, I suppose, it was sort of post-Genesis and a lot of the other musicians I knew weren't really into that sort of thing, wearing masks and stuff like that. Which is probably why The Shots didn't take off at that point! But Bruce was always singing with that same kind of high, falsetto vocal thing – that was always there, right from the start. In fact, in many of the songs that we did, you can [still] hear it's Bruce – even if you compare it to what he does today, you know it's got his trademark stamped right on it.' Times, as ever, were rather sticky for a young band. Not least financially. 'When nobody had any money, we used to go to rehearsals at Monster Music in Streatham. We used to rent a PA, but we couldn't afford the mixer in the room so all's we

25

had was that PA, so I used to plug Bruce into my Coloursound Overdriver, which was just sort of a pre-amp for the guitar, but it had treble and bass on it so his microphone had some sort of gain going into the PA system. I still have that overdriver now and they're actually worth a lot of money, but it's probably more famous because Bruce sang through it in the early days.

'I wasn't actually in The Shots for that long,' continues Liesegang. 'I auditioned for them – I think they'd had another guitarist and he'd disappeared. So I auditioned for them and Bruce was in the band then and we kind of got quite friendly, did some recordings and rehearsed for, like, a few months. I don't think we did any gigs as such.' Liesegang subsequently went on to form a band called Xero, who got themselves into rather a sticky situation during 1983, which we shall deal with in due course. The Shots, in fact, were beginning to attract a little attention. Bruce's onstage antics, as much as his vocal capabilities, were to bring him into the orbit of an artist whose career was another step up the ladder, one who in many ways is one of the most underrated and overlooked forces in hard rock during the 1970s and 1980s.

CHAPTER 3

SAMSON

Born on 4 June 1953, Paul Samson started his musical career way back in 1969 as vocalist and guitarist for Dartford rock act The Innocence, at a time when the shadows of the Summer of Love, the Woodstock and Monterey festivals were still affecting bands the length and breadth of the musical world. It was the time of Hendrix, Led Zeppelin and The Rolling Stones' return to their R&B roots with the previous year's *Beggars Banquet* album. The year 1969 also saw the Stones – and the 1960s – lurch into deep darkness after the death of their founder member Brian Jones, and a free concert at Altamont that was tinged by the sour atmosphere engendered by the heavy-handed and violent nature of that festival's 'security': the local Hell's Angels. The well-documented death of Meredith Hunter at the concert is seen widely to mark the point when the hope and hippiness of the 1960s ended. That the Stones had just released an LP entitled *Let It Bleed* was a horrible irony.

Musically, Paul Samson's heroes were those who ploughed the rhythm & blues furrow. 'The main one is Hendrix for me,' he told *Battlehelm*. 'I was also into Mountain and when I was a kid, Cream. There's also the blues side, 'cos my dad was a big R'n'B fan.' But as the 1970s developed, The Innocence evidently fell by the wayside. Samson's growing maturity as a player made him in demand as a session guitarist. As the decade developed, he sat in with Noel Redding – which, for a Hendrix acolyte, must have been awesome – as well as the likes of Slowbone and Atomic Rooster. His next serious band was Kelly, which he originally joined in March 1973. The gigs were mainly centred round the growing pub-rock circuit, and although there were tours mooted for South Africa and US air force bases in Germany during 1974–5, in the end both fell through, somewhat ominously, largely due to behind-the-scenes politics. Paul was by now a vocalist, and though he parted company with the band after they started to go in more of a funk-jazz direction, he was to perform in various line-ups of Kelly, on and off, all the way through to February 1976, when the band finally split (due, in part, to the drummer – one Roger Hunt – leaving to form an act called Scrapyard along with guitarist Bernie Tormé and bass player John McCoy).

It was March 1977. With the spectre of punk rock looming large, Tormé left Scrapyard to form his own band, and in one of those curious rock 'n' roll coincidences. McCoy and Hunt asked Samson if they could borrow his very fine amplifier so they could audition a replacement guitarist. Paul wandered down to the rehearsal room to pick said amp up a few days later, only to find a rather disconsolate McCoy and Hunt somewhat disappointed by the lack of quality of applicants for their new project – which was to be called, simply, McCoy. More for fun than anything else, Samson and the pair held a jam session and inevitably Paul became a McCoy. The bassist and the guitarist got on extremely well as musicians and on a personal level, and wrote a considerable amount of material together during the subsequent months, the first song of which was 'Big Brother'.

'We got Paul in as the guitarist from then,' says John McCoy, with a chuckle. 'We changed the name from McCoy to Samson depending on where we were playing, 'cause if either band had played there the previous month, they didn't want us back! We just changed our name and went anyway, and played the same songs.' The gigs would come thick and fast over the next six months or so, as things hotted up for hard rock and heavy metal acts. The three-piece was not to last as a viable unit, however, and despite their having written some seriously decent blues/rock tunes together, McCoy was to leave for pastures new – the band John DuCann beckoned, as did studio work on the other side of the mixing desk.

'It was just a three-piece rock band, old-style British rock,' continues McCoy. 'But I got very, very busy; I was doing a lot of production work and sessions. I was *really* busy, and at the time I had a young family and needed to live.' Thus shorn of a band, Paul Samson recruited bassist Chris Aylmer, who had actually been working behind the Samson band's sound-desk, but also moonlighted as four-string hero in the band Maya. Later in 1977, Hunt also left this very early Samson line-up, to be replaced by Maya's drummer, Clive Burr. The trio instantly found a good, locked-in musical relationship and by December of that year were so proficient that they were confidently touring USAF bases throughout Italy with a view to using the generated income to fund future recording sessions, the logical next step. This proved to be a lucrative enough tour, and with their growing momentum, the band were able to ramp up the live appearances in and around the London area, rapidly gathering a following. The trio were steady and slick, with Paul developing a singing style that was suitably manageable for the material that comprised the set of the time. This line-up headed into the studio in the spring of 1978, the recording session yielding the subsequent single 'Telephone'/'Leavin' You', a pair of hefty blues-rock bruisers with Paul's guitar to the fore, the seven-inch being produced by none other than John McCoy and released by the small independent label Lightning Records, in September that year.

Although the three-piece Samson was making great inroads into the rock and metal circuit, and were generally considered to be ahead of a lot of contemporaries including such bands as Bruce's Shots, Paul was slightly frustrated with his dual role, feeling that the pressure of being lead vocalist as well as handling the guitar licks alone was to the detriment of his lead playing. And that had a real effect on the band as a whole.

'I know that at the time Paul wanted a singer,' confirms Rob Grain. 'They'd tried a short period in 1978 with a singer called Mark Newman, who lasted about six gigs, and what you noticed was although Samson worked really well as a three-piece, Paul's playing developed when they had a singer in the band because he wasn't having to worry about both singing and playing. You really noticed the standard of the band go up when they had a frontman – not just visually, but musically'

'I actually thought the three-piece band was pretty hot,' says John McCoy, 'and the songs were really written in keys and melodically in a range that Paul was able to handle. It was like, "This band need a singer", and I could see that, yeah. I could see that they *needed* a singer, but they needed a *good* singer.' Paul Samson himself was under no illusions, commenting later that, 'as Samson started to play larger venues I knew that I was getting out of my league.'

Even as the new breed of spitting punks were making a mockery of the initial spirited independence of the 1976 movement, the unreported underbelly of bands that were drawn more toward acts such as Led Zep, Deep Purple, Black Sabbath and the like were finding venues of their own in which to frolic and flail. The most important of these was The Bandwagon, home to an influential rock disco that was run by Neal Kay. Having cut his teeth, Beatles-style, in an eighteen-month stint at raucous rock clubs in Germany (Berlin, in Kay's case) during the early 1970s, he returned to London and found himself running a rock club in Kingsbury's Bandwagon venue memorably described by *Sounds* magazine journalist Geoff Barton as a 'cheap B-movie set saloon'. It was a gathering place for those souls isolated and marginalized by the punk movement (which Kay described to me as, 'the eternal enemy of all time'). By mid-1978, the venue had begun to attract hairy lunatics from all over the country – and beyond. The growing movement was bereft of supporters in the media, however – that is, until the aforementioned Barton was finally enticed down to the club, where Kay had been bringing down rock royalty including Ted Nugent, Rainbow, Motörhead and Whitesnake.

'In the end, I managed through sheer bloody perseverance and aggression on the phone to dig out old Geoff Barton from *Sounds*, and he came down and was so shocked at what he found he put us as the centre double-page spread. On the front page of *Sounds* that week was, "A survivor's report, would you believe it – from a Heavy Metal discotheque". And, oh boy, that did it. It told the whole world we were there. Geoff Barton was the man who put The Bandwagon on the map. That's not even up for debate, he was the man. And after that it was never the same, things started going mad, insane – things I never even dreamed of. It was like I was the unwitting and semi-frightened leader of a mass that was being dragged up the High Road by something bigger than I could even see. And behind me thundered the heavy metal hairy hordes with The Bandwagon. Suddenly, other journalists start phoning up wanting to come and see what the hell was going on.

'One of the greatest reviews we got was from my broadcast buddy, Malcolm Dome, who was writing for *Record Mirror*,' Kay affirms. 'He declared his article "By appointment to HM (Heavy Metal)". The press were always there – I made sure of it, 'cause this is business. And this is where, really and truly, it starts with the bands because of all this that was going on and the increasingly bizarre behaviour of the punters.' These included Rob Loonhouse, for a while an honorary member of Iron Maiden, jumping onstage to jam with his cardboard cut-out Flying V guitar. He subsequently formed his own cardboard band, Willy Flasher and The Raincoats, complete with cardboard bass and drum kit and in which he also, according to Kay, was a 'cardboard keyboard virtuoso'. Another chap revelled in the self-explanatory moniker Superloony, and had a penchant for public nudity. The atmosphere was fuelled by a heady mix of bikers and longhairs, and with the heavy-metal megastars giving it the seal of approval, it was clear that something major was going down.

'The music press by now were aware, with all these comings and goings and all the mad shit and everything else, that something's happening in Kingsbury,' continues Kay. 'And they continued to come down; the phone never stopped ringing: "What are you doing this week then? What's happening, what's next?" and the pressure was huge. Man. It was going worldwide and *Sounds* decided that they would take from me our punters' requested chart that I did every week from the stage. They'd write it down, I'd take it home and compile a Top 20 every week and *Sounds* took that and started printing it. And that was it: demo tapes started arriving from everywhere and that was how it all happened. But to make it happen, I first had to make The Bandwagon what it was. It was a business venture. I mean, it was music of my heart and my soul and my spirit, but it had to be properly organised and it was very hard, in all honesty, because I was on my own and had no help.

'So into this electrically charged atmosphere dropped all these demo tapes, and the stories were heartbreaking. They were from all over the world saying the same thing: "Nobody wants to listen; we're from Norway, we're from Oslo, we're from Germany and nobody wants to listen – please help us." And I suddenly realised something needed doing and I thought, "I'm a DJ but I have to do something about this, this is why I've been put here. And now I've got the power and I know the people, it's time."' The intent was clear: to publicise this new movement as much as possible. With the tireless work of Kay to add to the mix, the *Sounds* chart and the near-critical mass of artists, fans and hirsute lunatics on board, it was rapidly approaching the point of no return. Bands coming through included Praying Mantis, White Spirit, Iron Maiden – still at this stage of 1978 looking to stabilise and settle into a line-up that truly suited them – and Angel Witch, whose former drummer in their Lucifer days, Steve Jones, had played with Bruce Dickinson in Speed the previous year. Jones remembers the period as being rather a state of flux for those whose music had suddenly become as unfashionable as the flares of the punk era's hated hippies.

'[It was] perhaps a strange time for die-hard rock musicians,' he muses. 'Many of the bands around at the time were in the Thin Lizzy/UFO vein. Some bands that were really pretty good but never quite made the big-time were others such as Magnum, Dirty Tricks, Heavy Metal Kids, Trapeze, Knutz and Paris, etc. Punk-related bands smashing their way onto the scene had a real effect. In particular, bands like The Clash, The Stranglers, Squeeze, Ian Dury, Dr Feelgood etc really shook things up for the traditional rock fan and musician alike. Whilst many of these lasted the course, the punk scene itself soon gave way to 'New Wave' and mainstream rock was quickly back on the agenda, hence the New Wave of British Heavy Metal. Other important DJs of the time were Andy King and the lesser-known Karen Doyle, who used to be known as Karon after some journalist mis-spelt her name. Both Andy and Karen used to DJ mainly at Crackers in Wardour Street, which was a very popular haunt just up from the old Marquee.'

By now, Samson were playing five times a week, able to tour everywhere from south Wales to the south of England, and come September 1978 they were also regularly playing at The Bandwagon, where Kay had recently added live shows into the Soundhouse mix. But it wasn't for the faint-hearted: this was an audience who had a deep appreciation for what was put in front of them. 'They loved to laugh, loved to joke,' notes the DJ. 'But they were the best musical audience of their day. The Bandwagon was not an easy place to play. I'd made the audience one of the hardest in the country, with an eight-thousand-watt PA to listen to recorded music through. They were not gonna be easily fooled. They'd met Ted Nugent, Whitesnake, Judas Priest *personally*, so they were very tough to please and if you were a shit band you never got on. So I never put shit bands on. There was a lower limit which I had to impose because if you weren't good enough you'd get a mauling by the crowd and that was the old Bandwagon Whistle Test.

'Paul Samson came up and gave me a demo, and he used to come up and play at the 'wagon too. I liked him. It was a strange relationship, 'cause I suppose we used to do the same illegal substances once in a while, you know? And his wife Jane and my first wife Michelle were really good friends. We used to go down to south London, where he lived, and spend the night listening to music and chewing the fat and stuff. He was also not very extrovert, very quiet, preferring to strum on his Gibson SG. As time went by, there was a kind of a problem that you could only sense at first, and then see. I met John McCoy and he and his wife became good friends as well, we used to go there sometimes with Paul. It was a kinda afterhours social club – fuckin' hell, some social club! Many a brew went down and bottles of other things too! Paul used to come up and play at the 'wagon too. I liked him.'

Paul Di'Anno was vocalist with Iron Maiden at the time, and he described the scene as, 'absolutely fucking amazing', in an interview for this book. 'There was a lot of social unrest in England at the time, with power cuts and all that, during the punk era. I came from punk music myself and it all seemed to rub along together. The atmosphere was electric; a good forty-five per cent of the bands you'd see were really quite good. You know, the New

Wave of British Heavy Metal thing was coined for Iron Maiden because [the press] just didn't know where to put us. Angel Witch, Samson, Saxon, they'd all had albums out but they didn't know how to categorise us.

'Because Maiden had this punk-rock-looking lead singer, this was "New Wave…" and I thought, "What the fuck?" And all these other bands, they all jumped on the bandwagon after that. You know, Saxon, they'd had about three albums out, Judas Priest had been going since fucking Jesus was born. But it done the cause good so it was all right in the long run. I get quite miffed about that because it was just Iron Maiden to start with. But we just wanted to go out and play music: you can call us what you like. Didn't really give a shit.'

The rest of 1978 saw a growing number of quality bands performing in front of one of the hardest-to-please, but ultra-loyal audiences in the country. In the case of Samson, the year drew to a close with recording sessions for their second single, 'Mr Rock & Roll'/'Driving Music', recorded by John McCoy once more, at Ian Gillan's studio during November; McCoy had by now hooked up with the Gillan band as a performer, and Samson completed 1978 by appearing as special guests of that band on tour. The final gig of an exceedingly busy year – Samson played more than two hundred gigs during 1977 and 1978 – was a New Year's Eve appearance at The Soundhouse, which, as it turned out, was Clive Burr's farewell to the band. In Iron Maiden–land, meanwhile, the band used 31 December to ignore the festivities, preferring to get themselves into Skyward studios to record a serious demo for the first time.

'Samson were all right, actually,' says Di'Anno. 'We'd see them around on the circuit, play the same shows and all that. Paul Samson was a mate of mine, although we'd mess around more with Motörhead and Angel Witch, all them fuckers. [Samson were] one foot in, and half out [with the Maiden camp]. But you can't sit on the fence forever.

'We were so caught up with what we wanted to do we didn't listen all that much to the other bands around us, I heard a few bits and pieces of Bruce with Samson and it wasn't too bad. It wasn't all that operatic back then, but that's what you get from [taking singing] lessons.'

By early 1979, Samson had acquired management courtesy of Ramkup and one Alistair Primrose. Neal Kay was ramping up activities still further, as one of the central movers of the scene the next step was inevitable. 'Alistair Primrose bounced this off my head,' recalls Neal Kay. 'He wanted to put me together with some unsigned acts to do some touring, and his raison d'être was very simply to promote Samson.' The band had sold out of 2,000 copies of the 'Mr Rock & Roll' single that February, and were shortly to launch their debut album, *Survivors*, which had been recorded by McCoy during April. Barry Graham Purkis had by now joined Samson to replace Clive Burr, and the former was to have a little fun, donning a featureless canvas face-mask and renaming himself Thunderstick, as Samson's stage show upped the ante. In their March/April pre-recording session tour, they added a host of pyrotechnics to bolster the blues-based hard rock so beloved of Paul. 'The songs that we did were basically the songs that we'd been playing as Samson and McCoy as a three-piece out on the road,' remembers John McCoy. 'We recorded that album very, very quickly. Probably in about a week, from beginning to end. It was with Thunderstick, the new drummer. I played bass and Paul did the vocals and guitar. Then Chris Aylmer took over from me. Well, you know, [as a vocalist Paul] had his limitations, but on those particular songs, he handled them well. He'd been singing them for about a year before that, so he should've done. He found his way around them. Singing and playing guitar is a difficult thing at the best of times but he coped pretty well.

'We had a lot of fun making that album,' he continues. 'I can't believe that we actually recorded it as quickly as we did, but it was a good time. It was a question of finance, we just had to do it in the time allotted and just didn't sleep for a week; we actually took it in turns to sleep on the couch in the studio while the others kept on working.' At this stage, there was no record label lined up to release the LP, something which the management were to begin working on rectifying.'

'We were the first band that had put out an album of the NWOBHM,' Thunderstick told me. 'It hadn't been termed that yet but we were the first to put something on vinyl. That was because Paul had a lot of songs knocking about from the time he was playing with John McCoy. Clive had gone, I came in and we just went straight into the studio. I had about two days' rehearsal, then we went straight on the road. You don't wanna be hanging around rehearsing for ages, you want to go out there and do it and see how it goes. *Survivors* was a John McCoy album. He produced it, he'd been in on the songwriting. John oversaw the pre-production, everything about it. It was something I had nothing to do with whatsoever.'

The band prepared to join Iron Maiden and Angel Witch on Neal Kay and Ramkup's UK tour – now known as the 'Heavy

Metal Crusade'. But even now, Paul's uncertainty over his ability to perform both frontman and guitar hero jobs was at the back of his mind, as cohort Rob Grain, Gravesend and Northfleet's finest rocker, recalls. 'I used to talk to Paul on the phone a lot at the time,' he explains. 'And in the course of the conversation, I'd always tell him which bands were worth catching, because at the time he was busy gigging five nights a week. Occasionally he'd get a day off and want to go out with his missus for a beer, or whatever, and he'd often come down The Prince of Wales, to have a quietish night out and see – not necessarily the competition, because he was up a level – but see how the other local bands were doing. Paul came from Sidcup, fifteen miles away, and because Gravesend was always a good circuit for him, he'd pop in and let the locals see his face, really. One of the bands I'd told him about a few times was The Shots, 'cause they were really good. All of a sudden he turned up one night with this big guy with a mass of reddy-ginger hair and a Kiss jacket on, and Paul said, "This is my new drummer, Barry." And The Shots happened to be on. I think Barry – Thunderstick – went to the toilet and Bruce collared him on the way and had a bit of [a laugh] and all that. If it hadn't been for Paul and Barry going into The Prince of Wales that night who's to say Bruce wouldn't have finished his history degree, become a teacher, and never sung again in all his life…'

'In late March,' says Paul Samson in his as-yet unpublished autobiography, 'I went down to one of our old gigs with Barry one evening for a drink at The Prince of Wales in Gravesend. There was one band on called The Shots who were very entertaining and theatrical, especially the singer. Even though things hadn't worked out with Mark Newman, my dissatisfaction with being the vocalist and the guitarist hadn't quite gone away. The album sounded fine to me, but half the material had been written in the studio, and I found that I couldn't sing and play some of it live as there was too much to do at the same time. Consequently, I had always had one eye open in the hope that one day I could find someone who could fit in. The guy in The Shots impressed me, and he came over afterwards for a chat and tried to get a support slot with us. We exchanged telephone numbers so we could keep in touch and he told me his name was Bruce.

'I took Barry down to see him with The Shots a few days later, and again we were quite impressed with his voice and stage antics. He even got me clapping and singing along with the audience, a feat in itself. After seeing him a second time, we were becoming quite interested in asking him to join us.' Thunderstick himself explains that it was by accident and design that things came together that fateful night. 'We didn't actually know that Bruce was there,' he told me. 'Paul used to go there quite a lot, not as a local but to go there and hang out and go and see bands; he obviously knew the promoter, Graham. Paul had played there a coupla times as the three piece with Clive and by the time I was in the band it was a case of, "Look, fancy going out for a drink down there and we'll go out for the evening."

'By this time, we'd already been pushed into the idea of finding a vocalist. It was record companies: our management company had CBS come to see us a couple of times when we'd played the Music Machine and done the *Survivors* tour, 'cause it was all about trying to get a major deal at the time. And they said, "Yeah, it would be a lot better if there was a singer involved." The reason being that they liked the band, and thought it was great but it definitely needed that centre of attention at the front of the stage. The other candidate for the job was Gary Holton. He was just about to get into acting, hence the reason he wasn't available. But he had always been my idol in the Heavy Metal Kids because he was totally such a showman, and because at the time we were kinda going down that route, it wasn't a conscious decision to do so but it just happened that we started going down that theatrical route. I'd always been in theatrical bands, I'd loved Kiss, The Tubes, Alice, HM Kids. Any band that put on a show and gave you your money's worth.

'So we went down there and Shots were playing. At that time Bruce, as part of his act, would pick on the audience, a bit like a stand-up comedian as it were. He'd interject the songs with comments aimed at or about someone in the audience. And because I looked fucking mad, I had bright red standy-up-type David Bowie/Ziggy Stardust hair at the time and was dressed totally bizarre, he picked on me. I used to just dress in a bizarre way that wasn't of that kind of time. It was kind of weird. In fact, in interviews Bruce has turned round and said in the past that we were all over the place as far as an image was concerned as we didn't have one! I just dressed accordingly to whatever I felt like.

'I've always been quite sizeable as a guy – I'm quite well-built, six foot tall – so I suppose I kind of stuck out a bit. He was using the toilet, actually, as a changing room, to go in and do his little bits and pieces – costume changes. And we thought he looked totally mad, 'cause he had this tiny little pencil moustache! And he picked on me [that night]. But there was no intention of going down and finding this guy and asking him if he wanted the job in Samson – it just happened that way. We went down, thought,

"Blimey, he's got a loud voice and is a real showman with it," and that was it. 'I went into the toilet with Paul afterwards and [Bruce] went white 'cause I think he thought I was going to go in and beat him up! But that was it, we spoke to him after the gig and the rest is history!'

Had Paul Samson not come into Bruce's life, his main career plan may well have taken rather a different turn, as he explained to Valerie Potter of *Metal Hammer*. 'My plans involved trying to hire a railway arch, putting Portakabins in it, starting a rehearsal studio and living in one of the Portakabins for free,' he revealed.

Bruce's renowned audience heckling was something he credited to his college days. 'Generally, going to school and learning about weird and wonderful Greek legends was of value to me,' he told the *BBC*. 'If you are observant about the outside world, it's all a help in writing lyrics. You can only write lyrics from your own experience or from observation of things that have happened to other people that you want to comment on.' Bruce's humorous schtick, of course, was one of the more compelling parts of the Shots experience. Refined through the months, and run through with a dose of sharp intelligence, he could hold his own with anyone who crossed his orbit.

But there was another reason why the final-year college student was drawing attention to himself. 'We noticed Bruce 'cause he had this Gillan scream: "Aiiiii!!"' Paul Samson told *Battlehelm*. '[He] was very theatrical and worked the crowd well. He noticed us, too and obviously knew who we were – 'cos right after the show he came over to get a support slot from us for his band.' That support shot was not to be forthcoming. On the contrary, following an invitation to join Samson onstage for an encore of a particular gig at Bishop's Stortford, Bruce had successfully transferred his showmanship and growing confidence to his new friends' act. Paul and Thunderstick were eager for Dickinson to join their act as that elusive fourth member that would enable the guitarist to soar with the freedom he so craved from his beloved instrument, and immediately offered him a job as their full-time frontman.

'He couldn't join there and then because he had to finish his history degree,' remembers Thunderstick. 'He would come down and do a couple of encores, we used to do "Rock Me Baby" and he'd come down, do the encore and get the crowd going and what have you. We took that as a kind of audition, thought it worked all right so that was fine.' The rest of Samson raised their collective eyebrows but nevertheless acceded to this puzzling request. After all, they had a Crusade to complete.

CHAPTER 4

BRUCE BRUCE

While Paul Bruce Dickinson was delighted with this development in proceedings, he would not allow himself to throw away the previous years of education so close to attaining a modicum of closure to his university career. 'I did my three years at university,' he said, 'and got the same as everyone else, a 2.2 – which means you did an adequate amount of work and then you do what you are going to do in life afterwards,' he told Spencer Leigh. Almost immediately after finishing his exams, Bruce hit Greenwich's Wood Wharf studio with his new bandmates and began learning the *Survivors* tracks. Very quickly, the band were ready to get out there and hit it live. The music itself was necessarily changing under the new frontman, whose predilection for Purple was grafted atop the influences of the guitarist and founder. 'The trio were kind of Hendrix, Rory Gallagher and metal,' said Paul Samson, 'Except we did these extended jams like Cream and

Mountain. When Bruce came in, we became more song-orientated with structured solos, although we still incorporated some jams.' The Heavy Metal Crusade gigs were still rolling on. The hope was that Bruce would be ready to make his debut with the band for their appearance with Iron Maiden on 2 July 1979.

At that time, it did feel like there was a groundswell of change in music, according to Thunderstick at least. 'It felt like it was a new thing, a new surge,' he says. 'But you're not aware of it at the time. You're not thinking, "We're turning the tide." It was only when we were doing press interviews and the way they angled their interviews you could see that this was something that was beginning to materialise as a body, rather than separate things happening. All the bands I loved were suddenly discarded as being dinosaurs. Zeppelin had always been huge, and the likes of Sabbath, Uriah Heep, the list goes on. And then punk came and really kicked that up the arse with this huge great push of energy and there were other bands who thought, "Well, we need that energy." Sure, there were other bands who fitted into that niche – bands like Rush that were hard rock. 'Heavy metal' hadn't even been coined yet. We were a hard rock band. I still insist that we were a hard rock band. We never fell into that heavy metal idiom, but unfortunately that's one of the things we got labelled with.

'[At the time, booking] agents were no good, the reason being that we were on the tail end of punk and everybody was still booking punk bands all the time: "What kind of band is it?", "Well, it's a heavy metal band." "No, we're booking The Snot, and The Cum" or whatever, you know. So it was a hard thing. So it did feel like a crusade, we were breaking down barriers within Student Union groups that up until then had been undecided and suddenly there was an audience for it. Gillan were doing the same, they were doing universities and colleges, around that time there was *Rock Goes To College* on television and more and more bands were breaking into that, it was good.

'Ramkup had a lot of good intentions at the time,' notes Thunderstick, 'and they had money, which was the most important [criterion] because [a] band cannot survive without money. So they were able to put the band on a retainer wage, they were able to put the gigs on – sometimes at a loss cause even at that time we were burning up sixty or seventy pounds of pyrotechnics every night – which, in 1979, was expensive! As well as putting the whole thing together and taking it out on the road. So they had a lot of money but they had [limited] knowledge of the music industry and the processes with which you had to work within the music industry. At one time, CBS, who later became Sony, were really interested. They had The UK Subs too. That's why, in the end, John McCoy ended up producing one of the Subs' albums. [The management] were members of a place called The Golf Club, which was all Fleet Street journalists. We would go down there and cause havoc. The UK Subs with bright pink hair, Charlie Harper and Samson. There'd be these Fleet Street hacks and people of supposed good standing in society – it was an exclusive club! And we were all going raving mad, and then later on with me wearing the mask in there and doing the full image thing – that was quite amusing.'

Contemporaries Iron Maiden had hardly been quiet themselves. By the time the Heavy Metal Crusade dates came about, their 'Skyward' demo had soared to the top of the Soundhouse chart, and their growing excellence in the live arena meant that not only were they building a large and enthusiastic fan base, they'd also begun to negotiate with a potential manager – one Rodney Smallwood.

'One day, Steve came to me and said, "We've got management, a manager who I'd like you to meet,"' remembers Kay. 'And of course, that was Rod. He and I became friends back then for a while. Rod was a very funny, droll Yorkshireman who took no nonsense from anybody; he'd already managed Steve Harley and Cockney Rebel, and worked for NEMS, so he knew his stuff.' And throughout 1979, Maiden continued developing their stagecraft, sound and aesthetic accordingly, with growing confidence and driven by the single-mindedness of their founder, Steve Harris. With mercurial vocalist Paul Di'Anno barking, growling and prowling up front, Maiden's stock was ever rising. Musician and metal fan Tony Miles – of various bands including Tush and, later, Gibraltar – was there at the time. 'I went to see Maiden in 1979 – when Tony Parsons was in that band and Paul Di'Anno was singing – because Tony's brother, Steve, was a bass player and I was trying to start a band. Most of the bands came out of the pub scene, hard and fast music venues with a band every night, and the goal was to get to the Marquee Club if you were at that level. Bands would bump into each other, as you do. There was no internet, so the only way you got to hook up with people was to go to the gigs, watch the bands, strike up a conversation or walk away in disgust thinking, "That was rubbish." But you'd know everybody on the same level. You'd go from pubs and clubs to the college and university circuit and then you'd know you were going somewhere.

'The scene was quite healthy and dynamic. During that period, Iron Maiden and Samson were [doing well] and we played the same venues from time to time; they came to see us, we went to see them. It was an exciting time.'

Thing were getting exciting too for the new Samson singer. As things turned out, the very first rehearsals went so well that the group wrote four new songs in just under a week, namely 'Take it Like a Man', 'Too Close to Rock', 'Walking out on You' and 'Hammerhead', all of which were later set to tape. 'We went back into rehearsal and wrote some more new material including "Manwatcher" and "Vice Versa",' said Paul Samson. 'The management began to feel that the elusive major deal would only be achieved if we presented the labels with the songs that we had written since Bruce had joined. Def Leppard were reportedly signing to Phonogram for an enormous sum, and Saxon had signed to Carrere, so the release of *Survivors* on an indie label for no advance was not very helpful to our financial situation.'

It is also during this intensive rehearsal period that Mr Dickinson was endowed with the rather strange nickname 'Bruce Bruce'. The popular reading of how this came about is that it is a very specific reference to a Monty Python sketch, entitled 'Bruces', which was first aired on British TV in Episode 22 of that show on 24 November 1970. In that particular comedy short, four Australians from the Philosophy Department of Woolamaloo are sitting around chewing the fat – but as they are all Aussies, their names are all Bruce. When a new professor, Michael Baldwin, is welcomed on board to teach political science, the other four Bruces ask if they can't just call him Bruce, to avoid 'confusion'. Subsequently, they refer to him as 'New Bruce' for the rest of the typically surreal sketch, which plays with the idea of crass and raw-mannered salt-of-the-earth type Aussies swilling beer and proclaiming their very macho opinions to the world while holding down very intellectually stimulating jobs and careers, such duality being a familiar Python theme. So far, so good. Where the confusion appears to have arisen is in the retelling of the story of an exchange between Dickinson and Paul Samson very early in proceedings. Samson enquired as to Dickinson's second name and hence confusion occurred, as, of course, the singer's full name is Paul Bruce Dickinson. 'I'd meant his surname,' said Paul Samson, 'and he'd thought I'd meant his middle name and I said, "Wot, Bruce Bruce?" and everybody roared up laughing.'

'What probably got mixed up there,' according to Rob Grain, at least, 'was basically that within the Samson circle, if anybody joined – manager, road crew, soundman – they were referred to as "The New Bruce". So when Bruce joined, he was "New Bruce" and his name was Bruce. That's basically how the "Bruce Bruce" thing came about.' Regardless, the joke must have worn a little thin when Paul Bruce Dickinson attempted to cash cheques made out by Ramkup Management in his alter-ego's name.

All in good heart. The new four-piece was more than content with the way things were sounding, although not everyone was as immediately enamoured of the new set-up. 'When you saw the band with Bruce it went up a level,' recalls Grain. 'To be honest with you, the first time I saw them with Bruce I didn't like it. And I said to Paul, "What have you done?" Because when you get a new person in the band, the music changes, and I felt the music had changed for the worse. I didn't think he sang the original songs so well, but in fairness to Bruce that's probably 'cause I was used to Paul singing them. So my first impression was that it was a wrong move. And I think that was quite a general impression amongst Samson fans. I saw them a couple of weeks later at The Bandwagon, and they didn't die a death – but they didn't go down very well at all. The general vibe around the place was that people preferred them as a three-piece.'

Doug Sampson, at the time drumming with Iron Maiden, remembers seeing Samson several times pre-Bruce. 'Paul Samson was singing at the time but Bruce coming in really put a different spin on it. He had a lot more stage presence and it was a much better show when he joined. We did a few gigs together at that period.' Sampson also remembers chatting with Dickinson over a drink about his vocal heroes. 'He said that he had seen Arthur Brown [live] and it had completely changed him and his vocals. He started singing in different octaves and trying to do what Arthur Brown was doing.'

There was recorded material to get out there, and the 'Mr Rock & Roll' single (this time with 'Primrose Shuffle' as its B-side) was re-released on 29 June by Laser Music, who subsequently agreed to release the already-recorded album, *Survivors* in the UK, which they duly did in September 1978. The LP's cover, however, rather mischievously airbrushes both Bruce Bruce and Chris Aylmer into the recent history of the band; but, as John McCoy recalls, their credits – as vocals, harmonica and guitar, and bass respectively – are less to do with what they actually contributed to the album recordings, and more to do with their forthcoming roles in Samson.

'It was a bit of a weird time,' recalls *Samson* producer and long-time collaborator Big John McCoy. 'The whole thing was very strange. There was actually a release on Lightning Records, and that picture was without Bruce, and when Bruce came in, his picture suddenly appears. I've always hated that cover, it's absolutely atrocious. It was difficult for the management; I suppose they wanted it to seem that the band that they managed, and was going out on tour, was the band that recorded the album. So on the back of the album, it didn't actually specify who played what, and when. Bruce wasn't around at all when we recorded that but I suppose it made sense to them to have his name on there, and make it seem like he was involved. Paul had a lot of new stuff, but I wasn't able to work on it with him. He wanted to continue our relationship into writing the next album, but I was just so busy at that time, that had to be left by the way. I think it was right that the guys all got involved in the writing. You've got to go out and play it, you've got to feel involved in it.'

'When Bruce joined,' remembers Rob Grain, 'They virtually went straight out on the road on the *Survivors* tour. But what happened was that because they'd started writing new songs it was probably frustrating – they were doing a tour promoting the album that had just come out but they wanted to get on with the new stuff that they were writing, so when they did the *Survivors* tour there were four new songs in the set which eventually went onto the next album, which was [to be] called *Head On.*'

Bruce's familiarity with the *Survivors* material was one thing, but the tracks were simply not written for him, some of them even pre-dating the renaming of Samson itself. As McCoy rightly notes, they were written for Paul and as such they didn't really suit Bruce's range, or provide him with a basis from which to really soar. And while the band were trying to incorporate new material into a set that was supposed to be linked to the sonic aesthetic of the blues/rock vibe of *Survivors*, there was a collision course waiting to happen. Much like Rob Grain, and the Samson fan base in general, McCoy wasn't hugely impressed with the Bruce experience at first. 'The management and record company were very keen for them to have a singer,' he says. 'I think the first time I really saw Bruce, Paul was raving: "I've found this singer, I've found this singer, he's absolutely brilliant!" blah, blah, blah – and me and Bernie Tormé [fresh from supporting Boomtown Rats with his own band, and now employed as guitarist for Ian Gillan] and someone else from Gillan went to Crackers, a club in Wardour Street. It was just a little gig, they did some numbers with Bruce and it was fucking horrible. The whole band was horrible, it was a naff gig.' Tormé was similarly underwhelmed. 'It was the old Vortex club that I'd played in as a punk,' says the guitarist. 'When NWOBHM began, it kind of changed its colours and became a NWOBHM club. I knew Paul but I hadn't seen him in a while, so John dragged me down because you know the band had changed and our Paul had a singer now. To be honest I don't really recall an awful lot about him – I always liked Paul anyway, I suppose. What Paul had done up till that point was blues. It was poppier, rockier blues. The main thing I remember about Bruce was that most singers in bands – and this goes continually up to today – are fairly mouthy people and confident and generally fairly aggressive. And Bruce wasn't, he was a fairly quiet, laid-back bloke.

"At the time they used to use pyrotechnics and one of the pyros exploded in one of the punters' faces – that's the only thing I can recall basically out of the gig; the most spectacular [thing being] almost blowing up a member of the audience!' Following the prevailing winds of the time, the initial reaction to the expanded Samson family had been a little hesitant. But it soon began to click into place a little more. 'They played the following week at

The Music Machine,' recalls McCoy, 'and I went down to that and there was the sort of inkling of the Bruce we now know coming out of his shell there. It was a big gig for him to join that band at that time. He'd done hardly anything [in music prior to joining Samson] and he tried his hardest to fit in the band's sense of humour and just to do his best, but I'm sure he wouldn't mind me saying, he used to look very, very silly. He has leopardskin tights, a lovely moustache – a sort of Peter Wyngarde moustache – and a bowler hat. It's not exactly the image of a heavy rock singer. And he sort of just ran around stage like a demented monkey! But he obviously had an incredible range and the couple of new songs that they played that night I remember as being really good and being quite impressed. I talked to Paul about it afterwards and he said, "We're committing to the guy," and I said, "Basically he just needs to learn his stagecraft. He needs to know about handling an audience 'cause that's what you've got this guy for – to involve the audience in the gig."'

Samson may have been growing into their status as a quartet to be reckoned with, but not everybody would rate the music they were doing as progressive. Enter Neal Kay once again: 'The problem with Paul is that his heroes were in the past and the kids' heroes were going in the future. Paul's music was very, very Hendrix, Frank Marino, Rush-styled influence. Iron Maiden and Praying Mantis and others represented the future and not the past. Paul was an awesome guitar player, to hear him do "Talking About a Feeling" live at the 'wagon was an experience. He was, to me, one of the great blues/rock guitar players of NWOBHM. He would say if he was alive today [Paul Samson died from cancer on 9 August 2002] that there was no such thing as the New Wave of

British Heavy Metal – he was around before it but he couldn't understand what all the fuss was about. He couldn't see it. In desperation to try and win the crowd back, he started resorting to these pyrotechnical displays where it was more bloody pyros than music.'

The stage show was, nevertheless, attracting attention; from the antics of the gimp-masked Thunderstick to the bundle of nervous energy that was Bruce Bruce, topped off by the free-riffing Paul Samson himself, the only steadying influence was the Ox-like Chris Aylmer, holding the groove down manfully even as the stage was beset by explosives from all angles. And it was time to take the show out on the road, old mates McCoy and Tormé helping to secure Samson a coveted support slot during October 1979 with Gillan. For Bruce, this was an unbelievable development. As a major Deep Purple fan, his musical taste and even vocal style owed a massive amount to Ian Gillan; to go on tour with one of his heroes so early in a career was simply astonishing – although his first meeting with his hero didn't go exactly to plan, according to Thunderstick.

'The very first time he met Ian Gillan, he was sick,' says the drummer, with a laugh. 'He literally went into the toilet and threw up with nerves. We were in Kingsway, I can't remember if we were recording or if we were just down there for a night off with the rest of the Gillan band, 'cause we all kinda mixed together. In came Ian and Bruce disappeared, we didn't know where he'd [gone]. The next thing we knew, Ian came into the control room and said, "You'd better go and have a look at your singer, he's in the toilet throwing up, he looks really ill." It was 'cause of the nerves of meeting Ian Gillan, which is quite amusing.'

'[Bruce] – he really loved Ian completely,' says John McCoy, laughing. 'He was quite overawed, you know.' As you would be. The tour featured full support from Randy California, and then, as Tormé recalls, 'The Speedometers and Samson on about half [of the dates] each.

'I mean, to Bruce I think it was even more of a big deal because he idolised Ian. One of the things I also remember is that he tried to keep up with Ian in terms of drinking and this wasn't a clever idea because there wasn't anyone on the planet who could keep up in drinking with Ian. Having come out of Purple who were, you know, a fairly hard-drinking band. I can remember on at least one occasion of Bruce being [very pissed] and Ian not even being slightly drunk!' 'I think he liked him,' offers Torme. 'He did – all of us did, because Bruce was a nice bloke. There wasn't any second agenda; he was just a nice bloke, basically.'

'We rehearsed for the Gillan tour and wrote another new song, "Hard Times",' wrote Paul Samson in his diaries, 'which featured an a cappella section with Bruce and myself, and put it into the set. We all did something mad to our hair. I put a tub of red henna on mine, Bruce had his cut by his grandmother, who put a bowl on his head and cut round it, Barry had dyed his bright red and looked like Ronald McDonald, and Chris looked as though his had gone wrong. It started off yellow, then green, blue and red and he looked a right tit! Anyone else would have dyed it brown that night, but he rode the insults until it faded months later.'

'When Bruce came along, he was as green as grass; he was a college kid and he didn't know shit from breakfast time at the end of the day!' offers Thunderstick. 'Paul and I were streetwise south-east Londoners; we'd both been brought up in a similar background and had known each other from schooldays – we didn't go to school together but we'd known each other 'cause we both used to rehearse on a farm. There was one electricity point and boxes of Brussels sprouts all over the place.'

'Samson was a strange band in that it was a very "clannish" band,' notes Torme. 'The Gillan band was basically a lot of fairly diverse people. I mean, I'd been a punk, Colin Towns had been a jazzer and whatever else and there wasn't really an ethos of having to fit in as a band, you just had to play – and it was good in that it was fairly grown up in terms of that. We all basically talked about each other behind each other's back, "Oh shit, look at the clothes he's wearing!" you know. But basically, all of us did it and it sort of worked. In Samson there was a awful lot more pressure, I think, to have everyone in the band fit in and at the start off point I think Bruce felt he didn't. I can remember there being some major argument on the coach. They were always up the back of the coach and Bruce was down at the front of the coach, and Paul and Barry and Chris basically had Bruce's case and were taking single items of clothing out and chucking them up the coach at Bruce. And to us this was not acceptable basically, so we turned around and said, "Look, stop!" and it did. At the time I think there was kind of an element, that they felt that Bruce was a tiny bit of a middle-class kid. When there were temporary arguments it was extremely extreme, it was like a gang of kids basically having an argument. To be honest, looking back at it and even at the time, I was always of the opinion that Bruce handled it really well.'

'I left the tour bus the day after that and drove myself,' says McCoy, chuckling, 'because it was starting to get hard work. It was getting a bit stinky and a bit crowded with people that had been met at the previous night's gig. You know, you'd get on the bus and there'd be a body there, and [you'd] think "Who the hell's this?" Usually female. It was a good, old-fashioned rock 'n' roll tour, pretty bananas. But we had a good time on that tour, it was a lot of fun. It was like being on tour with the Marx Brothers, being on tour with Samson. They were just completely insane, every day. I think Bruce basically just tried to keep up with them all. It was a really crazy band and a crazy time.'

'We were the naughty schoolboys on that tour,' says an amused Thunderstick. 'We went to the joke shop before the tour and bought loads of masks and pea shooters and stink bombs and this, that and the other. Bruce let a fire extinguisher off on the very first night of the tour and we were threatened to be thrown off of it. It was the powder type, which didn't go down too well. It went absolutely everywhere. It was at the gig, after we'd played. After Ian had played he was doing an interview with some press and Bruce let this fire extinguisher off and it just went everywhere.

'Not only that, but Ian came over to me and asked me if anybody had any cigarettes, 'cause I smoked at the time. Ian was talking to all these record guys, a comparatively small record label, but it was important to Ian. I'd primed all these cigarettes with these smoke pellets and he handed them all out and all these guys were talking away, until all of a sudden all this flaky smoke type dusty stuff 's coming off their cigarettes. On the tour coach there was Randy California – from Spirit – Gillan, and us, at the back of the coach like naughty kids in class, firing peashooters at people, just raving mad, we had all these strange masks, stink bombs and all kinds of stuff. It was Bernie and John trying to be as professional as they possibly could, Ian was travelling on his own with his girlfriend in his Roller and these guys from America, Randy and his bassist and drummer thinking, "What the hell…?" We gave the bass player from Randy California some chewing gum, which made his mouth go bright red; he was chewing away and he looked at us and we were pissing ourselves laughing. He looked at us and said, "What's the matter with you guys? You guys are really into your own personal jokes, aren't you?" And we were just absolutely cracking up 'cause his mouth was bright red and foaming and he didn't know it.

'We were serious about what we did musically, but that didn't mean that we had to be really serious people all the time. And we weren't. We were headcases – we were raving mad. You read interviews with Mötley Crüe and the fans love it that they were raving mad. We didn't take loads of drugs, it was never chemicals with us all the time. It was smoking dope, yeah, but we were just naturally mad as well. There was a lot of pressure on at the time and we were kids, growing up, developing our styles and learning what it was like to be in a professional hard rock band and being out on the road. It came natural to us, we didn't feel we needed to live up to that kind of ideal of throwing televisions out of the window or anything, we were just naturally mad.'

Thunderstick is somewhat upset, however, by the occasional portrayal of the Samson gang as a bunch of hooligans. Which they weren't. 'It comes over as "we were never serious" and that's so far from the truth. We were serious about what we did. The way we went about it was probably wrong, in hindsight, but we were always deadly serious. The moment I sat behind a drum kit, or Paul strapped his guitar on, we were serious about what we did and we would always try and push the parameters as much as we probably could, musically.' It was a time that firmly set the group up as a four-piece band.

'At the beginning, I think it was kind of hard for them,' recalls Torme, 'because our audience was always kind of partisan. It was basically an Ian audience and at the beginning even I got a bit of stick – and I think that the support bands tended to generally get a tiny bit of a hard time. And I think that, coupled with Bruce's lack of experience at the beginning, it was a fairly steep learning curve.' But learn he did; mostly from the side of the stage, watching one of his all-time heroes work the crowd into a frenzy night after night. Being a studious chap, and a very bright chap, Bruce very quickly began to pick up some tips. It was the tour that cemented his place as a performer who could compete at a high level with the best of them.

'It wasn't an enforced thing, but Paul got Bruce to watch Ian Gillan each night and say "Watch this bit, watch that bit, look what they do here!"' remembers McCoy. 'It sounds crass now, but the guy was learning. Ian is a brilliant singer [more so than] in terms of winding an audience up; in fact Bruce is probably better at that now. But that was my memory of it, I mean, it was interesting to watch the band grow on that tour. By the end of the tour, it seemed like it was a band, and not just Samson plus a singer, they were locked in. And destined for big things. The audience knew the connection between us and them, all the gigs were sold out. It couldn't have been better for them to play big gigs at that time. I do believe if they'd stuck together, they would have been a lot bigger. Because as I say, Bruce slowly came into his own, and by the end of the tour he was like he was in charge. He was running the show, whereas at the start of his involvement with the band, he was just like a guy that was onstage acting silly.'

'And he had this bizarre haircut!' Thunderstick recalls. 'In actual fact, we went fucking mad at him because his girlfriend at the time actually cut his hair by doing the archetypal thing of putting a bowl on his head and cutting round the bowl! That first promo picture he has that haircut – we went mad: 'It's a heavy metal band, for Chrissake!''

The eighteen-date tour also featured a day off to record a radio session with the late, legendary DJ, Tommy Vance. Meanwhile, the album *Survivors* was gathering four-star reviews from the likes of *Sounds* and *Record Mirror* and peaked at No.3 in the Indie album charts, a great fillip for the group. Refusing to rest on their laurels, however, they stayed on the road for the rest of 1979 honing their craft with a headline tour, supported by the brilliant vocalist Nicky Moore and his band and ended it with the double whammy of both headlining their own gig in front of over a thousand souls in Folkestone, but also appearing on the front cover of *Sounds* – complete with a picture of Thunderstick, clad in his now-familiar leather balaclava, with the splendid caption, 'The New Face of Heavy Metal'.

A young aspiring musician by the name of Bayley Alexander Cooke was a big Black Sabbath fan, but he was well aware of other music that was knocking around in the period. 'I wasn't into Samson,' recalled the man subsequently known as Blaze Bayley, for this book. 'I liked some of the songs, although I wouldn't be waiting for the next [release], but I'd listen to it if it was around. I was aware of Bruce Dickinson from then on.'

Samson were not the only ones making progress. Elsewhere, Iron Maiden self-released the 'Spaceward' demos – sans 'Strange World' and retitled *The Soundhouse Tapes* – and promptly sold

5,000 copies. Subsequently, the record companies finally, belatedly perhaps, began to take an interest in Maiden, and the combined forces of Smallwood – not a man to be underestimated – and Neal Kay led to an EMI A&R man coming down to see Maiden in a gig at The Bandwagon. It was packed. 'The A&R guy was about as big as me, about five-foot five, if that,' says Kay, amused. 'He was right at the back and he couldn't see a fucking thing, he could not see anything! The legend goes that at the end of the night, he said, "Well, it sounded good and the people liked it so I guess we'd better 'ave it." And so they signed.' On 26 November 1979, to be exact.

Earlier in the year, however, a potential problem that may have delayed matters a little had arisen, caused by what amounted to nothing more than backstage horseplay on the Crusade tour. 'There was a falling-out between Samson and Iron Maiden,' explains Rob Grain. 'Not a person-to-person falling-out, it was just politics really. But what you've gotta bear in mind is that all the bands at the time were trying to headline the same gigs, get the same record deals. So obviously it gets a little bit bitchy, every-one trying to get one jump further up the ladder than anyone else. There was an incident where one of the Music Machine shows had Iron Maiden, and EMI were coming down to see them. So they'd laid on this spread of food in the dressing room. Well, of course, while they were onstage Samson's crew went in and scoffed the lot! So by the time Maiden had finished and invited EMI backstage for the banquet it had all gone. There was lots of that sort of thing going on, inter-band rivalry.'

Maiden's drummer at the time, Doug Sampson, remembers there being a cross-section of punters at the Soundhouse gigs.

'You'd have your headbangers, the rockers and a lot of bikers there. They looked quite intimidating, but they were as good as gold. Barton turned up, saw the crowd and shit himself. He kept out of the way a bit – the crowds could be quite rowdy, to say the least. But it was a really good gig down there, like a church or a religion. I felt from the beginning that there was something going to happen and it was just at the right time. Def Leppard, Angel Witch and Maiden all seemed to gel. People were fed up with the punk thing, and bands like Judas Priest were spending so much time in America you'd never get to see them. You could see a local band of your own age at a club; slightly faster and more energetic, more aggressive than Priest and it was very appealing to the kids at the time. It was more for them and the speed of it even appealed to the punks.

'We could see that with Maiden. We wanted to take it as far as it would go. I'd known Steve Harris for quite a long time and we knew what to expect from each other. When Paul Di'Anno came in, he just slotted in to Maiden with me, Dave [Murray] and Steve. It just worked straight away; we all just got along really well. Paul Cairns came in on guitar but he injured his hand and was out of the band for so long we got really tight, and kept it as a four-piece. Tony Parsons came, a good bloke, it worked out really well [at the time.] Big business came in later, but it was just a bunch of blokes having a bloody good time.'

Touring was gruelling, not least due to the fact that in these early days the band were largely still working in day jobs, and often had to sleep in the back of Steve Harris's seven-ton truck, warmly referred to (the only warm thing about it) as 'The Green Goddess'. It's not to everyone's taste; kipping in the back of lorries requires a certain kind of character. Doug Sampson was to depart the fold, to be replaced by ex-Samson kit-clanger Clive Burr. Of course, Thunderstick had previously been a member of Maiden for around eight months during 1977, and indeed, prior to Burr snagging the job, had actually jammed with his former bandmates once more over the 1979 Christmas period with a view to possibly returning to the fold.

'Prior to joining Iron Maiden [the first time around],' explains the drummer, 'I'd been in a professional band in Sicily and I was listening to a lot of prog rock, bands like PFM, Steve Hillage, they were all kind of King Crimson, I loved the time changes and that's what I loved about the early Iron Maiden stuff. So I got re-offered the job with Iron Maiden; it was after the Heavy Metal Crusade. I got a phone call and it ruined my Christmas. They said, "We've just got rid of Dougie Sampson, are you interested in re-joining?" and I went down and played with them after Christmas. I remember Rod Smallwood saying to me, "This band's going to be bigger than Led Zeppelin!" and I thought, "Well, that's really nice you've got that amount of confidence in your own band." Little did I know! I remember saying at the time, "The thing really is the Thunderstick character is really taking off."' So Thunderstick stuck with his gimp-masked alter ego and his current band Samson, rather than go back to the more sedate, controlled Barry drumming persona bashing out the steady beat at the back, which Iron Maiden required.

Maiden's continued existence was – and arguably, for many, still is – down to the dogged vision of one man, and that is the band's bassist and driving force: Steve Harris. It is, says Thunderstick, Harris's band, and he is massively responsible for keeping it going and instrumental in all decisions. 'It was always his [band], always. Without a doubt. Even in the early days when I was with them, Steve just had that definition of foresight. There was nothing that was gonna deviate him, he was gonna go for it. In his attitude and his playing. He was living with his grandma at the time, I had my own house in south-east London, in Plumstead, [when I was with Maiden the first time around]. I had one room in my house where the kit was set up and he used to come round and we'd go through bass and drum lines. He was very serious about it and I always thought it was his band. And it was; time has shown it has always been his.

'It was a big deal [to be asked to rejoin]; I was absolutely gobsmacked by it. Can you imagine how gobsmacked I was a few weeks later when we were in Kingsway, recording *Head On*, and John McCoy phoned up and said, "Guess who's just taken a gig with Iron Maiden – Clive Burr!" I thought, "Oh my God!" So I was playing in Samson with "Iron Maiden" still written all over my drum cases – and vice versa. Clive was doing the same with "Samson" all over his drum cases!' The links between Samson and Maiden, like those between the Gillan band and Samson, were very strong in this period – and would soon, of course, be even stronger.

But for the time being, Clive it was for Maiden, and Barry stayed as Thunderstick. It was becoming evident, however, that things were really happening in the New Wave of British Heavy Metal, and it looked like a definite vanguard was indeed emerging.

All in all, for Bruce Dickinson it had been a rather decent year. He was only twenty-one years of age, and had not only fulfilled his ambition of appearing on a major stage, he'd done it alongside one of his major inspirations. The music he loved seemed to be firmly back on the British rock agenda, and with a new decade looming, the only way was surely up.

CHAPTER 5

HEAD ON

The new decade in the UK began with the sharp realisation that the excitement and newness of both the emergent punk and NWOBHM scenes was settling down into something ready to be absorbed by a more mainstream audience. In the case of the metal bands, this meant the inevitable historical marker being put down to set the lid, if you like, on the era. After the triumphs and occasional pain of the Heavy Metal Crusade, the next obvious step was to release a compilation of all the bands concerned on vinyl.

'*Metal For Muthas* came about 'cause of all the demo tapes I had,' says Neal Kay. 'A bloke called Ashley Goodhall working junior round table A&R for EMI and myself got together and decided they'd put out this compilation of new bands. I wrote a set of sleevenotes for it, believing EMI was going to put up the money for all these bands to be rerecorded whose tracks I'd picked. Unfortunately, boy, was I wrong, 'cause they didn't, which annoyed me, and the artwork was absolutely disgusting. Terrible! Fuckin' tacky! But it's considered by many as a landmark album because it represents a point in time where it was recognised that there was so much happening with small bands in rock at the time.'

Represented on the disc, which was released on EMI in February 1980, are several of the more familiar Soundhouse/Bandwagon/NWOBHM names – Praying Mantis, Sledgehammer, Angel Witch all holding up manfully with their contributions – alongside the also-rans (hello Ethel The Witch) and some not-yets, including Xero, a group complete with Bruce's old sparring partner in Shots, guitarist Bill Liesegang. For Samson's part, their contribution is a ballad-esque hangover track, a McCoy production and a rerecording of the McCoy/Samson composition that duly appeared on the *Survivors* album. 'Tomorrow or Yesterday' is a piano-based and very classic workout that owes as much to 1960s soul as it does to anything 'New Wave'; it is, in truth, a timeless piece of music that could have been written at any moment between 1960 and today. Paul's solo in the third quarter actually has a tone and aesthetic to it that is, arguably, ten years ahead of its time – sonically, at least. Samson's offering, however, cannot compete with the dual assault of their contemporaries, compadres and – ultimately – competition: Iron Maiden. What turned out to be their second single, 'Sanctuary', not only opened the album with a breathtaking pace, but they are also the only band to appear twice on the LP (the other track being the storming 'Wrathchild'). Significantly, Maiden's new management and label were now allowing the band to begin to stand out a little – perhaps demanding respect by their invention, energy and professional approach.

Back in Bruce-land, there was the little matter of another UK tour to contend with, this time with Samson as support to Robin Trower (Maiden were out at this time on the road with the *Metal For Muthas* tour, along with Praying Mantis, Tygers of Pang Tang and Raven). Trower was a legendary English guitarist, whose stint in 1960s heroes Procul Harum is well documented. But despite his obvious influence on Paul Samson's career, for a group ostensibly keen on being part of the future of the British hard rock scene, Samson's support slot was, possibly, ill-advised, especially if they were seeking to place themselves within the context of being future heroes rather than aligning themselves with the classic musicians of the past.

It was also, inevitably, a series of gigs that were full of incident, as Paul Samson noted in his biography. 'The tour carried on to Liverpool to Glasgow Apollo where Bruce nearly fell fourteen feet off the front of the stage 'cause we had so little room, then Edinburgh, Birmingham and Hammersmith Odeon. We went down well every night, although we found it harder work in the seated theatres, while Trower's crew did all they could to wind us up. I took to watching Robin's gig each night sat on a flight case at the side of the stage and learnt a lot. He was definitely the master of the understatement and in some of the spacier jams you could hear a pin drop in the gaps though they played loud. Jimmy Dewar the bass and vocalist was always nice to us, but Trower and the drummer barely came near us. I tried several times to have a conversation with Robin, but the most I could get out of him was, "Alright?" as he shuffled past in his anorak. At Sheffield, things blew up a little bit with the crew when at the soundcheck the monitors were feeding back so much... in the ensuing fracas, [Bruce's] microphone got broken and we were presented with a bill for three hundred pounds for damaging the equipment, and told we would have no monitors for the rest of the tour... we'd had enough, so we told the tour manager we were going home and pulling off the tour. He went into a panic and said, "Robin will go mad if you pull off the tour," and the outcome was that there was no [three-hundred-pound] bill and there were monitors for the rest of the tour. Although God knows what the out-front sound was like.'

The band were well received wherever they played on the tour, which was completed at Newcastle City Hall on 12 February 1980. 'It was an unbelievable mix between the two [audiences],' remembers Thunderstick. 'Stoned hippies for Robin Trower, and young kids hanging onto this NWOBHM thing – it was a total mismatch of audience, it was very interesting... and we got very laid back toward the end of the tour in soundchecks. It was great, kind of going into these spacey jams and things. Yet again, we almost got thrown off the tour on the first night; we used to make it a kind of recurring incident that would happen. The first night would always be the worst night. We did "Rock Me Baby" as an encore, Robin's guitar tech came back afterwards and said, "If you do that again, you're off the tour." We said, "What. Do an encore?" and he said, "No, if you do 'Rock Me Baby', 'cause that's Robin's encore! He does that." Which we were supposed to know. I remember Bruce unplugging a wedge, and passing it to the first guy in the audience and saying, "Can you pass that to the guy who's doing the sound engineering at the back, and tell him that all I'm getting is screaming feedback through it." And we just watched this wedge make its way back to the control desk at the back! I loved it. I was having a whale of time and enjoying myself.

We were gathering momentum no matter which tour we were on, we were still getting a large amount of audience turning up to see Samson, which was great.'

By now, Bruce had f irmly cut his teeth as a frontman, confident in the material the band were offering as well as having won over the previously sceptical fans that had greeted his addition to the Samson line-up with some initial bemusement. And just in time too – Samson almost immediately went out on tour supporting Rainbow, with a series of huge concerts pulling ten thousand people or more; no place for the weak and certainly no place to hide. 'We had a great gig [on the Edinburgh leg of the tour] and the sound onstage was excellent,' Paul Samson wrote. 'The crowd were with us all the way and sang their heads off in the participation bits, and Bruce led us well. All too soon our forty minutes were up. The Rainbow tour manager was full of congratulations, and was somewhat surprised at our reception. He said that even Ritchie had enjoyed it. Evidently he watched the set through the one inch gap between my amps and speaker cabinets.'

Samson were performing so well during this period – pyrotechnics, and gimp-masked drummers and all – that when the crowd demanded they perform an encore at the Wembley Arena date, the band duly obliged – but unbeknownst to them, this was not a popular decision backstage. Jennie Halsall was the major freelance PR of the metal scene at the time, and she remembers the incident well. 'I was known as the Heavy Metal Queen of PR, which sounds ridiculous now!' she told me. 'I looked after Ritchie Blackmore's Rainbow, Cozy Powell, Purple, all those bands. Samson were like the fledgling, new, exciting young band.' But after the headliners did not play an encore, 'The punters started to break up the place and I never ran so fast from the box office as fast as that! The audience kicked off and started to smash the place up.'

Surprised, but undaunted, Samson entered the studio during March 1980 for initial sessions for their new album, and to record the first single to feature Bruce as vocalist – perhaps fuelled by a sense of renewed urgency following Iron Maiden both appearing on *Top of the Pops* performing their 'Running Free' single, and playing it live on the famous show to boot, which was unheard of at the time. In Samson's case, the unavailability of McCoy due to other commitments meant that the band would be recording and producing the songs themselves. All new tracks were credited to the quartet that now comprised Samson. Initially, the intent was to come away from Kingsway Recording Studios with a three track single – 'Vice Versa', 'Hammerhead' and 'Manwatcher' were the tracks initially mooted to be put down to tape – but as it turned out, the band were sharp, on a roll, and in fact blasted through enough tracks for an album proper. The previous six months of bedding Bruce Bruce into proceedings had clearly added a vigour and focus to the music, which had put a real edge on a band doused in hard rock. And if there's one thing that great hard rock bands can do, it is ramp up the excitement and work quickly. Once the vibe is there and rolling, a band with the technical ability of Paul Samson, the steadiness of Chris Aylmer and the Keith Moon-esque thudding invention of Thunderstick can fly very high very quickly.

Thunderstick maintains that, in his opinion, he produced a lot of that album. 'I don't care what anybody says, I know that I was there longer and more hours than anybody else. I was the one who sat there with Chas the engineer and did Bruce's vocals. Paul and Chris went home, night after night, and I spent ages on that.

I've actually got tapes here, outtakes of Bruce doing "Walking Out On You", different tracks. I'd always loved production and Paul had always been more about the live aspect and playing. I loved Brian Eno and those kind of people who'd gone into the studio and pushed the parameters a little bit. So all the backwards stuff, and the bits and pieces of percussion and gongs and tubular bells like on "Take it Like a Man", countermelodies and madness – that was all mine. I pushed really hard for a production credit on it, and all I ended up getting was "Additional Ideas by Thunderstick", which was quite a bone of contention. It became a standing joke although it hurt a lot inside because I always felt I should have had a production credit on that.'

Thunderstick remembers the actual recording process very clearly. 'We put the backing tracks down, bass and drums, the three of us playing live and Paul either playing from the control room or somewhere we wouldn't get overspill on the mics,' he says. 'As soon as we thought the drums were okay, and there might be some bits and pieces that needed patching, we'd do that. The bass wouldn't be redone, we'd hope to get bass and drums down in the same track. Then we'd put down the overdubs on the guide guitar track we'd recorded. A lot of the time Paul would play in the control room, we'd crank the monitors right up and he'd stand there and just play. We all took part in backing vocals and, as I say, I did the sessions with Bruce on vocals and all the kind of madness was last on the list. Alright, it may sound a bit dated [now] but more than anything else, it is a band, the sound of a band finding its feet, and I love it for that, I really do. I'm going absolutely mad all over the place on it, playing-wise. Paul was pushing himself in different directions and using different sounds and techniques; he had the SG he used all the time but then on a couple of tracks he used a Strat… we were just pushing it. *Head On* was our *Sergeant Pepper*.

'It was Bruce's first crack at doing it for real, and we wanted to get the best vocal performance out of him. Some of it came easy. Some of it didn't. "Walking Out On You" was hard to get. We actually ended up looping one of his choruses, because by the end of it… even though we were able to push out the boundaries, we were somewhat limited on time and still gigging between it as well, so we still had to get things done as quickly and efficiently as possible. "Walking Out On You" is actually the chorus, one take of the chorus that was the best, then we looped it and put it in on each chorus because he'd shot his voice by the end of the night.'

Bruce Bruce also had rather an innovative way of warming himself up to get the vocal tracks done, as the producer/drummer remembers. 'He used to go and scream at the walls, he'd go and stand in the corner,' he laughs. 'Bruce used to walk around, he'd get that look in his eyes, walk about and become somewhat distant and removed, and just go to the wall and go "AAAAAAAAAAAAA" in the corner! I wouldn't say it was hard, but I wouldn't say it was easy either: it was his first "big thing" and he just wanted to make the best vocal performances he could. And also, to become a member of the band, because it took him a while to actually integrate into the three-piece; we had our humour and all that kind of thing, he came in and we had to make it a four-piece. It takes time, you go to a new college, a new school, a new job – it takes you a while to integrate and become part and parcel of what the whole thing represents. And that was his opportunity. That album was his vehicle, "Alright I'm gonna show you that I am the lead singer of Samson." And he did. We [eventually] got great reviews for it.'

The plan was to release a single, 'Vice Versa', on 9 May 1980, but negotiations between Samson's management, Ramkup, and the label who were interested, EMI, had stalled. Added to a company-wide pressing plant strike causing further delays, this was a huge blow to Bruce and the boys, who could only sit back and watch as Iron Maiden's stock grew ever larger on the back of their astonishing chart placement of No.4 for their own full-length eponymous debut, a thrilling and rampant metal album of power. It had one foot in the Deep Purple camp, and – perhaps due more to the lyrics and vocal delivery of Maiden's cheeky-chap, street-urchin singer, Paul Di'Anno – more than a hint of punk rock about it, in attitude at least.

'[Life] monumentally changed for me. I love that first album,' Di'Anno remembers. 'Although someone should remix it, because the actual production is absolute dogshit. The songs were brilliant and have never been beaten as far as I'm concerned. I know I'm saying that because I was singing on it. But when Steve presented me with what was going to be on that first album – fuck me, it blew me away. The songs were absolutely fantastic: fast, complex with lots of time changes.'

As an aside, Tony Miles has an intriguing addition to the genesis of that first Maiden LP. 'The story goes – and it's only anecdotal – that he came in with probably his own ideas but most of the songs on the first Iron Maiden album have lyrics that were not written by Steve Harris, or anyone else in the band for that matter, but were written by Dennis Willcox. He is a bit cheesed off […] but it's a bit difficult [to prove] when you have got no hard physical evidence.

There is a lot of early Maiden history that has been, shall we say, "adapted", which is not uncommon [for long-standing bands].'

Still, while Maiden were pushing forward on all counts, frustrations were evident in the Samson camp, as Bruce Bruce commented in a *Sounds* interview. 'All kinds of things were apparently going to happen but none of them ever seemed to get off the ground. In the end, there was a gap of several months after we recorded *Head On* when we'd ground to a complete standstill, we were out of the press, out of everywhere. So we missed whatever sort of boat that happened to be sailing around at the time.' It was a touch-and-go decision as to which company the band would sign with. Thunderstick recalls that it was a management decision. 'EMI had promised to do an album deal,' he says, 'but it became, "we'll put a couple of singles out and see how they do". They were in the market for the band and we would have got the spot that Iron Maiden had. And it didn't happen because they wanted to put the singles out, and our management being the way they were, really quite rambunctious about the whole thing and said, "Well, stuff it, we'll go with Gem 'cause they wanna put an album out immediately, and finance the tour and make the film", so it was all over the music press at the time that we were stolen away from EMI. And part of the deal was this film, *Biceps of Steel*, 'cause they owned Gem, who were a film company and had made things like *Phantasm*, and they got hold of John Roseman and we were given scripts.' So activities resumed on 6 June 1980, with the release of the 'Vice Versa' single, now on Gem – a subsidiary of giants RCA – although there was a growing sense of unease between the band and their management.

'Bruce never signed a contract with Ramkup,' notes

Thunderstick. 'He was the only one that was never, ever actually officially signed. All three of us had put pen to paper and signed.' The frustration with the management situation, and the constant flux in which the band found themselves, almost had an incredibly dramatic effect on the group. Bruce himself was on the verge of walking away from it all in early May 1979. 'He said, "I've had enough of all this,"' says Thunderstick, 'because… we really were losing ground, and we were aware of that. It wasn't for the fact that we weren't very good, nothing to do with the performances or the music, if you'll forgive the pun we were still "head on" with all that. It was becoming quite obvious that we were losing ground. It was just something that happened, I can't remember the logistics of it but he said, "Fuck it, I've had enough – I'm going to go, we'll see how The Marquee gigs go." And of course they were great, and so he stayed and that was it.'

During June, they spent three long days recording that afore-mentioned curious short film at the Rainbow with none other than Julien Temple, director of both the Sex Pistols' film *Rock 'n' Roll Swindle* (1980), and later his own more objective *Filth and the Fury* (2000) on the same band. The short movie, *Biceps of Steel* (filmed in 1980, but released only in 2003) was financed by Gem/RCA and is a curious, and often hilarious fifteen-minute piece that is based loosely on the biblical Samson. Basically, the story goes as follows. Samson (*Biceps* version) is a roadie for the band who are busy strutting their stuff onstage. For some reason, the orange-jumpsuited security staff begin to beat up a headbanger. Samson steps in and saves the day, to universal acclaim. The baddies, being baddies, don't like it so hatch a plot for a harpie to seduce Samson, which she does so effectively that while he is in (presumably) postcoital slumber, she cuts off his hair, sapping his strength in the best traditions laid out in the biblical Book of Judges. Cue derision from the security guards in the next gig, upon whom Samson gets his own back by managing to tear down the Marshall stacks by the stage onto everyone's heads. It is, in short, pure nonsense (the tracks used in the film by the band onstage are 'Vice Versa' and 'Hard Times') but from another point of view the *Biceps of Steel* short is nothing short of a full-narrative video, the likes of which would become commonplace with the advent of MTV, which began broadcasting in 1981. Its running time of fifteen minutes was one minute longer, in fact, than Michael Jackson's much-vaunted *Thriller* piece some two years later – and anyway, *Thriller*'s weirdo zombies were much less convincing, and a hell of a lot less scary, than some of the crowd members in *Biceps*. The film was intended to be the preceding short to the Hazel O'Connor movie *Breaking Glass* (1980), an often difficult tale that follows the career of the main character, Kate, on her journey from nobody to pop star, and the long and painful descent into nervous breakdown. It is a piece of its time that both reflects the 'new wave' aesthetic in terms of music, but also the paranoia and growing sense of helplessness as Margaret Thatcher's Tory government began to make its presence felt in the UK.

The Samson character was played by Thunderstick, and he enjoyed the experience immensely. 'It was totally mad! Great for me, 'cause I was able to play Thunderstick and then the roadie! With a very dodgy moustache and wig. It was an ideal vehicle for me,' he continues, 'because I was Thunderstick anyway so they'd only have to do close-up shots of me doing rolls around the kit or whatever, and the rest of the time I was free to be able to play the roadie. When I'm in shot and there's Thunderstick at the back, the guy playing Thunderstick is my then brother-in-law, who later ended up being my bass player in the band, also called Thunderstick. He'd followed my career and he'd been there right from the start of Samson, so he was able to dress as Thunderstick and do the appropriate movements in "Vice Versa"."

The humour of the band was still intact, in their usual streetwise, piss-taking way. 'Originally they had Dana Gillespie lined up for the Delilah part, but it didn't happen, so this girl came out of no-where. In the bit where she's feeding me the grapes and what have you,' continues the Stick. 'You see the band in the background; it was great 'cause they were at the back, she comes and leans all over me and I sit up and look at her and all that kind of thing. And you can hear from the back – 'cause they were playing the music on the stage – you can hear them shouting, "He's got a hard on! He's got a stalk on him!" It was one, big, mad, few days, because it was kind of before the time of videos so it was an idea of doing a short film and it ended up going out as a B-film for *Breaking Glass*, I wish we'd gone and seen it, but we never did.'

Immediately following *Biceps of Steel*, Samson swiftly recorded 'Angel With a Machine Gun' – intended to be a B-side – and prepared for the release of the new LP, *Head On*, on 27 June. The album, great though it was, needed something of a boost sonically, which was provided by Tony Platt – fresh from engineering AC/DC's legendary album *Highway To Hell*.

'My managers were Zomba,' Platt recalled when I spoke to him, 'and Samson were published by Zomba. [The recorded tracks for *Head On* were sounding reasonably] okay, but hadn't been properly sorted out – I went and remixed the entire album and toughened it up a bit 'cause they hadn't had time to bring out the best in the songs.' And he did just that. Bruce's full-length long-playing debut is an album that blends a sense of classic rock while launching the unearthly screams of a major talent on to a wider world. Not just as a vocalist – his growing control and delivery was occasionally still prone to veering into Ian Gillan territory – but also as a collaborating and solo lyricist.

Take opener, 'Hard Times' for example. Musically, it's as classic melodic hard rock as you can get, albeit with a definite punky edge – think AC/DC meets The Skids – but lyrically, when Bruce Bruce sings of fighting and drinking, he could be referring to those rough old Sheffield pubs of his youth. Conversely, the references to going down, being head over heels and wanting to teach a lesson to whomever the song is addressed, have definite sexual overtones. 'Take it Like a Man' details the punishment of an errant lad; again, it would be tempting to read this as a song about S&M. The heavily sexual 'Vice Versa' displays the influence of the early 1970s more than any other on the LP, a mid-paced and taut Purple/Sabs-influenced workout that stands strong against anything recorded during this period. Paul Samson contributes a jerky solo here, while Thunderstick and Aylmer sound like they're having the time of their lives throughout. 'Manwatcher' is a forgettable, sexually charged mid-paced rocker. 'Too Close to Rock', meanwhile – with its lyrics referring to college, missing lectures and music as a career – is obviously resonant as a self-affirmation of Bruce's choice of lifestyle and work. The instrumental 'Thunderburst' follows, partly written by Thunderstick. It bears some similarity to 'The Ides of March', which was to appear on Maiden's second LP, *Killers*, the following year. It is, hence credited to Samson/Purkis/Aylmer/Bruce/S Harris.

'I came up with a drum pattern that did that constant rolling,' explained Thunderstick. 'I would have ideas and Steve [Harris] would then transpose that, because I don't play guitar. It was the same with Samson... I'm unable to pick a guitar up and show my idea, I have to sit there and go, "Duh-duh-duh-duh-duh – no, that's the wrong note" – and we'd go through it like that. So that's how it came about. And I had a drum pattern and I was trying to explain the chords to go down on the drum pattern, 'cause the whole thing goes around the drum pattern. I think we played it a couple of times with Iron Maiden as an opening track. Just an intro, it was a throwaway thing, not really a track.'

'Hammerhead' is pure Bruce, however – the lyrics dealing with the forging of Thor's hammer, Mjöllnir, and referencing ancient Norse tradition. The laid-back, Saxon-esque 'Hunted' – with its rather silly lyrics about nailing brains to trees – follows, before Bruce comes back to the fore with 'Take Me To Your Leader', an inventive, and very punky/psychedelic track that – on the surface – deals with flying saucers, astral plains and mother ships, but is also a call to arms. It happens to feature some of the most astonishing vocal performances of the LP. Bruce's incredible range is shown off to its full effect in the post-choruses, a statement of intent and a real marker for any other vocalists on the scene. It's a real head-banging, silly, busy showcase for every member of the band. One moment, Aylmer's romping up and down the neck, then Thunderstick rolls raucously round the kit; the next moment it's Paul's turn for a trademark fluid solo; and then it's Bruce taking the reins, working through the octaves magnificently. It's everything Samson could do at their very best – in one four-minute piece of music. As the album comes to a close with 'Walking Out On You'

– which veers between Hawkwind–like psychedelic rock, Beach Boys-esque backing harmonies, a tinge of the epic as purveyed by Queen, and AC/DC devilry – it's clear that, on form, this is an act with much to offer.

The extremely influential *Sounds* eulogised over it, Geoff Barton happy to note that the 'ace musicianship is an outstanding feature' of the album, something that had 'hardly been in abundance' over the course of the NWOBHM releases to that date. Impressed as he was with the band's musical qualities, he also conceded that this relatively accomplished (rather than balls-out raucous) approach was possibly one of the reasons that Samson had never 'been among the trendiest of the new metal bands'. Praising the vocals particularly, and comparing Bruce to Free's Paul Rodgers, Barton gave the LP a full five stars, and – perhaps surprisingly, given the album's classic rock feel – memorably called it 'more metal than the entire fleet of Russian battleships'. Gushing reviews from one of the most influential movers and shakers on the scene may be one thing, but when the chips are down, it takes a lot more than just good press to make a band a viable success. Although the group set out on tour to promote the release, they had largely booked the concerts themselves – Paul and Bruce sharing the workload – and despite the album peaking at a very creditable No.34 in the charts, all was not well between Samson and their management, Ramkup. The group were becoming disillusioned by what they perceived as a lack of support.

Rob Grain feels the management's relative inexperience – compared to someone like the revered Smallwood – exacerbated Samson's slowing momentum: 'It was because of that that the other bands started overtaking. Samson were getting much better reviews in the press. They had a huge stageshow, with big rigs and loads of pyrotechnics and stuff, and the very first feature in *Sounds* that Geoff Barton did was mostly about Samson's stageshow.'

That stageshow was being taken around the country when Samson made the decision to sack their management, on 4 July 1980 – Independence Day, which must surely have appealed to Bruce's sense of irony. Things had begun to unravel very, very quickly – just as, musically, Samson was starting to thrive – and in order to get back on track, something had to give. Ramkup were not to be shaken off quite so easily, however, taking matters to the high court and obtaining an injunction preventing Samson from working until the law courts' decision had been made. The immediate knock-on effect of this was that the final ten gigs in the *Head On* tour had to be necessarily cancelled. Although the band tried to keep it going from their own pockets, it was inevitable that the group themselves would ultimately suffer.

'At the time,' says Thunderstick, 'we had [another] manager [who had professional freelance connections with the band Gillan] saying that he'd take us on as a manager as long as we got out of the Ramkup deal. He turned round and said, "Look, if you can get out of the Ramkup deal, I'll look after you and I'll make sure you can get to the places that you wanna go to, and start working in Europe." And because we'd always had this big huge tie-up with Gillan all the time, we were using Kingsway studios, I was doing offshoot stuff with John and Bernie, gigs at the Music Machine and The Marquee, and there'd always been this inter-band tie-up… it was a logical thing for us to do.

'This was the tour, where the routing was all over the place. Aberdeen one day and Cornwall the next! It was literally like that, it was unbelievable. At the beginning of the tour [the potential new manager said], "I can't do anything; it's gotta be down to you guys." So we wrote an official letter to our management company.' The consequences of this legal disagreement were severe for both the band's profile and – literally – their wallets. 'We were all absolutely piss-poor, absolutely skint, we had no money whatsoever. We were doing Radio 1 interviews with Tommy Vance and the like, and he would say, "The band's doing really good, it's really progressing" and this, that and the other, and literally we didn't have ten pence in our pockets. But it was awful: we started the tour with all the accoutrements you take with you and we finished it out of the back of a local hired transit, with a local PA, somewhere up in Scotland. By that time, we were well and truly losing ground – I mean, the fans were promised the big show and the cage and the pyros and all they got was four guys that by this time were feeling rather dejected.'

As Rob Grain, Samson's tour manager and confidante, puts it, 'Whilst all this was going on, all the other bands were still playing, touring, building up a following and Samson, to all effects, were defunct.' So, ultimately, there was only one thing for it, as Paul Samson himself acknowledged. 'When it was discovered that it was us who were in breach of contract,' he said, 'we were all threatened with bankruptcy… we had no option but to go back to Ramkup.' When a new Heads of Agreement was drawn up, Ramkup then paid the band back-pay retainer wages. In theory, the financial difficulties were over and Samson could plough on. The band had played two major live events, headlining Lowestoft's Norfolk Festival and joining the legendary 1980 bill at Reading Festival on 24 August, alongside headliners Whitesnake, UFO, Sheffield's

Def Leppard, Wishbone Ash and a confident and fabulous, speedily rising Iron Maiden. It was also one of only a handful of occasions that Thunderstick's expensive cage was used – most of the time it had been too big to fit onstage (he also played inside it in *Biceps of Steel*). The two gigs, however, were a rare pair of happy, sun-soaked moments amid a dark time for the band – although Bruce was bullish enough to see a light at the end of the tunnel, telling *Sounds* that, 'as long as you've got something really good to offer and you've got people behind you who believe in you and are willing to give you support, then you can't fail to win through in the end. And Samson will win through, mark my words.'

The management situation may not have helped the band's gigging career to any appreciable amount, but one knock-on effect was that they'd had plenty of time twiddling their thumbs while off the road to come up with a new set of tracks – approaching an album's worth, in fact. And it was Tony Platt to whom they turned to work on the new material. Platt had just completed work with Iron Maiden, who'd curiously chosen to agree to follow up their Judas Priest tours and chart positions (their first two singles, 'Running Free' and 'Sanctuary' had got to No.44 and No.29 respectively) with a cover version of a song that – let's face it – was hardly a feminist anthem, a rather dunderheaded macho rocker entitled 'Women in Uniform'. It was an old Skyhooks number, which had previously been released by that Australian band down under, some two years earlier. Platt recalls the events leading up to his working with Maiden on that track. 'The only reason I was doing that was because [Maiden's original choice] Martin Birch was finishing off the Whitesnake album,' says the producer, who has also worked with Bob Marley and Cheap Trick. 'They had to make this single, and Martin wasn't available. They were running out of time rapidly and I happened to have time spare so I said, "I'll go and do it if you want." They sort of got talked into [recording that track]. I feel somewhat sympathetic in that respect.'

'Women in Uniform' is widely regarded as being a rare error of judgement from Iron Maiden. Admirably, perhaps, they'd not wanted to mine their debut LP for another single – but they'd not wanted to dive into the material earmarked for the follow-up album, either. Still, the band themselves went with the idea, not least because Platt at that time was being considered for their second album, and it seemed an ideal opportunity to suss out each other's modus operandi. 'I kind of started this whole thinking process that having a singer who had a higher range would be a good idea,' he says. 'At the time, I'd just started to work with Samson, and one of the things about them was that the way the songs were was a good sound picture. And obviously, coming off the back of working with AC/DC, that was fairly prominent in my mind as well – as an arrangement and production technique.'

But Steve Harris was not impressed with the results. The mixes, he felt, were weak and commercial compared to the original sound the band had attained in the studio. So when Martin Birch became available, Maiden started a relationship with the Deep Purple/Black Sabbath producer that lasted many glorious years for all concerned. These days, Platt is philosophical about 'Women in Uniform', noting that, 'On one hand, it's been quite good because it's earned me a bit of money over the years – on the other hand I got a pasting from Iron Maiden.'

Back in 1980, Samson and Platt began to chat about how the new material might shape up in the studio sessions for the forthcoming album, which would eventually be called *Shock Tactics*. The producer found that he immediately gained a rapport with the band as musicians, and understood their context within the hard rock and heavy metal scene of the time.

'The total idol that Paul Samson had was Hendrix,' notes Platt. 'So he really came from that blues/rock side of the feeling. In that respect, Samson were a much more stripped-down band than Maiden, and it has to be said, actually probably more adept musically; then again they were competing in exactly the same arena, so there was no point Samson trying to do exactly the same thing that Iron Maiden did. *Shock Tactics* had some serious pre-production; we really got stuck into that. The whole idea was to really, really get the songs up to scratch.' The term 'pre-production' refers to chatting about the songs, rehearsing them, playing with different arrangement ideas experimenting and refining how the final versions might be recorded when the band gets to the studio.

The feeling was that, at least musically, Samson were moving forward, although it all could have ended in disaster, according to Platt. 'We did all the pre-production in Easyhire Studios, and it was fantastic. It was crazy, right from the start, the whole thing. We were recording stuff, fine-tuning the songs and deciding what we were going to do, that sort of thing, until one day we all started feeling a bit weird and drowsy and we discovered that the room was being heated by gas heaters – one of which was not actually burning the gas which was going into the room. Either that, or the exhaust was blowing into the room – either way, we all started to feel heady. When we went outside and the fresh air hit us we realised that there was something decidedly untoward going on. It was wintertime, so you had to have heaters on 'cause it was bloody freezing!'

The year 1980 began to draw to a weary and confused close for the band, with a small stop-off for a studio session during which Bruce dubbed his vocals onto the master tracks for *Survivors*, the intent being to release that as a free limited-edition album as an extra bonus with the forthcoming new release (in the end, the idea was shelved). Remarkable things also happened when the band finally began to gig again. However, in contrast to Bruce and the boys' avowed wish to tour Europe to promote *Head On*, they found that they had been booked by Ramkup as support act on Uriah Heep's own tour of the UK, playing venues that Samson had headlined in their own right merely months earlier. For many involved, this seemed unwise, as Rob Grain recalls. 'There were arguments between the band and the management all the way through. In the end, it all went too far: *Head On* was out, *Shock Tactics* was just about to [be recorded] and what should have been a headlining British tour to support the album became a support tour to Uriah Heep – who weren't particularly pulling people at the time. The line-up [was weak].'

'It was weird,' says Thunderstick, with a sigh, 'because all the progress we'd made headlining on our own... I didn't know what was happening and I didn't get involved with decisions like that. But we needed to go and do another tour, and really by this time we should have been hitting Europe. That's when we lost ground – and it was a dramatic loss of ground. Uriah Heep was a great tour; it was playing places that we'd played in our own right, headlining a few months before, hence the reason we felt we were losing ground because we were opening for them. It was a three-band package, Spider opening the show, Samson in the middle and Uriah Heep closing it. There were a few more punters there, but not really that many, not really. We were still playing to a real hardcore Samson audience every night. Uriah Heep treated us with a lot of respect and Nick was a great guy to be around with his anecdotes and what have you, because he'd been there, done it and got the T-shirt quite a few times. But we lost out on making progress.'

A year – and a decade – that had begun, with Samson rubbing shoulders with many of the aspiring acts of the NWOBHM, had ended in confusion, frustration and depression. While Bruce was learning valuable lessons about the vagaries of the music industry, they were lessons learnt at a high cost – namely, and perhaps most significantly, watching his band's main rivals, Iron Maiden, surge ahead of the pack and become the 'Most Likely to Happen'. Vocally, and as a writer, Bruce Bruce had begun to mature, though, and while 1980 had descended into something of a fug, with sessions scheduled during January to record a new album, and the band finally being free to extricate themselves from their management contract in February 1981 in accord with the high court judgement, there was yet much to look forward to. It seemed quite possible their collective hair was not yet fully shorn, after all.

CHAPTER 6

SHOCK
TACTICS

The year 1981 began with Samson shutting themselves away from management problems and outside influences. They were ensconced at Battery Studios in West London, with a producer who was genuinely enthusiastic for their music. January promised to be a month that reaffirmed the band's status as musicians. Regardless of all the hassle going on elsewhere in their chaotic career, there was one place where the band still had control – and that was in the recording studios.

Producer Tony Platt recalls the sessions with a great deal of fondness. 'The sessions were in the strange Battery Studio Two, which ceased to exist shortly after!' he says with a chuckle. 'It was downstairs in the building that became the main Zomba building, and in order to get to the control room, you had to go through the studios, so once everybody was playing you couldn't get in and out of the control room. By the time we got to the end of those sessions, they were refurbishing all the upper floors, so the building was almost completely deserted a lot of the time.' Leading, no doubt, to less distractions from the task in hand – namely, making the definitive Samson album. *Head On* had been written, in part, while the group were getting to know each other as musicians and people, but by the time it had come to the end of 1980, the enforced inactivity of the previous months had led to a verdant period in terms of songwriting. The musicians had worked together for long enough to know each other's strengths – and weaknesses – and as a result of the time they'd had spare, thanks partly to the court case, they'd also had a significant time to work on the songs and their sound.

'We had a really, really good time making that album,' says Platt. 'A *fantastic* time – and we had some riotous, riotous nights in the studio. We worked bloody long and hard on that album, we really did.'

Famously, Iron Maiden were concurrently working in a nearby studio on their own new album, and the paths of the bands occasionally crossed. At the time, there was also a growing amount of rivalry between the two camps, although in the case of Samson it was confined largely to their 'cuttings wall', as Platt explains. 'There was huge amounts of competition between the [bands], of course. Maiden were in the other studio, so there was all the usual banter going backwards and forwards. All the way through the session there were these big sheets of paper on the wall and we used to cut bits and pieces out of magazines and newspaper captions. And this collage grew over the period of making the record. We'd got all sorts of comments about Maiden stuck on the wall, and somebody told us they'd done the same about Samson on their wall. Certainly from the Samson side it was quite friendly!'

'We nearly got chucked out of that studio,' says Thunderstick with a laugh, 'because Bruce let a powder fire extinguisher off in that studio as well. It used to be his thing – it went everywhere. You can imagine a powder fire extinguisher inside a recording studio! Fortunately, it was not in the control room, it was in the actual studio but – Jesus – it was all in the piano and everything was covered in white.'

'There was [also] Bruce's girlfriend Jane,' continues Platt, 'who, 'cause nobody had much money, she would turn up every night with a few beers, a load of Chinese food, something like that – and keep the sessions going quite well. It was quite rock 'n' roll and lots of fun.' And you can undoubtedly hear the relaxed atmosphere in the recordings. The irony of *Shock Tactics* is that it is a blaster of an album, performed brilliantly by a group totally at ease with the material and each other. The events that were to follow also make it one of the great lost opportunities of its era. But at the time, the focus was firmly on enjoying bringing the rock, and creating perhaps one of the more bizarre (and rare) bootlegs that is somewhere in existence.

'I still have a cassette that Paul made of all sorts of stupid outtakes of those sessions. Bruce probably still has one as well, 'cause Paul made a copy for everybody,' continues Platt. 'That started because somebody had left two sweets on the edge of the desk. I was the mug, and one day I asked, "Whose are these, then?" and Bruce, or Paul, said, "Yeah, they're mine, you can have one if you want." So I said, "Thanks," and ate one. Then I realised that everybody was sniggering and I said, "What the fuck's this, then? What's wrong with them?" and they said, "Well, they're fart sweets." We all said. "Nah that's impossible." And then around ten minutes later we discovered that they were in fact incredibly effective – which meant that everybody then had them. Everybody was then in the studio letting fly with these *amazing* farts. So we stuck a microphone up and hotwired it straight into one of the tape machines – and all the way through the day you'd be able to see somebody, all of a sudden break off halfway through a conversation, run across, set the tape machine up and let fly into this microphone. You can hear all the background stuff of people talking and going, "Oh no!" and all that sort of stuff. That's the "fart tape". There were the phrases that used to go through the session, everything that was bad was, "Really Dad's"… "That's really Dad's, that!" All these phrases that went on, it was a very happy album to make, we had a lot of fun.'

From the opening chords of the album's first track, 'Riding With the Angels', it's evident that this is a band as tight and together as anyone could hope. To open the LP with a cover version is perhaps a surprise, but the choice of track – which Samson turn into an anthemic, dynamic monster – is a great one. It sets down a huge marker as to the quality of what is to follow; stomping backbeats, great guitar playing and vocals that range from gravelly to soaring when the mood demands it. '["Riding" was suggested by] my manager, Ralph Simon, who was their publisher,' explains Platt. 'I said it would be good if we got something in there that had a little bit more of a singles-y vibe to it, and this song came up. Being a Russ Ballard song we thought, "That's got a very good chance." This is the unfortunate thing. There was the usual thing from the band, "Why do we have to do someone else's song?" We talked very long about whether we could do something with it. But once we decided to do it, everyone got in there and gave it a bloody good seeing to! And we worked very hard on it. I think we came up with a very, very good version of that song.' In fact, Samson's version of 'Riding With the Angels' was such a success that Ballard himself subsequently sent a congratulatory telegram to the band after hearing it.

Following 'Riding' is the galloping, lead-heavy 'Earth Mother', another strong track, beautifully recorded and with melodic feedback and layered guitars introducing a Dickinson vocal streets ahead of anything he'd previously recorded. Salacious and eyebrow-raising, screaming and flailing, it is the sound of a man growing into his voice in every sense. The riff-tastic 'Nice Girl' keeps the pace up – a track inspired, said Bruce, by sympathy for 'prostitutes, with the fact that women have to go to these lengths to earn a living and it's also about their clients. These blokes who don't get on with their wives or whatever so they settle for a ten-minute wife, a ten-minute hypocrisy.' 'Bloodlust' features one of the great guitar performances of Paul Samson's career; always controlled, incredibly tight, he's able to play with harmonics and control his tone in a way that lesser guitarists could only dream of. Bruce, meanwhile, uses the space atop the sparse licks to layer squeals and squalling vocal lines full of doomy dread, revelling in the darkness – the personality of the song comes out with an aplomb that speaks volumes of the time they'd spent in pre-production.

More sleaze follows on the insistent 'Go To Hell', with another great solo, before Thunderstick's rain-dance tom-toms introduce the singalong 'Bright Lights', a classic early 1970s-style piece of melodic blues-rock – complete with plenty of space for guitar histrionics – that was so close to Paul Samson's musical heart.

Bruce's lyrics and delivery were developing to a point where he could step into character at will, 'Once Bitten' showcasing a fictional character firmly in accusative/self-destructive mode. You can almost feel the fingers being pointed – a track with the hefty simplicity of Motörhead, with whom, of course, Samson share musical roots in many ways. 'Grime Crime', according to Bruce, 'is about one night when, recently girlfriend-less, I went down to The Music Machine at two in the morning, got rather drunk and spotted this apparition in the corner which, in the half light, looked quite attractive. By the time I got home, though, she wasn't as attractive what with the streetlights and everything but I – ahem – didn't have any option because she said that unless I did the honours, she was going to scream and call the police.'

In one sense, the last track on the album is the most prescient of the lot, given what was later to happen. The lyrics of 'Communion' mark it out as an end-of-life, end-of-career, homeward-looking piece of work; it surges into an epic, swirling musical soundscape that speaks of freedom and breaking out, resting with peace and searching for contentment. It's a remarkably expansive and evocative work, full of regret, passion and hope for the future. The only real failing the track has is fade-out after a mere six-and-a-half minutes. To go from the stomping statement of intent 'Riding With the Angels' through to the dénouement of 'Communion' shows a real understanding of the narrative power an album can have, placing *Shock Tactics* as one of the greatest albums of 1981.

Surprisingly perhaps, Thunderstick himself enjoyed the freedom of the previous LP more, as did the guitarist and driving force behind the band. 'Paul didn't like it as an album,' reveals the drummer. 'He thought that his playing had been suppressed quite a bit, he didn't like the guitar tone that Tony got. It was never really kind of rated as his favourite album. I think, out of the two, *Head On* is my favourite album because of the fluidity of it and the ability to be able to let yourself go and create in the studio, whereas *Shock Tactics* was less of a creative experience, it was more of a workload, if you like. In terms of my own playing, the real Thunderstick is on *Head On,* but *Shock Tactics* taught me so much – in as much as by the time I eventually arrived in the band Thunderstick, I was actually able to use the knowledge that I'd got from both. I was too Keith Moon in *Head On* and too Simon Kirke in *Shock Tactics*, so I needed to kind of fit somewhere between the two, pull out the mad bits when I need to and [for] the rest of it, keep it regimental. So it's a learning process and you learn as you go along.'

It was an album that was absolutely instrumental in the development of the singing style and vocal control of Bruce Dickinson, a vital part of the continuing learning process he was going through. 'Bruce has gone on record a couple of times saying he learned a lot about singing during that period,' says Tony Platt, 'and I think his voice developed quite dramatically during that period of time. He stopped shouting and he really became an excellent singer.' Indeed, twenty-four years later, Bruce was to credit Platt's influence on his style, during an interview with *Grantland.* 'Tony got me to sing way out of what was my natural range,' he revealed. 'I actually hated it, but everybody else who heard the record loved it and said, "Wow, your voice sounds so much better." I'm like, "But I hate that voice. That's not me." And then I realized that actually, what I hated about the voice was it actually was me, and I just didn't know how to reproduce that voice reliably.' He would belt out the numbers until he lost his voice, before he had a word with himself: 'I went, "Well, you schmuck, you spent all this time doing breathing exercises and learning all this technique and da da da da da da da. What do you think you learned all that technique for? Why don't you learn to copy yourself?"'

Having recorded an LP of such a high standard, it was perhaps inevitable that something was going to have to give. The news came through that Gem, the record company who were to release *Shock Tactics*, was going to the wall, thus taking away any potential cash for touring support. Secondly, even as Samson were finally freed from their Ramkup management contract and were auditioning at the Marquee for potential new management, it was going to cost the band to extricate themselves from their old contract, as Rob Grain explains. 'In the end there was the final court case and the only way Samson could get out of the management contract was for the management to retain the rights of the first three albums. So at the end of it Samson came out of the management deal but they didn't own *Survivors, Head On* or *Shock Tactics*.'

It was another blow to the band as a whole, but very nearly had unfortunate repercussions for Samson. During March 1981, Paul Bruce Dickinson decided to shake off his double-B persona, hooking up with an old friend of his by the name of Stuart Smith, to whom he'd been introduced after a concert at The Marquee the previous year, while Samson's future once more looked shaky as a band. 'At the time he was very dissatisfied with Samson, simply because I don't think they had a record deal,' Smith told me. 'Bruce was a very big Deep Purple fan and of course I was as well, so we started getting together, really just to hang out at the time, and then eventually we ended up writing some material together and we got a bunch of people together and we went into a studio and rehearsed this stuff, just sort of laid it down on cassette. And it was really good, it was great stuff. I mean Bruce's voice, of course, has always been incredible. He was very creative as well. I think the first song we wrote was "Rosetta".

'We just got together with some people and just played,' he continues, 'I can't even remember who we had playing with us at the time. But I do remember Bruce really well because it was really him and I who got these people together. But it was great, it could have done something if we'd had a chance to develop it.'

'Stuart and I spent some time attempting to get a band together,' recalls Steve Jones, 'and the three of us got together in a basement flat – I can't recall whether it was Bruce's or Stuart's abode. Anyhow, we had a small practice amp for Stuart, and Bruce sang without amplification. And they threw together "Rozetta" [sic] – I am sure I have a very short mono recording of it somewhere in my loft.'

At the time, of course, it was just two mates playing music together for the sheer fun of it, but had circumstances been different, could the project have *really* got somewhere? 'It could have,' acknowledges Smith with a smile. '[Because] you knew whatever Bruce was involved in it was going to do something. I mean, he just had so much drive and so much energy. And so did I, and we got on really well, we were great friends and it could have gone further. But in those days we were both just trying to survive, living around London, musicians hanging out trying to make it happen, hanging out down The Marquee and The Ship. You know, we were all young, we didn't have real jobs, doing the couch tour a lot of the time. I do remember that as a joke for my birthday he gave me a cheque – he was with the Midland Bank – and he gave me a cheque for a million pounds. I should probably try and cash it now, the money's probably in the account!'

Smith and Dickinson's project was going so well that they decided to try and drum up a little publicity for themselves, so they went to Jennie Halsall, PR extraordinaire, for advice. It was a bad move for Stuart's growing project, but ultimately very good for Bruce's 'main' band of the time. 'I took Bruce down to meet Jennie because I wanted to tell her that we were going to try and get this project together,' Stuart recalls. 'Bruce was dissatisfied [with Samson at the time] and he felt that they should have a record deal – which they rightly should – certainly with Bruce fronting the band, who was great even back them. Which is I think why he tried to take the reins and got Jennie in to try and do publicity for the band. And I think she saw a going concern with Samson, and offered her PR services, and that was it. Basically, I guess Bruce thought that they [Samson] could possibly do something if they could get some good publicity – Jennie was really surprised that they didn't have a deal – I think it was about three weeks later that they suddenly did have a deal. It was great for Bruce and Samson, of course, but it basically put an end to what we were doing. But you know, we carried on hanging out during our time in London. Great singer, and a really, really smart intelligent guy. He was always really bright; I think he'd just got out of university at the time we originally met and he was really young. And even back then he was talking about if he makes it he was going to get a swimming pool with heat exchangers in and all this kind of thing. Really bright guy, great sense of humour, we got on really well.'

RCA, who were the sister company of the struggling record label Gem, were the lucky chaps to pick up on Samson's stunning new music, and 'Riding With the Angels' hit the charts in May, peaking at No.54. *Shock Tactics,* also, was finally released to coincide with a major tour of the UK in June 1981. *Sounds* gave the LP the thumbs-up with a four-star rating; that magazine's reviewer, Robbi Millar, called it – rather verbosely, but also pertinently – 'a monolithic masterpiece of musical might… and subtle too!' (unlike the alliteration, possibly). *Record Mirror* also loved it, Malcolm Dome going one better and giving the effort the full five marks available.

The tour, part one of which began at the Forde Green Hotel in Leeds on 11 June 1981, had been largely booked by Paul and Bruce, and some of the dates were packed tightly – but not necessarily with an eye on the geographical implications. It was immediately dubbed 'Don't Give a Fuck About the Petrol Bill Tour', thanks to the often bizarre schedule and often tortuous distances between gigs as the band criss-crossed the country day after day. They'd also gained a new manager at this stage, one Terry McClellan – coincidentally, the owner of Easyhire Studios. Unfortunately, his tenure was to turn out to be rather a brief one.

Samson were as prolific as ever, writing and demoing more tracks in the run-up to the June dates. 'Turn Out the Lights', 'Firing Line' and 'Red Skies' continued the musical momentum that the band had built up. But things, as ever, were not straightforward in the hallowed halls of Samson. Thunderstick's cage was too big for most of the venues – which turned out to be a symptom of a rather deeper malaise, and one that Neal Kay, for one, had sensed two years previously. 'The Samson shows were overblown,' declares the larger-than-life DJ. 'They were completely and utterly overblown and the press reported them in a variety of overblown ways. Because no one knew what the hell Paul was trying to sell. Was he selling fireworks, or was he selling music? His ability was never questioned, and quite rightly, because he was a good guitar player. [But] the roots were wrong and the trouble was that Bruce, in my view, never could really develop the horsepower and performance and use his ability to the full when he was singing the wrong sort of songs. Bruce, in actual fact, was more powerful than Samson could ever have been. It was the wrong vehicle for him, but it did put him in the right place at the right time.'

Thunderstick's love for the more theatrical side of performance was beginning to cause a small problem. Bruce and Paul, for all their own love of stage histrionics – and Paul's own fixation on pyrotechnics over the previous two years – were largely pulling in the other direction. The album they'd just released was a ballsy, brilliant success and the music was strong enough to stand or fall on its own merits. The band were strong and tight enough to deliver a stunning set, Chris Aylmer's rock-steady bass playing enabling the rest of the band to float round the rhythm with freedom and groove. Speaking to *Record Mirror* at the time, Bruce said that the band wanted to attain the reputation of being an outfit who were, 'visually great because of what we do onstage, not because of what the stage does to us. Besides, if I had to sing with lungfuls of smoke and bangs blowing me eardrums in every night, I'd be a wreck inside two weeks.'

Thunderstick recalls that, 'Bruce and Paul were quite emphatic at the time that it was to become more of a bluesy, "We are serious", Blackfoot type of band. I was into heroes that I'm still into now, like Alice Cooper. I love The Tubes – anybody that put a lot of money back into the show and gave the audience what they wanted. Look at Iron Maiden: people go to see the shows when

SHOCK TACTICS

they go to see Iron Maiden, they wanna see the Eddie [character], and they wanna see the [big stageshow and props], whereas Paul was dead against that… other bands were gaining on us at the time and overtaking us, [and] he thought that it was probably due to the fact that [the character of] Thunderstick was holding it back, basically.

'I decided I'd had enough because we were then squabbling amongst ourselves, they wanted to go in a much bluesier direction,' he continues. 'In fact, the last Marquee gig I ever did with them I felt [isolated] because they weren't gonna dress up anymore and Bruce wanted to do the jeans and T-shirts things and said, "Fuck all this theatrical thing, I'm sick and tired of it, it's a pain in the arse." Rather than [Thunderstick] being a motif for the band and a selling point for the band, it was actually holding it back. By that time I wanted to take it in even more of a theatrical direction, so we decided to part company and I went [on to start] up [my new band] Thunderstick.' His final gig with Samson in this incarnation was on 8 July 1981, at Wigan Pier.

Samson's great rivals, Iron Maiden, were – on the face of it – forging ahead at a thunderous pace. On the back of their stunning 1980 debut album, the band had undertaken another reshuffle. Guitarist Dennis Stratton had been replaced by one Adrian Smith, a long-time mate of Maiden's other six-string player, Dave Murray, continuing an instantly recognisable twin-guitar attack that meshed together beautifully. After the 'Women in Uniform' single, the band had been out on the road ripping it up left, right and centre, and followed their debut up with the excellent 1981 album, *Killers*, although the press reaction was noticeably more muted this time around. Paul Di'Anno recalls that he wasn't wholly into the new LP: 'We'd gone upmarket a bit, I suppose. Well-known producer in Martin Birch, more money behind it, stuff like that. I thought the songs were crap. I only wrote "Killers" and for me the whole mood set in and I started losing interest, to be honest with you. The album is a great album, but it doesn't have the bite of that first one, which really done it for me. I talk to peers all around the world, like Metallica grew up on it and stuff, and those first two albums were pivotal in their careers. So we done something good!'

Undoubtedly, Di'Anno has all the attributes of a great frontman: cocky, confident, cheeky and with a sharp tongue and appetite for life that could be both a blessing and a curse, as Neal Kay recalls. 'Paul was like a kid let loose in a chocolate factory; his eyes were bigger than his stomach,' he says with a chuckle. 'I remember in Newcastle, at the Mayfair where we played on tour [during 1980]. Paul had a penchant for wearing a mod hat, a pork pie hat, and he'd go out on stage in it – which annoyed Steve no end, anyway. This is not the way a rock band portrays itself! In the middle of Newcastle-land, in a late set, about half-eleven at night, Paul rolls out onstage and then announces to the world that West Ham are gonna knock the shit out of Newcastle. That did it! In one gig we did, I think it was Mansfield, Paul lost his voice and couldn't sing – Steve did the best he could with the vocals… and promised everyone the show would go back there when the vocalist had recovered. Clive Burr got very sick on that tour; he had a temperature and everything and was throwing up while he played. They carried him behind the kit, gave him a bucket to throw up in, and as soon as the gig was finished, back to bed he went. It was a tour for heroes; it was a time for real men. It was the forging of the legend of rock 'n' roll. I'm proud to have been there to have seen it.'

SHOCK TACTICS

If there was one thing that Harris insisted upon within Team Maiden, it was that – no matter what happened the rest of the time – when the time came for the band to take care of business, they had to deliver. Anything that jeopardised their stage performance was an absolute no-no. As 1981 rolled on, Paul Di'Anno began to lose his voice regularly, as well as increasing the intake of his preferred recreational fuels. Maiden had gone through so much under Steve Harris's guiding hand over the years, and any unpredictable behaviour that threatened to destabilise them as they stood on the cusp of *really* making a go of matters in the music industry was anathema to their ideals and ambitions.

'It was all a little bit weird for me,' Di'Anno says these days. 'It seemed to have lost the magic. It was down to the music and me being too stupid to do too much about it! I'd messed around in punk bands before Maiden, but this was the first real thing I'd ever done. No matter what I said, nobody listened, so I said "fuck it" and became increasingly unhappy in there. And you turn to "other things" for amusement, don't you? I was really fed up.'

By the early autumn of 1981, Paul Di'Anno was out of Iron Maiden – something that was kept rather quiet; the press had little inkling as yet. But he'd wrung as much of a good time out of it as he could. 'Every gig was a brilliant experience and a great night for me to show off to everyone and fuck and get blowjobs from as many birds as was possible,' explained the rampant Di'Anno to *Classic Rock Revisited*. 'Steve would be planning world domination and putting the fifteen pounds that were made at some shows towards the next show while I was trying to get as many birds' names in my little dirty black book as possible.' And as Maiden's stock rose, so did the demands on the singer. 'At that age, I wasn't also handling things as well as the other guys who were older than me. One minute I was a kid off the street and the next I was expected to handle things like it was sliced bread. Needless to say, I started drinking a lot and I must've done half of Peru up my nose. I screwed up… I wasn't happy, both with the [*Killers*] album and myself and I really didn't wanna be there. And if you can't give one thousand per cent to a band like Iron Maiden, the best thing to do is get the fuck out. I just walked in and told them how I felt and walked away.' The full story in Paul's own words was to later come out in his autobiography, entitled *The Beast*.

Tony Miles, whose band Gibraltar briefly featured Dennis Willcox, Di'Anno's predecessor in Maiden, said that when Di'Anno departed it was, 'no surprise'. 'We'd heard the tales, he was a difficult guy, he was on the booze, on the drugs, et cetera.'

Samson, meanwhile, had signed a talented new drummer, Mel Gaynor, to replace Thunderstick, and were busy bedding him in for their high-profile appearance at the Reading Festival. Samson took the stage at Reading on 29 August 1981 – and absolutely ripped the place apart. Coincidentally, the headliners that year were none other than Gillan. Mel Gaynor's immense talent was a massive fillip for the band, whose RCA contract was about to expire. The record labels knew it, having seen what Samson were capable of on the *Shock Tactics* album. The Reading set – which was recorded for posterity by the BBC's *Friday Rock Show*, and included another new track, 'Gravy Train' – was an affirmation that this was a band worth investing in. From the new drummer to the steady bassist, the fluid and often fast-fretted guitarist and the remarkable singer, every element was at last surely in place. It has been mooted that it was the sound of a group who were one hit single away from a breakthrough. The Reading performance was subsequently released as an album some nine years later, and the energy and belief emanating from the band is spot on. From the nine-minute 'Walking Out On You', to a near-incendiary '... Angels', it's a set that rarely dips from its fizzing rock zenith. It's not without humour, either: when Bruce introduces Mel Gaynor, he draws attention to the fact that, although he is in fact Samson's drummer, Gaynor has nothing on his head or obscuring his face. But the greatest cheers, and they are many, are reserved for Paul Samson. One can only imagine how that must have felt for the guitarist after so many years of near-misses and frustrations.

When an exhausted but hyped-up Bruce Bruce, Chris Aylmer, Mel Gaynor and Paul Samson came offstage, shook hands and parted ways for a much-needed two-week break, Samson's stock was once again rising high. They were back from the brink once more, and the record companies were lining up at last.

CHAPTER 7

A VOYAGE BEGINS

'**W**ith any band, you gotta try and get as many components right as you can,' says Tony Platt. 'Circumstances did prevail against Samson; some were beyond their control and some totally within their control. Paul was a difficult bloke, in a lot of respects. I told him on many different occasions that he had a very negative attitude to things. He tended to take the viewpoint that he was being prevailed against, rather than take the viewpoint, "Well, fuck the bastards, I'm gonna get on with it," you know? The problem in any circumstance like that is that you can see that people do have a point. You can see that for some people it gets tiresome, banging your head against the same brick wall week after week and month after month.'

Samson had, in a very real way, both predated and outlasted the NWOBHM. Come their triumphant appearance at Reading 1981, they'd closed the chapter on rather a strange period in music.

Although the band were rightly credited as being a force in hard rock during 1977–1981, there was always something about them that didn't ring true alongside contemporaries such as Saxon, Def Leppard, Angel Witch and Iron Maiden. Perhaps it was the classic rock approach. *Shock Tactics* has certainly stood the test of time, without question, and is in a sense timeless; *Head On* also, albeit a little less so. But the Bandwagon crowd, in particular, weren't hugely enamoured of their style.

One oft-referenced gig that was sadly memorable for all the wrong reasons saw Samson leave the stage at The Music Machine to total silence from what was a packed crowd, prompting a row between Paul and Neal Kay, who had been previously good buddies. 'Samson had top slot on the bill, with Iron Maiden under them,' says the DJ with a sigh. 'But Maiden took the stage and basically wiped out anything and anybody with their honesty, their music and their delivery. When Paul Samson took the stage, people were polite enough but he interspersed his whole old-fashioned style set with explosions and pyrotechnics and all sorts of bizarre things; and at the end of the set not one person clapped. Not one.' After the unfortunate gig, which took place in 1980, Paul confronted Neal and accused him of somehow manipulating the audience so they would show no response. Kay replied in the negative. '[I told him] "You stand or fall on your own merits, mate, and it's your music they don't like. It's not that they don't like your playing; they admire you as a guitarist, but you ain't going where they wanna go and Iron Maiden are." That was the problem and he couldn't see it.

'Maiden reminded me of Slade,' Kay continues. 'I don't mean musically, but Noddy Holder's prime directive is "No Mercy and

No Prisoners". If you've ever stood twenty feet from Slade and watched them do a show, it's one [song] straight into another. There's no fucking around, no long verbals; in those days there wasn't much chat. Maiden were in for the kill, they played their set like I played records, one after the other, bang! And the way Steve and the boys went at it was kinda like that. You were awake, you were being assaulted – visually and by audio. And Slade were like that, completely. They mesmerised me and at Christmas they just shot on stage and killed people. They were so damned good. So Slade were never that pop group you see on *Top of the Pops* all the time, they were a *fucking rock 'n' roll killing machine*, and so were Iron Maiden.'

Samson's performance was being watched with interest by other bands, though. 'Steve and Maiden were working under them. I was right there in the middle as well and we could all see what Bruce could do,' concludes Kay. 'I remember Steve coming up to me one night and turning round and saying, "What do you think of Bruce?" and I think I said something like, "I'm non-committal, Steve, because I think he's with the wrong band." And Steve said to me, "I think he's an *animal!*" Those were his words.' Animal or not, perhaps the problem was the dynamic within the band Samson, none of whom were prepared to fade into the background. 'Bruce was a major showman,' Tony Platt says. 'The one thing that never settled with me was the hooded drummer, which I always thought was a bit stupid. They should've let Bruce be the showman all the way, all the time – but, then, it was Paul's band.'

One of the major aces that Iron Maiden had up their sleeve was their management: Rod Smallwood was an innovative and dynamic character who meshed in with the band's (and ultimately,

Steve Harris's) vision. While Samson were floundering from court case to injunction, booking gigs themselves or supporting unsuitable bands, Maiden were larging it round Europe setting fire to audiences onstage and rampaging off it.

'Basically, the thing that Maiden had that Samson didn't have,' offers Tony Platt, 'was a bloody good manager and a much bigger record label. Samson were on Gem Records, a small label, and Maiden by that time were getting the support of EMI. Maiden had Rod Smallwood, but Samson [had] Ramkup… they needed to be properly promoted – and *Shock Tactics* was not properly promoted by any stretch of the imagination.'

Being a bright chap, Paul Bruce Dickinson would have been more than aware of Samson's failings behind the scenes, and the relentless feeling of kicking against the odds requires a massive amount of energy. Even in the immediate afterglow of absolutely nailing it in front of a massive festival crowd, the underlying problems were not going to fade so easily. And so, after that Reading performance Bruce was approached by Rod Smallwood, given the chance to audition for Maiden, and after a quick rehearsal at Hackney the deal was done.

'Rod was very much a fan of having a singer who could really pump it out,' says Platt. 'And, of course, you've got other bands like Whitesnake, already in that arena of having the voice up high – AC/DC were very successful at having that aspect. It made a significant amount of sense for Iron Maiden to have a vocalist who was giving the same kind of edge to things.' It was a sound they'd flirted with in the days of Paul Mario Day, to an extent.

During August and September 1981, Samson were being courted by a number of record labels, including A&M, and were on the verge of being offered a *significant* advance against future album sales that would stabilise things somewhat for them. Neal Kay declares his part in proceedings. 'I was doing the Green Man in Leytonstone or something. Steve Harris phoned me and said to me that if Bruce turns up that night, would I get him to call Steve. And Bruce did turn up and I did say to him, "Phone Steve, 'cause he wants to talk to you, here's the number." And that was it, I did my bit.' Bruce did his and made the call.

The 'time off ' after Reading was rapidly becoming a major headache. Bruce was so much in demand at this time that whispers abounded that he was also being courted by Ritchie Blackmore's Rainbow as a vocalist. Samson publicist Jennie Halsall was one of the many people whose advice Dickinson sought at this confusing time. 'I can remember one key issue: we were in Henrietta Street the month he joined Iron Maiden, basically. Bruce and Samson had just been offered a deal at A&M [and] Bruce rang me up in a bit of a panic. He said, "Can I come and talk to you?" and I said, "Sure." So he came in and I said, "Let's go to the boardroom," which was the caff across the road – we used to do all our meetings in there, sat down with a mug of tea. He said, "I've got this problem, we've just been offered this deal with A&M but it's taken ages, and, well, I've just been offered the lead singership of Iron Maiden." And I went, "Oh, Christ, that's tricky…"

'I remember the conversation really plainly. I said, "I've come to those sort of crossroads a lot of times in my life and I've done what's right – but not necessarily what's best for me. You'll never get this offer again; it's amazing, it's fantastic, it's where you should be. But the Samson boys are going to hate you, because their deal is going to fall through." And he knew that, he said that. And I said, "But there'll be an opportunity for you to pay them back at some point, which obviously won't be the same, but it'll be the best you can do. So you've gotta take it because these offers don't come around very often, and you'd be brilliant at it." It was frustrating [for Samson] because visionary managers who were business-like in those days were pretty few and far between. That was the problem. Rod Smallwood, and his partner managing Iron Maiden, were meticulous, studied, focused.

'Not long before that, I was looking after [a very famous rock trio], and particularly the band's new drummer, who told me when he joined that he'd taken his own lawyer and accountant with him. One time, a royalty cheque came through to him from Japan. He used to give the cheques to his accountant, send him on a plane, and quite a few times the accountant would go into the record company, do an audit and [the cheque] would be short. But once you cash the cheque, you accept the audit [and therefore have accepted the cheque].

'It was totally the right thing to do for Bruce, although I knew it would cause casualties. But a business decision is often a tough decision to make, and you have to leave your own personal feelings out of it.'

Even guitarist Dennis Stratton, who had recently parted ways with Iron Maiden for non-playing reasons, says he told the twenty-four-year-old vocalist that this was an opportunity he could hardly afford to pass up. 'I did tell Rod Smallwood there was no way Maiden would ever break America while Paul Di'Anno sang in the band,' he recalled on the official *Preying Mantis* website. 'I was in The Ship in Wardour Street when Bruce Dickinson told me he had been offered the gig. And I said, "Yeah, take it. And if you take it, Maiden will be big in America," because he had the range to go up against your Robert Plants and Sammy Hagars and people like that.'

Ex-Shots bandmate Bill Liesegang also recalls speaking with Bruce about the options in front of him at the time. 'Bruce came over to my house; we were still quite friendly even though we weren't playing in the same band, because I had gone from Shots to Xero, and he had gone on to Samson. And when he came over he said, "I've just had this offer from Iron Maiden, do you think I should take it?" And I was like, "Well, you've answered your own question there, Bruce, go for it."'

It is a decision that Bernie Tormé, Gillan guitarist, has sympathy with. 'There was kind of a residual attitude in the Samson camp that Bruce was responsible for the band not really cracking it, because he left,' he muses. 'But the point is that anyone would have left. If you'd have been asked to join Maiden at that point, basically anyone would have. [Samson] had ended up… they didn't have a situation at all, really. And Iron Maiden had probably the best management in the country at that point and they were also on EMI, I mean, who'd turn that down?'

'It was a good decision on Bruce's part,' agrees John McCoy, so instrumental in the early career of Samson. 'I've been in bands and been offered much better gigs, and because of loyalty have stayed with my original band and then that's all fallen apart, and I've regretted not taking the offer of a better gig. I think Bruce did the right thing, because [Samson] were kind of floundering. And there wasn't any money there to support everybody, and Maiden had their career already planned out for eighteen months to a couple of years ahead. And they had probably the most sensible management of any band at that time. [Maiden's management] made sure that the guys were all comfortable, and spent money advertising and getting them on the right tours and, let's face it, they were a good band compared to a lot of their contemporaries. Angel Witch had a couple of good tunes, but they weren't in the same league. There was an energy about Maiden that came through, even in the early days. You know, Steve just had that buzz about him.'

Years later, Bruce was to work with bass player Chris Dale. A student of rock 'n' roll history with a penchant for an entertaining left-field tale or two, Dale unearthed some interesting information for his constantly brilliant *Metal Meltdown* column. Dale: 'Go West are a British pop band that were formed in 1982 by the songwriting partnership of guitarist/keyboardist Richard Drummie and vocalist Peter Cox. They had a string of UK and US hits such as "We Close Our Eyes", "Call Me" and "The King of Wishful Thinking" in the eighties and early nineties. [...] Richard Drummie and I were chatting about Iron Maiden, as most people do from time to time. [...] Richard told me that he'd recently been looking at some old diaries of his from around the time he was trying to get various projects together before Go West hit the charts. He'd been trying to find singers to work with and had no doubt been placing ads in *Sounds* magazine and suchlike, as people did back then.

'He said in one diary he had a singer named as "Bruce" noted down, a phone number and next to it he'd written "Too heavy!" I wonder,' he mused 'if that was Bruce Dickinson from Iron Maiden?' Bruce joined Iron Maiden in September 1981 after Samson famously played before Maiden at the Reading Festival. It has since been widely publicised that Bruce was unhappy with the band Samson, due to differing professional attitudes long before the chance to audition for Maiden arose.

'London-based guitarist/songwriter in the early 1980s talks to London-based singer. It's possible, isn't it? So, the next time I shared a pint with Bruce, we talked about Go West. [...] I asked if back before Maiden it was possible that he'd ever called a guy called Richard about a song writing collaboration or project? That's a tough question, isn't it? Can you remember every conversation you had in 1981? If you were old enough to talk back then...

'Bruce said he had had chats with different people, some promising and some not so. But of course, he didn't remember all their names. I told him the reason for the question – which, of course brought a twinkle of mirth. [...] Really it could have gone either way in that one conversation on their landline phones. I know Richard Drummie and Bruce's musical tastes, so this is how the conversation probably went in our universe: Richard: "So what kind of bands are you into?" / Bruce: "I dunno, a bit of Deep Purple maybe some Fr–"

'As Bruce says this, Richard takes his pen and writes "TOO HEAVY" in his diary, underlines it three times and interrupts with: "Oh, cool. I'm into more like, Smokey Robinson and stuff. But it's been nice talking to you..."

'But in the other alternate universe it could very well have gone differently. It all really depends on what band Bruce mentions first in that conversation: Richard: "So what kind of bands are you into?" / Bruce: "I dunno, a bit of Free maybe some De–" Richard: "Oh, cool. I love Paul Rogers. Actually I've been talking to a guy called John Glover who used to work with them..." And the so conversation goes on, they meet up, get along, write songs and form a band in that other universe [...]

'So what about Iron Maiden? Who ends up singing for them in the alternate universe? Well funnily enough, Peter Cox the singer from Go West (he is an incredible and soulful singer too, by the way) told me another time over dessert, that he was once involved in a jam with Nicko McBrain back in the day...'

Back in the real universe. Bruce rehearsed with his new band, and there was a massive sense of homecoming, musically at least. 'Samson was heading south, there was no two ways about it, there was nothing happening,' says Neal Kay. 'The thing was that Steve had a perception beyond my own in some ways there, because I never had the luxury or the opportunity of seeing Bruce try out with Iron Maiden – Steve, of course, after the phone call, obviously took him into rehearsal and Bruce finally realised where he belonged. And he belonged with Iron Maiden. There's no question of that.

'You needed some type of power upfront to combine all the influences and outputs and come up with the definitive lyrics that fitted what was going on. Bruce just gelled perfectly with Iron Maiden. It was a fait accompli. Bruce is the man who was the missing link, because once he joined it was frigging obvious what had happened – the balance was finally achieved. In Bruce, they not only had a consummate frontman who could be as funny as hell but he also told great stories that he managed to convey beautifully through the music. He was an Iron Maiden member all along – but I guess he just didn't realise it.'

'Arguably, one of the other things about Maiden was that they probably had a better handle as to exactly where they wanted to position their roots,' says Tony Platt. 'Samson didn't quite have a handle on that. Bruce's vocal heroes were in the area of Deep Purple and that kind of thing. Arthur Brown, very much so, and very much the drama of it all. Bruce was always fairly dramatic and that's what he brought to Maiden. Maiden had to do something more than just "bloke rock" or "bloke metal", but the problem was they were archetypically Spinal Tap in that they sort of didn't see the joke. There needed to be a bit of humour in what they did to make it go that extra nine yards... The thing about Bruce is that he was able to completely divert that, because his Sword and Dorkery lyrics were absolutely the perfect thing [to avoid being perceived as over-earnest].

'And because Bruce is intelligent, he was able to come up with lyrics that had an awful lot of bite and worked musically, lyrically, melodically, in a rhyming sense and everything. Because the guy's eloquent he was able to come up with those aspects quite easily, and make them believable.'

Tony Miles has an interesting theory. 'Stories have come out of the woodwork that Bruce Dickinson [was] very, very dismissive of the early Iron Maiden albums. He thought they were rubbish; *Killers* particularly.' Time can muddy all memories of course. Having come to one of the most difficult decisions in his young career to date – leaving Shots was simply not in the same league as the stakes involved here – there was one thing left for the vocalist to do, and that was the tricky and sticky one: to break the news to Paul, Chris and Mel Gaynor.

Rob Grain, closer to Paul Samson than most, relates the moment when a leather-jacketed Dickinson finally came clean. 'After a couple of weeks on holiday, Bruce went into a band meeting. Since they'd been away, the band had been talking to record companies and had two confirmed record deals on the table worth two-and-a-half million pounds. And Bruce came swanning in the meeting and said, "I've got a bit of news, chaps, I'm leaving, I'm joining Iron Maiden."' Both offers were subsequently withdrawn.

'[But] on one hand, it was a case of, "Good luck to you,"' continues Grain. 'Even at that point Maiden only had two albums out – but they had toured with Kiss and Judas Priest, and they were playing Hammersmith Odeon-type gigs. You could never knock anybody for wanting a bit of success. Quite a well-known Bruce quote is that when he joined Iron Maiden they had the next two years mapped out, whereas in Samson you didn't know what you were doing in two *hours'* time! So, fair play to him. Samson [subsequently] got Nicky Moore in, and got a record deal with Polydor. The two albums that they did with Polydor far outweighed the three they did with Bruce in terms of sales: they did bigger tours, played to bigger crowds, and sold more records.'

Paul had discovered Nicky Moore – a magnificent blues singer whose lungs are some kinda weird hybrid between Muddy Waters and Joe Cocker – at a gig at the good ol' stamping ground of The Prince of Wales down in Gravesend and, of course, must have known what he could do, Samson and The Nicky Moore Band having shared stages many times over the years. As Tony Platt says, 'It was an excellent decision: Nicky Moore's voice is fantastic and it really did suit the music they were doing.'

Later, Paul was to philosophise that Bruce was in many ways a slightly square peg within the band, in terms of personality at least. 'He tried hard but he was never really one of the lads,' he reflected. 'He tried to blame it on drugs, but all we did was smoke a little pot. Really it was that he was from a different social class and educational background. We're working-class lads like Iron Maiden, whereas Bruce was suburban middle class.'

When it really came down to it, it was all about the music for Bruce Dickinson. 'When I first heard Maiden I got the same buzz off them I did when I heard *Deep Purple in Rock*,' opined the singer. 'It was like a steam train coming at you and none of the other bands did that any more. I really wanted to be the singer in their band… Paul wasn't surprised when I left and it was a relief to him because he wanted to be more in control.' And if there ever was a band who were in control, it was Bruce's new group: Iron Maiden.

CHAPTER 8

RUN TO
THE HILLS

Sensibly, Iron Maiden's first gigs with their new singer were out of the UK. While Bruce had been rehearsing the set to get himself up to scratch during September 1981, the press began to get wind of what was still rather a shock to the system. Di'Anno had always been a larger-than-life character and certainly the eminently quotable focal point of a band of lads who still stood tall as the keepers of the heavy metal flame. Despite having raced ahead of (most of) the baying pack, losing such a strong personality from their ranks could have been perceived as very risky indeed, at least from those on the outside who did not yet know the quality of the new addition to Team Maiden.

So the band headed out for five gigs in Italy – beginning on 26 October in Bologna – prior to Bruce's official unveiling at the Rainbow club on 15 November, where they were supported by Praying Mantis, still plugging away manfully. Despite some initial nerves, by the time the band hit the UK for that gig, they were as united and forceful as if they'd been playing together for years. The rest of November and December were spent in the rehearsal room, writing tracks for Maiden's third album – Bruce's first with the band. But the spectre of Samson – or, more specifically, Ramkup – still loomed large over proceedings.

Due to the judgement in Samson's court case, if Bruce had written any material on this Maiden album, Ramkup would have had a claim on some monies – so Maiden's management reached a settlement with Ramkup. Restricted from official creative input into the new album sessions, Bruce later commented that he had a 'moral contribution' to at least three tracks: 'The Prisoner', 'Children of the Damned' and a little throwaway ditty named 'Run to the Hills'. Paul Di'Anno, though recently departed from the camp, confirmed for this book that he was "nowhere near" any involvement with the new Maiden record. 'I was on a beach in Antigua, mate,' he said with a laugh, when I asked him.

By the time they laid the album on to tape in the closing months of 1981, with Martin Birch at the helm, Maiden had become a remarkable unit. As yet, the only people to realise exactly how remarkable they could be were a few thousand lucky Italian chaps, the miscreant audience of the Rainbow, and the punters at the Ruskin Arms, Maiden's old stamping ground, where they played a charity gig on 23 December. The world was soon to sit up and take notice, though.

'When I first joined,' Bruce observed on the DVD *Classic Albums – Number of the Beast*, 'I thought that I could be the best damned singer the band had ever had. I knew that they were ready to do things properly, that the set-up was there. It really was a case of when things were going to happen. When I heard the material for the album that they'd been working on, I knew they were ready.'

'The Prisoner' stemmed largely from Bruce's experiences as a youngster. Not only was the eponymous TV series – in which Patrick McGoohan plays a secret-service operative kidnapped and imprisoned in a very strange village – one of Bruce's favourite programmes; as a youngster moving around from school to school, and prank to prank, he also deeply identified with McGoohan's character (referred to only as Number Six). 'I didn't really have anywhere I belonged, so when The Prisoner turns round and says, "I am not a number, I am a free man," I wanted that to be me,' he said during that *Classic Albums* interview. Musically, that song came together from a very simple beat that would-be drummer Bruce had been bashing out, while Clive Burr was elsewhere having a cup of tea. Then guitarist and bassist Adrian Smith soon joined in the jam, and the track was born. It only remained for Rod Smallwood to get permission from Patrick McGoohan to use the iconic quote with which Bruce had identified so much. Thus was born the classic, doom-laden introduction and the song was complete.

'Children of the Damned', meanwhile, is loosely based round the movie of the same name, which drew on the themes of John Wyndham's 1957 novel *The Midwich Cuckoos*, an early example of Maiden's love for taking musical and lyrical inspiration from movies, books and popular culture. The tale concerns alien children (hence the 'cuckoo' reference) whose powers of mind control quickly draw a typical Middle England village under their spell, motivation unknown. The track is suitably taut and paranoid before bursting into the familiar galloping, melodic choruses that Maiden do so well. Bruce commented later that it was heavily influenced – musically, in feel and in structure – by Black Sabbath's 'Children of the Sea'. Certainly, both tracks have a plaintive, eerie gravitas that ramps up the gothic drama with much skill.

'Run to the Hills' is, of course, not only a classic Maiden track, but a song that stands alongside anything ever written in hard rock. It has it all: a slightly political edge, rollocking, romping, William Tell bassline, harmonic guitar leads, solos, and plenty of room for Dickinson to exercise that remarkable vocal ability of his atop the swell. 'It's about American Indians and Western movies,' he revealed in a radio interview with the *BBC*, 'and the way that American Indians are always seen as cannon fodder, which is not always the case.' All in all, the LP is not only light years ahead of *Killers*, but galaxies away from anything anyone else could manage at the time. If ever there was vindication of Bruce's decision to join the band, it was there in black vinyl. And while his 'moral contribution' may or may not have impacted on any particular tracks, the fact remains that Bruce's range and technique freed Maiden's songwriters to explore sonic territories previously undiscovered. Of the previous work of Maiden and Samson, the closest either had previously come to a track as atmospheric, dark and hefty as *Number of the Beast* closer 'Hallowed Be Thy Name' was Bruce's previous outfit, Samson, whose 'Communion' shares many qualities with that song.

For Bruce, 1981 had begun with recording sessions for one of the best rock albums that the New Wave of British Heavy Metal had produced. It ended in recording an LP that was to have rather more significant an impact even than that. The year 1982 had one hell of a lot to live up to.

CHAPTER 9

NUMBER OF
THE BEAST

Paul Di'Anno is strident as ever on Year Zero for the new Maiden line-up. 'What a great year for music, not only *Number of the Beast* but *Back in Black* and the *Black Album*. *Number of the Beast* is a fantastic album.'

Thanks to an inordinately tight schedule between the recording the album and the planned tour to promote it, mixing was not completed in time for the LP to be available during the UK phase of the group's tour, which took place during February 1982. Happily, however, producer Martin Birch was able to complete the master for 'Run to the Hills' in time for it to be released as a single on 12 February. It soared to No.7 in the charts, a remarkable achievement by anybody's standards. The first single released by the group with its new singer is rightly heralded as a timeless classic. Blaze Bayley remembers buying it as a young man just starting to think about his own potential career in music. 'It wasn't just Bruce's voice but overall the band just felt so fresh. I'd been listening to a lot of Sabbath and Zeppelin up to then. I liked Judas Priest, but it didn't seem too exciting to me. But when I got "Run to the Hills" and then bought *Number of the Beast*, I just played it back to back all the time. It was [then] that I started to really appreciate what Bruce could do. Ronnie James Dio was one of my biggest influences, Bon Scott, David Lee Roth. I've always been more interested in singers that are individual and have attitude rather than technical.

'They all sounded like themselves, and that is how I wanted to sound [when his band Wolfsbane started]. Bruce's power and majestic feeling was completely original and when I was eighteen, working nights, I used to listen to it over and over again. *Back in Black*, *Highway to Hell* and *Number of the Beast* then the next Maiden album plus those two Sabbath records with Ronnie. That's what I got through my life with when I was eighteen; those records kept me going.'

Maiden duly embarked on their *Beast on the Road* tour, which would eventually take in 180 dates worldwide. It was a major step up for Dickinson, who had never previously played outside the UK – not through want of trying, of course. But with a professional, clued-up and innovative management team, visionary and strong-willed Steve Harris pushing matters and the support of EMI, Maiden's stock was higher than ever before. They'd outgrown the loose confines of what used to be called the New Wave of British Heavy Metal, and were now – in the words of Rod Smallwood – a worldwide proposition. When the LP was released on 29 March, it slammed straight to the top of the UK charts. Famously, the group were told of their success during a rather mundane moment: trying to push-start their tour bus, which had broken down in the snow on the way to their concert in Zurich. In such moments are band relationships cemented.

The gigs were well received throughout Europe, although across the water there was trouble ahead. It began in France during April, when Bruce contracted a chest infection, forcing the cancellation of three concerts – something that the band had always hated doing, but needs must when the illnesses of singers intervene. The American assault was the inevitable next step, and to that end Maiden had an astonishing 104 gigs set up, mostly as a support act to the likes of Judas Priest, Rainbow and The Scorpions. Given the album's title, and the rising tide of what would become known as the 'moral majority' in the States, it was unsurprising that a furore started up, casting this quintet of rockers as devil worshippers. The ludicrousness of the laughable accusations centred round the subject matter of the album's title and lead single, which had been inspired by a dream – in turn inspired by *Damien: Omen II*, a film that Harris had seen – rather than anything of any further occult significance. Nevertheless, Maiden records were burned and Maiden vinyl smashed en mass, along with all sorts of other nonsense. Of course, as this involved buying the LPs in the first place, quite possibly it didn't harm the Maiden cause as much as the protestors intended.

During the May dates, Bruce – perhaps unused to touring quite so heavily – had injured his neck, forcing him to don a surgical neck brace for several dates. A succession of doctors prescribed painkillers – one even going as far as recommending surgery – before the singer finally found relief under the tutored hands of a chiropractor. By now – and if you look for these kind of things, you're going to find them everywhere – the misfit majority were looking for all kinds of satanic messages hidden within the album, with its memorable artwork by Derek Riggs depicting Maiden mascot Eddie manipulating the devil. Bruce was later to comment to *Enfer Magazine* that the problem was that our American cousins were bereft of 'the same sense of humour', prompting certain sections to take it all too seriously, and demand stickers be applied to the LP, 'warning people of the so-called satanic aspect of the lyrics'. For someone of Dickinson's intelligence and education, this kind of dunderheaded response to art that is essentially slightly provocative, but also slightly tongue-in-cheek, was both puzzling and unexpected.

For now, however, there were bigger fish to fry, as the *Beast on the Road* tour thundered its way through the summer, the American audiences much enamoured of Maiden mascot Eddie's antics, as Rod Smallwood explained to the author for an Iron Maiden special issue of *Metal Hammer* in 2005. 'There was the story, don't know if it was a true one, but [Ozzy Osbourne once] bit the head off a [live] bat [thinking it was a rubber prop]. So we thought, "Eddie's always been a very good mate of the bats... we can't have that." So Eddie will take revenge on behalf of the bats. So we superimposed Ozzy's head [into the picture of the incident, indicating Eddie had in turn bitten off Ozzy's head]. And his manager at the time, Don Arden, called, and said it was "inappropriate" and could we withdraw it. So I said, "Okay, we'll withdraw it." So I sent a telex – in those days it was telex – out to all the record companies, asking them could they please withdraw it. But you know, it had pretty well all got out by then, so it created more of a "thing" about it. Meaning no disrespect to Ozzy, of course.'

By the time August 1982 came around, tour fever had firmly set in, and tales abound of various ways the band would let off steam. One such story, which is possibly apocryphal, places the band's singer entering a bar in Beaumont, Texas, on around 9 August. The manager of said hostelry took exception to the shorts-and-socks combo Bruce was wearing and refused to serve him unless he changed. Bruce went back to his hotel room, and returned with a different kind of shorts – denim, this time, although just as short – and a T-shirt with the rather lovely caption 'FUCK' emblazoned on it. He was subsequently served with his refreshments.

If there were any doubt whatever about Bruce as a member of the band, it had been dissipated by both the huge success of the new material and the growing realisation that the vocalist's range, energy and approach had ramped up matters massively. Following another visit to Reading, Maiden returned briefly to the States – as guests of Scorpion this time, who handcuffed Bruce's hands behind his back during one of the gigs – before the band toured Australia and Japan to complete an inordinately busy but ultimately massively successful year in their careers.

Looking back on 1982, Jennie Halsall reckons it 'was huge, absolutely massive' and, even at this stage, recalls Bruce had one eye on other creative activities. 'Bruce always did the cartoon stuff, the images and the writing,' she says. 'He was also talking about book ideas back then and always wanted to do so much more than just being the singer in a rock band. I don't think Samson, or indeed the Iron Maiden boys, had any other aspirations apart from making it in the music business. He could see the business for the business: as a career and not just the rock 'n' roll stuff. Which sets him apart from the rest, in my view.'

'If you saw that tour,' says NWOBHM expert, John Tucker, 'you'd see there was something really special about them. It wasn't like their third album, with a new singer; it was like a band who'd been doing this for forever and a day. It's a well-paced, well-put-together set. They had self-confidence, something about them that said, "We are superstars and we're not gonna look back." And they didn't. Something had to happen one way or the other, because *Killers* didn't do too well in the press. People didn't like the production [on the debut], and though there were good songs on the second album, and *Metal For Muthas*, there's a lot of things people didn't like about what was going on. Whether it was journalistic vitriol or what, I don't know, but the album didn't do particularly well [in comparison]. It was the age-old Make Or Break album, and – boy did it make 'em! What can you say? It's a great album.'

Neal Kay sums it up: 'With Bruce upfront, the band couldn't fail as far as I was concerned; it was very gratifying to sit back from a lower position and watch them. I wanted to go with them, 'cause I knew what was coming, but I had my own destiny and other things to do – they went off touring and I saw them when I could but it was really gratifying to read stories and see pictures of them. They opened up the possibilities for British rock bands of the time and those who might follow in the future, in so many ways. To the far ends of the earth, new territories, new venues and showing the world that no matter what political view you took, or religious stance you had, that nothing actually in truth ever became a barrier to rock 'n' roll. I know Steve thinks like me, and I like he, that in all honesty that's how rock 'n' roll should be.'

'I'd moved to the States and Bruce and I lost touch,' says Stuart Smith, who could've put a huge spanner in the works, had his and Bruce's project taken off only eighteen months previously. 'I remember hearing "Run to the Hills' – I think it was when I was getting the tyres changed on my car and it was getting played on the stereo system there – and I was "Christ, that's Bruce!" and I didn't even know he'd joined another band! The music scene in England wasn't really happening [for me],' Smith continues, 'and Ritchie Blackmore said, "Why don't you come over to America and give it a shot there," so I went and stayed with him in Long Island for a while. But in the first week of being there, I heard Bruce and I recognised the voice. You can't miss it!'

CHAPTER 10

PIECE OF MIND

First up was to appoint a new drummer, Clive Burr having vacated the hot seat following some issues on the extensive *Beast on the Road* tour. The band parted company with Burr in late 1982, replacing him with Michael Henry 'Nicko' McBrain, who had previously supported Maiden with his band Trust. To complete the merry-go-round, Burr would go on to fill the drum stool for... Trust! Bruce was standing as the voice of a new generation of metal fans, and yet was still unable to officially contribute to writing new material thanks to that settlement with Ramkup. On the back of the success of *Number of the Beast*, and the associated merchandising and tour memorabilia sales, however, the Maiden boys had suddenly found they were comfortably off financially. There was only therefore one thing for it. 'Iron Maiden's management, when Bruce became established within Iron Maiden, was able to go to Ramkup and buy the rights and the publishing and everything,' explains Thunderstick.

The practical effect of this was to free Bruce to take up his songwriting credits on the imminent new album, which was largely written in the Channel Islands during January 1983. Maiden manager Rod Smallwood remembers the concept behind the new long player well. 'Steve had the idea of Eddie being in a straitjacket,' he says. 'I thought, "That's cool but it needs a little bit more than that." So I got the idea of lobotomising him. And then we had to think of a title, and none of the song titles really seemed apt for it. We were down in Guernsey where we used to go to write the early albums, just trying to think of titles. *Food For Thought* was one for a while! In the inner sleeve, the brains are being served up to the band at the dinner table. And then we were in a pub and it just came out: *Peace of Mind*. Iron Maiden being for "Peace of Mind", in the normal spelling, was quite a fun idea. Then making it *Piece of Mind*, it just seemed to work.'

Title and tracks sorted, the band decamped to the rather more warm surroundings of Compass Point Studios in Nassau for the actual recordings, again with Martin Birch at the helm. Jennie Halsall remembers her part in the process. 'We stayed friends,' says the publicist. 'Maiden were recording the new album and he invited me out there so I got on a plane with Jane, complete with curry spices, which were an important part of the suitcase – [they really wanted] to make curry in the Bahamas! Robert Palmer lived down the road [from the studios] and I met a hero, 'cause I went out on a boat with them for the afternoon fishing, which was good fun. We'd stand in the house and watch the storms out in the Caribbean, which would flash along.' In that kind of electric atmosphere, Maiden recorded an LP that follows on from their massive hit of the previous year in many ways. Aesthetically, it is in many ways a companion piece to *Number of the Beast*, although the themes of *Piece of Mind* are less occult in feel, and more about conflict, war and resolution. In many ways, indeed, it is a superior album to its predecessor: the band – with whom the new drummer meshes as if he had always been present – are tighter and more together than on …*Beast*, the year of touring having brought them together as musicians and as people.

Bruce's first official contribution to the Maiden canon is the ambitious 'Revelations', a six-minute extended discussion of religion that features typically over-the-top references. The entire first verse is a poem by the social theorist and paradoxist Christian philosopher G K Chesterton, but there are also nods to Hindu and Egyptian philosophy, materialism, mysticism and a character with whom the singer would grapple throughout his career, the atheist philosopher Aleister Crowley. It is an entirely Bruce curveball to throw into the mix, although no doubt the subtleties were lost on those all too keen to paint Maiden as downright evil – as witnessed during the previous year's American clashes with the religious right. 'I take a lot of interest in all the religions of the world and the different forms they take,' the singer offered to interviewer Philippe Touchard, 'because I think that all the religions are the mirrors of the various possibilities and opportunities of life that could benefit mankind.'

Following this marker, Dickinson's collaboration with Adrian Smith, the anthemic 'Flight of Icarus' is self-explanatory, yet its references to touching the sun, and flying on the wings of dreams, are also a powerful reference to the huge rise that Maiden – and the singer himself – had experienced. It was the first track to be released as a single – on 28 April 1983, and reached No.11 in the UK charts. After this mini-classic comes the call to arms of 'Die With Your Boots On' – a three-way effort between Smith, Dickinson and 'Arry 'Arris. The sentiment is as impeccable as the control of the arrangement. Bruce's final contribution as a credited writer is 'Sun and Steel', again written with Adrian Smith. It features a rather unconvincing Harris-pastiche galloping verse structure, and a very Smith/Dickinson venture into a poppy chorus work that, while setting nothing alight, sets up a natty guitar-harmony section and keeps the album rolling along. 'It's based on Yukio Mushima, who disembowelled himself,' explained Bruce to Spencer Leigh. 'He was a Japanese novelist who started living the Samurai code, took up a course in bodybuilding and did the whole warrior bit. He stood in front of the Japanese Ministry of Defence and decided to start a revolution. It didn't work, so he went inside and disembowelled himself.' As you do. 'His partner chickened out and did a botched job of cutting his head off, but finally someone decapitated him; all a bit messy… [it's] a pleasant little ditty.'

Piece of Mind was released on 16 May, reaching No.3; Maiden could do little wrong, and the singer was enjoying himself. The concerts continued to come thick and fast as the well-received new LP spread to all corners of the globe. The inevitably named *World Piece Tour* was to all intents and purposes Maiden's debut headlining world jaunt, and its 140 gigs spanned the globe. There was the occasional controversial moment, such as the band's concert in Buffalo on 15 August 1983. A local model named Suzette Kolga had won a competition to appear onstage with the band. Subsequently, while dancing around the band cracking a whip, she alleged that Bruce had exposed her to the audience by ripping off her top, and sought punitive damages in court for damage to her personal and professional reputation. The matter did not reach the courtroom.

Under tour pressure, every band is prone to occasional tear-ups, of course, and Bruce captured one particular disagreement between Harris and McBrain on cassette, having stumbled upon an argument over a drum solo after a gig at Allertown, Pennsylvania. McBrain clocked that Bruce was, in fact, whirring away with his Walkman getting the shouting match on tape, and jumped on the cassette in question. However, on the B-side were sketches of new material that Dickinson had been working on!

It was a punishing, gruelling schedule, but by the end of 1983 Maiden had retained all the momentum of *Number of the Beast*, and added to their stock through their consistently hard-working approach; *Piece of Mind* was later voted by *Kerrang!* magazine readers as 'No.1 Metal LP of All Time'... with *Number of the Beast* at No.2! Bruce himself was happy enough, although he did concede that it was tiring. Approaching fast was 1984 – Orwell's year.

CHAPTER 11

A TEST
OF STAMINA

After a couple of weeks off at the start of 1984 to recharge the batteries a little, Maiden reconvened during February and March to begin rehearsing and jamming out new material for their fifth album, and Bruce's third as vocalist for the group. In many ways, the material that eventually became the *Powerslave* album draws a line under a trilogy of sorts that began with the breakthrough …*Beast* album. Certainly, when it came to returning to Compass Point during April 1984, the collection of tracks the band had assembled were as assured as anything they'd come up with during their accelerated and hectic schedule of the previous two years.

Bruce's collaborations with Adrian Smith were beginning to sound mature and easy. His knack of marrying singalong choruses to Smith's insistent riffing is shown off immaculately in '2 Minutes to Midnight' – an horrific but glorious anti-war diatribe that takes its title from the conceptual Doomsday Clock, which is 'set' at closer to, or further away from, midnight – the hour of destruction – depending on the development of world events. The first time the hands of the clock had been 'set' to 23.58 pm had been in 1953, when the United States Government decided to pursue the creation of hydrogen bomb, a weapon that was many times more powerful than its predecessor, the atomic bomb. In 1984, the clock was set at three minutes to the hour of doom. The track makes no bones about its subject and relishes in its pull-no-punches lyric throughout. It was released as a single on 6 August 1984 and reached No.11 in the charts, continuing Bruce's good run of chart placings for tracks he'd been involved with as a writer. This was despite a modicum of controversy that was whipped up by certain sections seeking to somehow link parent company Thorn/EMI's military material-building section with other sections of their company – including the record label and therefore Maiden, by implication – and suggesting that the group were hypocrites.

Bruce's writing is strong throughout an album which – while allowing for such relatively weak moments as the instrumental yawn, 'Losfer Words (Big 'Orra)' – is also notable for the genius tour-de-force, near-fourteen-minute epic 'Rime of the Ancient Mariner', not only one of the greatest songs that Steve Harris has ever written, but also a truly timeless moment in rock history. Ironic, too, that a track whose lyrical narrative sticks very closely to the poem of the same name by Samuel Taylor Coleridge should be released by a band of supposed 'Satan worshippers'. The poem, and the song itself, has one message writ large: have respect for all of God's creations or be damned to ever walk the earth telling your sorry tale to passing strangers. Musically, each member is playing to their best of abilities, the time changes, outstanding musical arrangement and drama are meticulously worked out – and yet there is room aplenty for the Iron Maiden vibe to come through.

Such heights are rare in music – for a band to have one mighty peak in a career is an achievement – and yet this is an album with two moments where the band touches heaven. The other is Bruce's title track, which not only marks the aesthetic of the subsequent stage show, artwork and Egyptian references, and also discusses obliquely the iconography of celebrity and the rock star lifestyle, but is also, brilliantly, a logical extrapolation of some of the concepts discussed on the track 'Revelations' from the previous year's *Piece of Mind* LP. As was becoming clear, one set of Bruce's lyrics can tell a story on the surface while concurrently raising more questions to explore. That is the mark of a true artist – although it's fair to say that the song was written in a slightly more prosaic situation than its academic context would indicate. Bruce was sat at the breakfast table thinking about 'Revelations', and its references to Hindu or Egyptian mythology and discussions of mortality, when he suddenly hit upon the crux of the matter. 'There was something missing; the power of death over life, which is a theme you find very often in Egyptian mythology,' he told *Enfer*, 'I basically wrote "Powerslave" while listening to "Revelations", a cup of tea in one hand and bacon in the other.' Dickinson's other contributions to the album are 'Back in the Village' – which is, to all intents and purposes, the sequel to 'The Prisoner', being a slightly dotty but still rather natty collaboration with Adrian and another anti-war workout that builds to a rollocking chorus – and, perhaps most intriguingly, the paean to fencing, 'Flash of the Blade'.

'...Blade' is a track that revisits one of the singer's main interests:

the sport of fencing, with which he had become more and more involved over the previous year or so, since taking it up again after many years. He'd first become interested in fencing in his Oundle days, as he told *Sports Illustrated*. 'A workshop teacher turned up to school one day with an Excalibur-type sword he'd made,' explained Bruce. 'We were like, "Cool. Can we make one?" He also mentioned he was a fencing coach and we persuaded the school to buy some kit and I got hooked.' The young Dickinson found himself drawn to its cut-and-thrust blend of skill, movement, energy and physical poetry, winning the school tournament and becoming Oundle captain at the age of fifteen, in 1975. He described himself as a 'ham [who] was immediately attracted to fencing because it seemed like a romantic, melodramatic form of combat'. Stuart Smith recalls talking with Bruce about the sport back in the late 1970s. 'We were talking one night over a couple of pints about what we thought a good lead singer was, what sort of stage moves he should make. And both of us were big Purple fans and [fans of] the way that Ritchie Blackmore would move on stage. I think I even said something to Bruce like, "A frontman should hold the stage like how a fencing swordsman would move," and, of course, Bruce later went into fencing and became an instructor.'

Although Maiden's schedule had been exhaustive (and increasingly exhausting), Bruce had found time in-between the bouts of hedonism and rockaround to try, at least, to indulge himself in the sport as early as the *World Piece* tour, although it could be rather tricky explaining to customs officials exactly what a heavy metal reprobate was doing with a fencing kit, as he noted in September 1984. 'You can't imagine the problems I had with customs! I'd learned how to say "fencing" in ten different languages! And every time I was asked the same question, "Oh I see, you're a professional fencer!" And my answer was always the same, "No, I'm a singer!" They look at me pretty suspiciously!' Although Bruce would enter regional competitions when time allowed over this period, opportunities to pursue this interest were necessarily limited. The *World Slavery Tour* was the most ambitious the band had yet undertaken: rehearsals beginning as early as 20 June in Florida, with five days of production rehearsals in early August in Bonn, Germany, before the tour proper started on 9 August 1984 in Poland.

It was, says Neal Kay, a typically brave move by an act who were still seeking to break down boundaries wherever they found them. 'They were the first band to take a full show behind the Iron Curtain in 1984,' he notes. 'And they went to all the countries back then that were terribly starved and the youngsters were terribly ill-treated: Poland, Czechoslovakia, Hungary. They took a full three truckloads of gear there and released a four-track video, *Behind the Iron Curtain*. It's wonderful to see; there's all these Polish guards in Krakow standing with their guns by their sides, headbanging, while outside on a concrete pillar sits a 1949 Mig-15 – and the kids are just un-fucking-believable. Maiden have truly gone places and touched people that only a mega-successful act has the privilege of doing and I feel incredibly proud to have known them.' That concert, at Torwar Sports Hall, Warsaw, was the first time that a Western band had played a full show – complete with Egyptian Eddie and lights – on that scale. Fourteen thousand people turned up, with five thousand locked outside.

Bruce himself had been thrilled at the prospect, welcoming the change in itinerary from the band's usual practice of beginning their live activities back at home in the UK. 'We never toured over there,' he told *Metal Attack*, 'and our fans need to see us because they feel frustrated, forgotten by the rest of the world. They hunger for Heavy Metal, they've never seen any hard rock band and we thought, "Why not us?" I think it can bring a very positive experience; basically, it's not about selling more records in those countries.' As a history graduate, however, Bruce was more than aware of the still fairly recent atrocities that had taken place in those countries during World War II. The band visited the Auschwitz concentration camp, an experience that put everything into perspective. The trials and tribulations of a rock band struggling to cope with the odd late night and full schedule can only pale in comparison to such unimaginable man–made evil. Bruce later was – rarely for him – unable to articulate the experience. 'A black atmosphere just hangs over the place,' he began. 'I don't think I could ever write a song about [Auschwitz] – words couldn't sum it up. We all felt relieved to walk away.'

The tour rolled on for Maiden. In the light of the recently released film *Spinal Tap* – the legendary 'mockumentary' of a ludicrous metal–ish band on tour – it was gratifying to note that the stage set was still ambitious and somewhat overbearing, a huge Eddie behind the band mirroring the album's artwork, pyramids and the whole Egyptian kaboodle. It was deceptively simple too, with a minimum of complex technology to trip it up. In fact, more often than not the moving parts were actually powered by the stage crew pulling levers! Which makes sense if you are planning to be out on the road for the best part of a year. The *Powerslave* album crashed the UK charts at No.2 on its 3 September release, and was also well received in America, where the band were rapidly becoming a major draw. The intention after studio album three —with a group as together as any rock band could hope – was to release a subsequent double LP. To that end, Martin Birch recorded gigs at London's Hammersmith Odeon – during Maiden's four dates there between 8 and 12 October – and Long Beach, Los Angeles, on 17 March 1985, almost six months later. This LP became the magnificent *Live After Death*, which subsequently hit the shops in October 1985, and featured the first vinyl appearance of a new catchphrase, when, in the introduction to 'Flight of Icarus', Bruce exhorted the audience, 'Scream for me, Long Beach!'

The *World Slavery Tour* also took in the first-ever Rock In Rio series of concerts, which were to become synonymous with Maiden over the years. It was the biggest crowd to which Bruce had played to date, as Bill Liesegang – by this stage playing with Nina Hagen – recalled to the author in an interview for this book. 'At the first Rock in Rio [I was] with Nina Hagen and Iron Maiden were also on the bill, so we did run into each other,' Liesegang recalls. 'Bruce was very friendly and we had a chat. Obviously, he was a lot richer than the last time I met him!' The experience was best described, quite possibly, as 'unique', with the organisers putting together all the more raucous elements in one place, perhaps to try and contain the madness. Whether Bruce indulged himself in his well-rehearsed fire-extinguisher party trick, however, is lost to posterity. 'It was weird,' says Liesegang with a laugh. 'They put all the metal bands on the bill – AC/DC, Whitesnake, Ozzy and so on – into one hotel and all the other bands they probably thought were a bit easier, like Rod Stewart and Yes and all that, they put them in the other hotel. Queen were on that bill as well. But we were in the other hotel in the Copacabana. We had a great night out with all the metal bands.'

The event itself was impressive, however, both ambitious and well received in a country that is now renowned for its spirited enthusiasm for all things rockin'. 'It was twelve consecutive nights that one, about half-a-million people [sic] every night, so it was quite a big thing,' said Liesegang. 'We were there for the full twelve nights, we started it, played on the first night and ended up having the whole week and five days off and having another date at the end, which was quite good.' 'Quite good' being possibly the understatement of the century in this context.

And the gigs rolled on, and on, and on, and on. If anyone was under the illusion that being on the road was fun and games, or that Maiden did not work their proverbials off in this period, then a glance at the ridiculously full schedule of dates in the liner notes to the reissue of the *Live After Death* album would have very quickly provide a corrective. Maiden were on a mission – a mission from 'Arry, originally – and part of that was to conquer the States. The problem was that there was still a massive groundswell of 'moral' outrage directed against heavy metal bands in general – and Maiden in particular – during 1984 and 1985. Bruce was amused to find that a particularly fervent follower of TV evangelist Jimmy Swaggart had been sending him religious literature decrying the awful influence that rock 'n' roll was having on the younger generation. He was even more amused when he received one particular pamphlet that featured a rather rockin' picture of Steve Harris himself on the cover. But the tour – for all its good intentions – marked the first moment of real schism within the career of Bruce-era Maiden. As the days rolled into each other and the band travelled between hotel and hotel, a full year was passing by with the band members scarcely aware of anything going on in the rapidly receding farrago of protoplasm and mistakes known as 'real life'. By early 1985, the band was becoming physically – and mentally – exhausted by the pressures of their own success. The Maiden boys were so in demand that new dates were regularly being added to the end of the tour. It was a Sisyphean task, and one that was to very nearly have major consequences.

The exhausted band were sinking into a state of depression, having been burnt out by the concentration required in putting on such energetic concerts night after night with barely a day off and waking up from dreams of egg and chips back in Blighty to find themselves on another tour bus in the middle of America. It was as disconcerting an experience as anything that army training could have offered. The concept of breaking individuals down and rebuilding them as an unit is debatable at the best of times, but musicians are not necessarily the people best equipped to deal with it. Bruce was no different, and eventually went to Rod Smallwood – who had a background as a booking agent – to tell his manager that the group had reached their limits. For the first time since joining the band, Bruce was having second thoughts about matters.

'It had just worn everybody out,' he said in an interview with *Hard Radio*, 'And at the end we were feeling like we were going through the motions every night, which wasn't very satisfactory, since none of us are people who like going through the motions or faking it. And I did wonder whether or not, just for the sake of my mental health, to go off and do something else. Very ordinary things were really attractive at that particular moment in time.'

The tour finished, finally, after eleven gruelling months, on 5 July 1985, at Laguna Hills, California. It was the culmination of three years of unimaginable success for the band, three fantastic studio albums and one live LP to come, with a prospective tour to support it – one can only imagine how that went down with the band. In just under four years since leaving Samson, Bruce had pushed himself to emotional, physical and creative places that nobody could have predicted back in 1981. His band stood at the peak of their chosen field – and he was not yet twenty-seven years old.

CHAPTER 12

EXTRA-CURRICULAR

For the first time in half a decade, Bruce Dickinson had some time to think. The past few years had hardly allowed for introspection, being day after day of demands, travelling and tearing it up. Now that immense period was finally over, the long-delayed hangover began to kick in – and in spades. A power-slave indeed: Maiden was a monster raging out of control, and at the pinnacle of success there was to be found there only pressure, expectation and people seeking to shoot you down at every turn.

Bruce had married his long-term girlfriend Erica 'Jane' Barnett on 27 December 1984 at a registry office in Hounslow, London. No longer touring, he now also had time to train in fencing again. He would take it more seriously than he had for nearly ten years. 'I wanted to get back into fencing to do something outside rock 'n' roll,' he told *Sports Illustrated*. 'I didn't want to reach forty and have to say all I'd done was look out the window of a tour bus and get drunk.' To that end, he enlisted the help of British Olympic fencing instructor, Ziemak Wojciechowski, who specialised in the foil discipline that was Bruce's speciality. Bruce would spend several months training five times a week with Wojciechowski, refining his technique as much as was possible, and very quickly reached a level of skill in a sport that had helped him, rather obliquely but measurably, to reassert at least a modicum of control over at least one part of his life.

The band's four-month sabbatical had also left him with time to try and pursue other aspects of his musical aspirations. There was, of course, the little matter of the follow-up studio album to *Powerslave* looming on the horizon. Bruce's ambitions were not yet satiated on a pure musical level – the trilogy of ...*Beast,* ...*Piece* and *Power...* seemed nicely rounded off with the remorselessly brilliant *Live After Death*, and while the band were at the height of their popularity, they had surely bought themselves the right to explore other sides of their musical bent.

For Bruce, that meant ripping up the rulebook and chasing down the next challenge. After a period of relative musical inactivity, he found that he was gradually regaining some enthusiasm for working and living in music. However, the tours would have to be shorter, and the music would have to ask questions not only of the band, but – in a typical piece of Bruce logic – also of the audience, and further, stick two fingers up at the cultural pressures and expectations surrounding their success. He set about writing a set of mostly acoustic-based songs, searching for an aesthetic that would inject what was – to him – a much needed freshness into the Maiden machine.

When Maiden reconvened – again in Jersey, and again based there for tax reasons that kept them out of the UK for some nine months every year – the sketches, riffs and songs that Bruce would propose for the new album were rather different to what you'd expect from a Maiden record. His ideas were not pursued by the band. Martin Birch, again producing the new material, felt that they weren't true to the Maiden sound and approach, rather than being poor tracks in themselves, something with which Steve Harris concurred. And Harris always had a very strong sense of what was 'right' for his band, as Rod Smallwood noted. 'Steve is pretty obstinate, I mean, Steve knows what he wants,' he says, 'and is unbending. If he thinks something's wrong, he just isn't gonna do it. And it's like, you know, the record company come in and say... you know, EMI haven't been in the studio with us since 1980, I mean people aren't allowed anywhere near the band! They make *their* album. It's their album, not anybody else's album.' But there are, of course, limits to how far Iron Maiden can subsume stylistic diversions too. 'All the songs I'd written sounded very much like Spanish folk music,' Bruce told *Hard Rock* magazine in an interview in May 1986. 'I remember playing my serenades to Steve. Everybody was in stitches! So there's only one song from me.'

While the group rehearsed the material (sans Dickinson originals – that 'one song' was quietly also dropped) for the first time since 1982, the singer was spending any spare time he might have refining his fencing technique, having discovered to his surprise that his relative lack of progress was actually rooted in the fact that, while up until that point he had been training and carrying out bouts with a right-handed stance, he – like his father – was ambidextrous, and if anything, stronger leading with a left-handed stance. It was something of a revelation. 'It was strange at

first,' he acknowledged. 'Everything was so much more natural…
my coordination and timing had also improved considerably.' He
still had to iron out problems in his stance, but was more than
pleased with this new development in his growing career. By the
summer of 1986, Bruce had entered and made it to the last sixteen
of competitions both in the UK and the Netherlands – not bad for
someone who'd only just begun to sort out his technique properly.

The band themselves were torn over the subject of where to
lay the new album down on tape. The same studio at Nassau was
mooted, but Bruce, Adrian Smith and Dave Murray were less than
keen, feeling that the laid-back atmosphere and heat were less than
conducive to an edgy recording experience. Bruce was also keen
to change the routine, although he noted that the bass and drum
sound in the Bahamas had been good – hence the reason that
Harris and McBrain had happily returned there for that part of the
tracking process. The tapes would then be brought back to Europe,
with the rest of the lads recording their parts in Amsterdam (a
studio in Munich had been suggested – Musicland, famous for
being the place where Queen recorded – but it was already booked
out). The results, eventually, were mixed. While the album had a
rather different sonic character to it – and even utilised synthesisers
– the songs themselves seem to lack a certain nuance. Perhaps that
was down in part to the staggered tracking sessions, perhaps it was
down to the lack of material from its singer, perhaps the band
had simply exhausted themselves more than they realised over
the previous three albums' worth of excellence, but the general
wisdom suggests that the LP that was released on 29 September
1986 as *Somewhere in Time* is considerably weaker than anything
that had bore the Maiden stamp for many a year. Paul Di'Anno's

view certainly reflects that. 'I stopped listening after *Somewhere in Time* and that to me just killed it off. I haven't listened to an Iron Maiden album since. Just a couple of snippets here and there.'

Although the vocal performances are as soaring and full of belief as ever, the singer himself was perhaps still searching for answers. Unbeknownst to the rest of the band, the rebuff to his material had affected Bruce more than was initially evident. His feelings of rejection were strong, and at one stage, the thought crossed his mind to leave it all behind him. However, the crushing blow and nagging feelings that must have surely reminded him of not fitting in at school all those years ago, were tempered by a mixture of acceptance or acknowledgement that the *World Slavery Tour* had taken a lot out of him. He also had a growing feeling that being Bruce Dickinson quite possibly meant more than merely being the vocalist in one of the biggest bands on the planet. As he had done throughout his life, Bruce took a step back, took the outwardly painful blows on the chin, trusted his intellect, and retreated inside, undefeated while he schemed to reassert himself. Bruce trained hard to get into good physical shape before the tour started, running up to five kilometres per day and training five times a week in a club in Offenbach.

Tour life being what it is, there is many an hour to fill between those all-too-brief onstage moments of soundcheck and the gig itself. And while in the past, these long hours had been obliterated by means fair and foul – by liquid and by the romp of youth – Bruce's sharp mind would, during the *Somewhere on Tour* months, turn to an idea he'd had way back in 1981: writing books.

'[Just being the vocalist in a band] was never just enough,' says Jennie Halsall, friends with Bruce and Jane – who would sadly split up before too long. 'I think he's an incredibly nice guy, he has a brain that can do two or three or four things at once – which is quite unusual for a chap! Of course, as well as the book he was already starting to be into fencing then, he just wanted a balance I think. Many people found it very hard to identify the need for a rounded approach to themselves and it was rarely achievable, not least in the macho world of rock 'n' roll. I didn't get that balance out of the music business for another ten years, until the early 1990s I suddenly woke up and realised "This is not the end of the day," although I was freelance, I realised that you must come from the outside and look in, otherwise you get *fucked up*. Because the music business is a *very* bully boy culture, particularly the heavy metal department. If they didn't get a shag, things weren't happening. I used to go on the road quite a lot and [music industry people] weren't very nice to girls – especially girls in offices. But Bruce was different; a great mate.'

Bruce's self-awareness and sharp intelligence was demanding other outlets, and so, on his latest tour, he began to sketch out the plot to a novel. It would be a flight of fancy, one that would draw on his often rather child-like sense of humour, while satirising the quintessentially English class system – with which, of course, he had had his brushes down the years, not least at Oundle – and throwing in dollops of shagging and scatological humour. 'When you are on the road and working every night,' he explained, 'two hours onstage running around, you don't have much energy to do much else. You just want to get onto the tour bus and off we go to the next town. In Europe, you do get a bit more time because the distances are less, and I like to travel by train… you can hop on a train at eleven in the morning and be there by two in the afternoon, and you can get your mind in gear doing something – which is what I did when I wrote this book. I would write for two or three hours every day, and when I was on the train or travelling I would rough it out and then I would sit down and write it [when I got] to my destination.'

The book was eventually titled *The Adventures of Lord Iffy Boatrace* – the name of the main character being a play on words from the Cockney rhyming slang for 'face'. The basic plot, said Bruce, came together pretty quickly in a succession of hotel rooms and tour buses – and, given he'd been planning to get it together for half a decade or more, it's little wonder that it was so swift a process. Somewhere in the recesses of his skull, some of his grey matter had always been on book duty. Revitalised, he would insist on sharing the day's new words with the crew and bandmates, to the point of near-irritation, as Nicko McBrain explained. 'He was unbearable,' admitted the drummer, 'because you'd be doing something on the bus and he'd have just finished writing a new chapter and he'd want to read the whole fricking story to you! But he was so excited, you can't blow someone out the sky for that.' It was something that was for his own – and others' – amusement, more than anything else at this stage. 'I was just curious as to what would happen if I started writing a book,' he said. 'The only reason I continued is because it proved very popular with people – like the road crew – who would come into my room and I'd sit there and read them the next chapter. They'd all go, "Well, what happens tomorrow?" I go, "Well, I haven't written it yet, come back tomorrow."' And so he did. And soon – even as Maiden were whipping up noisy appreciation on stage after stage – the book was completed.

The Adventures of Lord Iffy Boatrace is a story that is inspired by the novels of English writer Tom Sharpe, a touch of the jolly what-ho style of the Biggles books, the absurdist, neo-Python humour of the man himself and a dollop of puerile nonsense straight out of the pages of *Penthouse*. The basic premise of the novel is that the protagonist, Lord Iffy, Laird of Findidnann, educated at Thigwell Boarding School, is skint. Thirty-five years old, a virgin, and a semi-transvestite with a thing for stilettos and stockings, he concocts a madcap scheme to introduce remote-controlled robot grouse into Findidnann Hall's grounds, in order that he will be able to offer grouse shooting the whole year round. He is in cahoots is his butler – named 'Butler' – who, unbeknownst to Iffy, has schemes of his own to fulfil: his primary plan for money-making involves creating a mechanical fucking machine he calls 'Pelvotron'. The hapless Iffy invites a group of old schoolmates to come and experience the shooting. They, of course, all have various sexual and behavioural hang-ups, and confusion and slapstick humour – often on the slightly sick side of bawdy – ensues. Iron Maiden's mascot Eddie appears – as a scowling, leering taxi driver – as the book romps around various plot devices shoehorned in to the shag-and-deathfest. To cut a long, and twisted (in both senses) story short, the book comes to a conclusion with a final car-chase-cum-showdown between Iffy and Butler and Wing-Commander Symes-West, master of disguise, whom Iffy had employed to keep an eye on his invited guests.

Needless to say, the novel ends with the door held firmly open for a sequel as first Iffy's half-brother, Alphonse, arrives in search of the famed lost treasure of Dub'lune – said to be buried under the castle's pantry. (Alphonse swiftly meeting his doom through a mixture of being first buggered, then blown to smithereens.) Finally, a letter arrives from the 'reverend Jimmy Reptile', inviting Lord Boatrace across the pond to become a missionary. No prizes for guessing who that represents. As a tale told on the back of a tour bus, it's salacious, extremely silly and laced with enough filth and squalor to keep anyone occupied for the duration.

Later, Bruce admitted freely that stylistically he'd been partly inspired by Tom Sharpe, although he also revealed that, 'I don't like him. He's too slow. I only ever read half a Tom Sharpe novel and I was bored out of my mind. They're much slower paced and I thought they needed to be jazzed up. You want a gag on every page. So I just went for the approach of doing a punk version of Tom Sharpe. I thought, there's no point in trying to be gentile [*sic*] about this. Let's just get as pornographic as we can, as graphic as we can, and a gag where you don't know whether to laugh or vomit. A book with a sort of emetic quality. You could actually hurl over the book at breakfast!

'It's certainly not aimed at the younger end of Iron Maiden fans,' he warned, 'because it is extremely rude; personally I find it funny. If you like Gary Larson's cartoons, or *Viz*, you'll find it funny. If you look at the cover [which is all primary colours, nudity, champagne and cartoonish], everything that is on the cover is extremely filmic. I'd love to have a shot at [making a film of it]. When I saw the trailers of *A Fish Called Wanda*, I thought, "Oh no! Someone's already done it." It's a farcical book, everyone's a caricature and outrageous, and if you find that funny, you'll laugh at it.' Bruce also enjoyed the process getting the story out of his brain and onto the page, referring to it later as something of a catharsis. 'It's completely lunatic,' he said with a laugh, 'so I think I've probably got it all out of me. If ever go through a period like that, something good usually comes out of it in the end, as long as you come through it with most of your marbles still intact.' Bruce went on to say that he had sketched out ideas for other short stories, which he was planning to develop as time went by.

As for his debut book – well, suffice it to say that on its 1990 publication by Sedgwick & Jackson, reviewer Mat Snow of Q magazine was in rather unforgiving mood. '[The] shock is not that Bruce is unlikely to be up for a Booker with his first novel, but how very bad it is compared to the worst piece of fiction this reviewer has ever encountered,' he intoned. But, to be fair, Bruce himself had admitted that, 'It's not going for a Pulitzer Prize, it's not Dickens.' *NME*, on the other hand, called it 'amazingly brilliant'. Sales were immense, and on its 1990 release, *The Adventures of Lord Iffy Boatrace* went on to shift 40,000 copies. Out of print now, it regularly commands a hundred quid in those online auction-type sites, and sales were so speedy-high that the publishers were to commission a sequel in rather quick time.

Back in 1986, however, Bruce's path was to cross once more with an old bandmate, the man who had done so much for his singing career. Paul Samson had again been beset by line-up problems in the early 1980s, and the band of his surname had effectively split up in 1984. Paul was still determined and full of ideas, however, and by the middle of the decade had settled down somewhat, putting together a new line-up to gig under the moniker of Paul Samson's Empire. The band released their debut LP, *Joint Forces*, in May 1986, and were subsequently invited to join Maiden's *Somewhere on Tour* jaunt during October and November of that year, some twenty-eight dates beginning Oxford and running throughout the UK to end with a rollocking six-night stay at the massive Hammersmith Odeon. Paul himself knew how to tour; his experience was as a professional. His band, however, were enamoured of the accoutrements of touring life, putting the line-up of Empire under pressure, despite the fact that Maiden's audience, rather ironically, had taken to his musical endeavours with a great welcome. Despite the regular four-and five-figure crowds, the Maiden tour brought the problems within Empire to a head and the line-up changed soon after, just as momentum was arguably once more building up for the band.

Head Tactics, a compilation of the two Bruce-era Samson albums, had just been released – something that caused a little soreness within the Samson camp, who of course had no say in the matter as the rights to both the publishing and the release resided now with Sanctuary and Bruce. Thunderstick admitted that, 'It hurt. It was awful,' when I spoke to him. 'None of us,' he continued – meaning Paul, Chris Aylmer and himself, 'were involved with it.' Actually, Paul and producer Jo Julian had spent some time re-mastering and mixing the tracks at Music Works studio during 1985.

The *Somewhere on Tour* gigs passed largely without incident, in as much as a mega-selling rock band's gigs can. Maiden managed a hefty 150 concerts altogether, including Japan and America – where Bruce would seek out fencing competitions to enter whenever he could find one. He did so well at one contest in Long Beach, California, that he had to dash back to the venue, with less than an hour to spare before he was due to actually begin the gig.

While in America, and in-between competitions and gigs, Bruce hooked up with an old mucker by the name of Jimmy Bain. The

Scots bassist had been a collaborator with Ronnie James Dio, Phil Lynott and a member of the band Wild Horses, alongside ex-Lizzy guitarist Brian Robertson – who went on to join Motörhead for their excellent (but critically panned) 1983 LP *Another Perfect Day*, which was coincidentally produced by one Tony Platt. By 1986, Bain was at something of a loose end, and when Dickinson ran into him at one of the American concerts, the two decided – for the hell of it – to jam some tracks out together. Although Bruce's writing contribution to the current Maiden LP was absent, the ideas were still there. He recalls that he 'went round to [Bain's] house one night and we wrote the bare bones of about five songs, recording the stuff on a little demo machine. It was quite good, quite different – a bit sort of Procul Harum-ish, soul-y.' It was a typical spur-of-the-moment collaboration between two friends, a refreshing change to the necessarily constricting boundaries of the Maiden camp. But although there were plans to expand on these casual sessions, they never came to fruition.

Although the band were less exhausted than at the end of the *World Slavery* tour, the camp felt different to the way it had been before. After the gigs were completed, and partly because to remain at a lower tax band meant living outside the UK for nine months per year, Bruce decamped to Bonn in Germany. There was another motivation, however: the (then) West German National Centre For Fencing was a world-renowned gathering place for the élite trainers, equipment and athletes. Bruce spent a lot of time training there with top foilist Justin Pitman, who was regarded as one of the UK's top practitioners of the sport in the 1980s, and the two spurred each other on to greater feats.

The aftermath of the previous tour had taken a huge toll

on all the participants individually and collectively. Ultimately, it resulted in an album considered to be something of a weak moment in Maiden's history, particularly when held up against the creative output of the growing groundswell of heavier acts such as Metallica, many of them directly influenced by earlier, gnarlier Maiden (and, in truth, by many of the other NWOBHM acts, including Diamond Head). The time off after the tour saw Bruce in a better place, although it was not as much of a break as he would have liked. 'What everyone needed [after *Powerslave*] was just a bloody good rest, away from it all,' he later commented. '[But] we didn't get that much of a rest, we went straight on to the next tour. I was in a very strange place, if I was going to go off on the treadmill again, I wanted to do something different – something to freak people out. If you're feeling bad about something, it must be somebody's fault, so you look for scapegoats, somebody to blame. And in part, at least some of it is your own fault, for doing it in the first place. But that never occurs to you, does it?'

By the end of the *Somewhere on Tour* gigs, Bruce's sharpness and enthusiasm for life had returned, having had a chance to manifest itself in creative ways outside the relentless schedule. Writing books and becoming something of an expert fencer returned control to his own hands; as it turned out he was, after all, much more than a man famous for merely being the singer in Iron Maiden – as he had told an interviewer from *Hard Force* magazine who had conducted the chat mid-air as the band flew between gigs. Bruce compared the situation in the United States, where money had an immense impact on the way that people conferred status and respect on you, with being in a successful rock band – where people jump to your every whim as you are the 'talent'. Finally, Bruce contrasted this with the grounding effect of being back in Blighty, where your mates can often bring you right back down to earth again.

'In order to keep sane,' he mused, 'you need this contact [with everyday reality and] the life most people live; we're not different people. Your mental balance cannot only rest on the name of a band, even if it is Iron Maiden.' He went on to explain that he needed to mark a very real compartmentalisation of, or demarcation between, his job with the band and the rest of his life. In order to do that, he reflected, he only needed to think back to those skint-but-independent early days working with Samson, where the pressures were rather different. For the singer, being financially well-off both, 'entices and spontaneously creates a shallow and meaningless entourage', which he studiously recognised and distanced himself from – a theme to which, of course, he would subsequently return. It is to Dickinson's enormous credit that the realisation of this came even while adulation was being placed upon his shoulders. Uncomfortable with the pedestal he was being put on, but also revelling in his hammy, dramatic side, the dichotomy was both recognised and to a large extent embraced.

There are many pseudo-intellectuals within rock bands – but few people have the intelligence and insight to *really* think philosophically about their place within culture, as well as their own place within a wider world as a creative individual. It's fair to say that Paul Bruce Dickinson – having been taken right to the edge during that intense four-year period of remorseless touring and, let's say, throwing himself into touring life as a young swordsman – had found something within himself as a result. That's not to say that what he had found provided answers to the madness and magic; in fact, the opposite is probably true. A thousand questions had presented themselves, but the difference is that he now had bravery and energy to pursue them wherever they led.

The 1980s were drawing to a close. Maiden and Bruce necessarily had one eye on the new decade. It was going to be, at the very least, interesting.

CHAPTER 13

SEVENTH SON

Iron Maiden's follow-up to *Somewhere in Time* was to capture the imagination of a refreshed Bruce Dickinson almost from the outset. When Steve Harris rang him, enthusing over an idea for a concept album, Bruce immediately jumped on board. While previous artwork may have led the listener to a certain frame of mind in which to approach the constituent musical pieces, largely it had been based on one particular song: *Number of the Beast; Powerslave; Somewhere in Time*; or a bit of Smallwood/band cooked-up mischief and play on words, such as *Piece of Mind* and *Live After Death*. Harris had begun to write a song – inspired by the death of spiritualist medium Doris Stokes – which would end up being 'The Clairvoyant'. Intrigued by the concept of second sight, he rang Dickinson to chew over the possibilities inherent in that general theme. As it would be Maiden's seventh studio album, the idea began to germinate as a full-length LP. Moreover, according to historical occultism, the character traditionally blessed with this sixth sense was the seventh son of the seventh son. It was an inspired moment that put a fire Bruce's heart, a singer whose performances on the *Somewhere on Tour* gigs had, while being perfectly acceptable by anyone else's standards, perhaps occasionally dipped below the 'incendiary' level.

By this point, Bruce had a well-stocked personal library into which he would retreat to read and study books that were perhaps a little more involved than *Iffy*... Collecting occult, magical and fantasy/decadent literature from Crowley to Rimbaud, Bruce would sit with his two dogs by his side in his library-cum-study in front of the window, chewing over themes and alchemic ideas and letting them develop into potential songs and narratives to be used when the time was right. On the back of having written his first novel, a world of possibilities suddenly seemed to be opening up again. Bruce had been chatting for some months with a friend, the horror author and major Maiden fan Shaun Hutson, who had brought a script to the table that dealt with Maiden mascot Eddie's back story. Based on the album covers, prehistoric shenanigans and a theme of Eddie returning to get his revenge, it was the very early stages of a screen treatment for a movie. Shaun and Bruce sat down during early 1988 and tweaked the idea. As with many plans for such matters, nothing came of it, although Hutson – who has appeared on stage with Maiden many times over the years – rejigged the tale as a short story. His books resonate with many quotes and references to the Irons – and why not?

Bruce had indulged himself in reading Anne Rice's novels, and was much enamoured by the second instalment of her *Vampire Chronicles* series, a doomy and gothic tale of the undead called *The*

Vampire Lestat. The protagonist is also an accomplished musician who uses his position as a member of a successful rock band in the mid-1980s to begin a war between the mortal and the undead which is only resolved in the third volume, *The Queen of the Damned*. Dickinson and Harris – at this time, getting on famously again, creatively speaking – discussed the possibility of recording the score to a future movie based on the *Lestat* novel. 'We'd love to do some film music sometime,' Bruce confirmed to Sylvie Simmons, 'so somebody should make a film about it and we'd like to volunteer our services!' Prescient, in a sense: the first volume of the trilogy, *Interview With the Vampire*, was later to become a Hollywood blockbuster in 1994, starring Brad Pitt, Kirsten Dunst and Tom Cruise.

So the singer was thinking in *very* narrative terms during this period. He had also begun work on a project that was a planned rock opera about the Italian violin virtuoso Niccolò Paganini, a controversial but stunningly talented 18th-century character whose life was beset by gambling, a series of love affairs, mad plans to build casinos, illegitimate children, secret affairs with royalty, many run-ins with the church, and all manner of insane and self-destructive rock-star behaviour. Paganini – like bluesman Robert Johnson, around a century later – was said to have sold his soul to the devil in exchange for his extraordinary talent, and there were rumours that he had also been imprisoned for murder. His nickname, 'The Devil's Violinist', no doubt contributed to the fact that he was not buried in consecrated ground until five years after his death. That such a character provided interesting subject matter for a rock opera was undoubtable, and Bruce would spend much of 1987 and 1988 trying to raise money to move the project forward, having written a synopsis that placed the project somewhere between the films *Tommy* and *Amadeus* – the latter, of course, being the story of another punk-classical artist-genius, Wolfgang Amadeus Mozart. 'The conflicts he had to resolve, the temptations he had to fight,' Bruce told *Kerrang!*, 'are all relevant today… on stage he dressed all in black, a bit like Ritchie Blackmore. He was an explosive Italian and would never play one note when fifty million would do!'

So, when Harris told Dickinson of his expansive ideas for a new LP, Bruce was already in the mood to make a larger statement with a full-length musical work than ever before. The album was to be called *Seventh Son of a Seventh Son*, and in musical and conceptual approach it was to take some of the synthesiser-based sonics that the group had established with *Somewhere in Time*, pair it with wider issues – musically, this meant delving back into the group's prog-rock past, with early Genesis and Purple's more psychedelic moments a major influence – and to take the theme of the seventh son's clairvoyance and magic as far as possible.

Recording sessions took place at Musicland in February and March 1988, and Bruce's contributions to the songwriting are significant. He was to comment that elements of his rejected lyrics for the previous effort were to find something of a home herewith, albeit in a different form, but it's clear that from the acoustic introduction to the album and the keyboard riff that sparks off the album proper, this is Maiden in full, epic flow. The first track, 'Moonchild', kicks into action – a Dickinson/Smith composition with the familiar anthemic chorus, plugging-bass and tension-building middle eight that characterised the pair's collaborations. The lyrics speak of birth – for good or for evil – of a new day, a new child, and are very close in a literary sense to (him again)

Aleister Crowley's notorious *Liber Samekh* – also known as the 'Preliminary Invocation'. The Beast raised his head in Dickinson's work once more.

Bruce's collaboration with Smith and Harris, 'Can I Play With Madness?' is a true three-way piece of work. Announcing itself with a harmonic vocal call-to-arms, it melds Adrian Smith's riffs with Dickinson's lyrical ideas (originally Smith had written the now-familiar, and extremely poppy, chorus as 'On the Wings of Eagles'); subsequently, Harris offered the time changes that are reminiscent of Led Zep, and the resultant track is one of the most satisfyingly realised songs that Maiden had put together for many years. It was subsequently released as a single on 20 March 1988, debuting at No.3 and remaining in the Top 10 for three weeks. It even made it on to daytime radio – a rarity for anything Iron Maiden ever released – and its running time of just three-and-a-half minutes slotted nicely into the ideal format for a 'radio single'. '... Madness' is followed up by another three-way collaboration, the pacy and edgy – but still extremely catchy – opus 'The Evil That Men Do'. This time, the lyrics hang on a quotation from Shakespeare's *Julius Caesar*: 'The evil that men do lives after them / The good is oft interred with their bones.' In this context, Bruce's lyrics frame the reference with a tale of lost love, a longing for redemption and living life on the edge. In terms of the narrative, the protagonist, the seventh son, has reached a rite of passage during which he begins to accept his fate. Bruce's final contribution to the album is also the LP's closing track, 'Only the Good Die Young', a collaboration with Steve Harris, and lyrically also referencing those Shakespearean lines, in spirit, as well as perhaps a pay-off to 'Die With Your Boots On'. It is an excellent ending to an album that regains some of the conceptual and musical ground the group had lost, and the lengthy knockabout ending and reprise of 'Moonchild' complete a very successful project for the group.

As ever, there was an extensive tour to promote the release, although on the back of the problems of previous years, Maiden would insist on more rest days, while Harris opted to travel in his own tour bus along with his wife and young family. Gone were the days of hedonism and harridans hanging from hairy roadies (most of the time); 1988 was, after all, the year that Bruce turned thirty years of age. And just under two weeks after the singer left his roaring twenties behind, Maiden finally fulfilled a prophecy of their own, headlining a huge concert to take place at Castle Donington under the *Monsters of Rock* banner. Also on the bill that day were contemporaries including Guns N' Roses, Megadeth, David Lee Roth and Kiss – with one Neal Kay deejaying and exhorting nearly 100,000 people to yell obscenities back at him. Not that they needed much encouragement.

The celebrations soon turned tragic, however. The inclement weather had muddied Donington considerably, and in the crush to watch G N' R's set, two individuals – Alan Dick and Landon Siggers – lost their footing and were trampled to death. What should have been a great triumph for the band had ended in tragedy, although Maiden were unaware of what had happened when they took to the stage for their headlining performance, which Bruce described as being, 'a fair old racket'. 'If you stood in front of the speakers,' he told the *BBC*, 'it was like standing at the back end of Concorde. You do have to be loud to get across to 107,000. The Beatles would have been a lot louder if the technology had existed in those days... they were using something you would find in a small disco or youth club as a PA for fifty thousand people all screaming as loud as they could!'

Maiden continued to headline the *Monsters of Rock* tour throughout Europe, the *Seventh Tour of a Seventh Tour* drawing to a climax with two nights at Wembley Arena – which were filmed for a planned video release – and a return to Hammersmith Odeon for three sold-out nights, ending on 12 December 1988. It was another gruelling jaunt, and although sales of the album had again gone platinum – *Seventh Son of a Seventh Son* had debuted at No.1 on its release on 11 April – the critical response had not been great from a music press pack who were head over heels over hell on earth for Metallica's bludgeoning album … *And Justice For All*, a gnarly, aggressive and thrashy effort that was in spirit and focus hugely different from the cerebral soundscapes that Maiden were offering. In truth, for all the excellence of *Seventh Son…*, and its huge sales, heavy rock music had moved in an entirely different direction. Although Maiden had put down a superb marker as to the possibilities inherent in the expanded narrative, a generation was growing up wanting the instant thrust of the noisier and grimier side of life. While Maiden tied off loose ends with a slick, epic and confident touch, Metallica, Megadeth and their ilk were roaring at the skies with an angsty malevolence that Bruce and the boys had left behind some five years earlier. Bruce himself, talking about thrash, labelled it as a limiting style, reminiscent of punk in that, 'as soon as it's born, it's dead… to most people it just sounds like a noise, they can't play their instruments properly and they can't sing in tune.' Next you'll be saying there's no tunes and you can't hear the words… 'and there's no tune anyway,' he mused to journalist Sylvie Simmons.

SEVENTH SON

As 1988 drew to its scruffy close, then, Iron Maiden were happy to – somewhat prematurely – say goodbye to the 1980s, having left behind them a body of work that was at turn aggressive, salacious, anti-establishment, streetwise, conceptual, ambitious, stodgy and fizzing. After the triumphs and the hard times, the band decided that 1989 was to be a year off from all official Maiden activity. For a certain singer, it was to prove a year that would allow him to explore further some of the passions that were growing in him, as well as hark back to simpler times.

CHAPTER 14

GOING SOLO

Freed from Maiden duty for a while, Bruce Dickinson – now a qualified fencing instructor – had time, among other things, to get to grips with the central heating in his new, smaller house, having moved out of The Mansion at Pednor Top after his marriage ended in 1988.

One of his major projects during 1989 was to investigate the establishment of a fencing centre for young people; he felt strongly that the UK was under-represented in that sense. 'I have to find the premises,' he told *Kerrang!*, 'it won't be in London because there's so much going on there... I'd like an old warehouse and try and attract a sponsorship deal. I won't throw money at it.' Sensible chap. Bruce went on to explain that the West German Government spent 25 million marks [around £8 million at the time] on fencing, allowing schoolkids to develop their skills while being tutored at the centres, and having all their equipment – and, for that matter, their upkeep as boarders in said schools – paid for by state bursaries. As an ex-public schoolboy himself, Bruce could vouch for the educative possibilities (and otherwise) of a set-up like that. His own fencing career was taking an upturn in the last year of the decade, and although his career record was average, during 1989 he was able to rise as high as No.7 in the British rankings from the previous season's ranking of eighteenth – which in itself wasn't a bad result for a man spending at least nine months of each year on band business.

'I fence,' he stated, 'and I don't see anything unusual about it. It would be nice if more people got the opportunity to do it, but until Her Majesty's Government sees fit to treat the sport in a proper way in this country and not regard it like *Chariots of Fire*... sportsmen today need to be professionals even if they are amateurs. You can't expect to have world-class sportsmen in any sport today unless the person can afford to train full-time – and that means at his peak. When he or she are twenty-four or twenty-five – they are going to spend most of their early life playing sport. You have to be able to create some structure whereby your most talented athletes can have a life after that and not just be chucked on the dole or mini-cabbing or something. It's not fair – and it's disgraceful.' Bruce was well aware of the potential inherent in the sport, citing that when cash had previously been injected into development of the sport, the results had been noticeable; and, he mused, not just for the received wisdom of fencers being mostly middle-class boarding school kids, but with results across the demographic board. '[They] were coming, not out of toffee-nosed boarding schools, but street kids were getting into fencing, the sort of kids who were getting into karate or kick-boxing,' he told a radio interviewer. 'You get the same buzz out of it – fencing is like boxing without the brain damage. It's a combat sport, it's really exciting and you have to be as fit as hell to do it. It's hard work, and very demanding.' Bruce also felt that with the correct coaching and financial support, British kids could end up competing at a very high level. A man fired up, if nothing else. In 1988 – on 25 July, to be exact – he had taken the first steps toward setting up a company to import fencing equipment from China to the UK, calling it *Duellist Enterprises*. Bruce's club, Hemel Hempstead, won the National Championships that year.

It was as a musician that Bruce Dickinson was still best known, however, and an opportunity was shortly to come up that would give the 1990s something of a remarkable change of focus for him. It was also something of a fluke; when the clarion call came out from Rod Smallwood searching for people to contribute a track to the film *A Nightmare On Elm Street 5: The Dream Child* (1989), Steve Harris demurred as he was busy in an editing suite, going through the live visuals and audio that Maiden had recorded on tour the previous year, to pull it together for release on video. Bruce stepped into the breach, looking for things to amuse himself in a musical sense – and looking for a project that he could work on with his old mate, Janick Gers, with whom he'd reacquainted himself in a musical sense by performing the Mott the Hoople classic 'All the Young Dudes' at a Prince's Trust benefit concert during 1987.

Gers, a near-neighbour of Bruce and a mate from the Samson days, was close to the vocalist, and had in fact replaced Bernie Tormé in the Gillan band, although by 1989 he'd been on the verge of chucking it all in after some years of inactivity from the live scene. The pair got on well, and in short order had pulled together a ripsnorter of a track with the lovely title, 'Bring Your Daughter… to the Slaughter.' The producer for the soundtrack project was the well-respected Chris Tsangarides. 'It happened because my management, Zomba, basically owned Sanctuary at the time and they were also Bruce's publishers as well as putting out the soundtrack to the film,' Tsangarides told me. 'They needed a song and Bruce had this "Bring Your Daughter… to the Slaughter" business, so they thought it'd be a good idea to put the pair of us together, and it turned out to be a right good laugh.'

It went down so well with the Zomba chaps that they immediately asked Bruce whether he had any other material that might make a nice solo album for which they could then possibly find a label. Bruce said that, yes, of course he did, and immediately put a phone call through to Gers, informing him that he'd better not sell his gear because they had an LP to write and record. For the sessions, they roped in Andy Carr, bassist for the band 3 Rivers, and Jagged Edge drummer Fabio Del Rio. 'I called Janick and went, "Janick we have to write another album of this shit, quick!" and he said, "What shall we do?" [And I said] "Oh well, we will write a freak sort of tune and a Rolling Stones kind of a tune and an AC/DC kind of a tune and we will just have a laugh because these guys just have loads of money and they will pay for us to make a record so just shut up and have a laugh!"' *Stormbringerzine* reported.

'We thought, "Well, why don't we make an album?"' says a laughing Tsangarides − who has worked with the likes of Judas Priest and Thin Lizzy as well as Depeche Mode and Tom Jones. 'It really was a natural thing, just like that, 'cause Maiden were not doing much and he was sitting around scratching his arse, so that's what happened. We thought, "Let's do a record where it's just fun and laughter", basically. Nothing to compete with Iron Maiden, because it's nothing like an Iron Maiden record. That was the spirit in which we entered into it, and also at the time we didn't have a deal other than the publishers, who happened to own the studios, manage me and Sanctuary etc, so they sort of funded it for us to go in and record it. And about halfway through it, EMI said, "Well, we'll release it." So, there you go! It was recorded in Battery Studios, in London, in the summer of 1989.' Returning to an old haunt meant, in a very real sense, revisiting the relaxed atmosphere of the *Shock Tactics* sessions – the polar opposite to the recent recordings with Maiden, and an unexpected opportunity to get down to writing and recording some classic rock tracks with mates.

'*Tattooed Millionaire* – as the album came to be called – was purely down to having a good time, making a good record and having a laugh,' says Tsangarides, smiling. 'It was eight weeks, something like that. And we just had a bloody good hoot every day. We set up that board game about war and battles on the pool table – *Risk* – with the armies and whatnot. We were playing that, so that was on-going at all times. We were also shooting lightbulbs in the studio with air guns. It started off just shooting the odd dead one, and ended up shooting everything! That was quite a laugh.' The back-to-basics approach ranged from the rock 'n' roll tracks that Janick and Bruce had swiftly written together – within less than a fortnight – all the way to the recording process, which, much in common with *Shock Tactics*, was the sound of a band doing what they do best. 'We set 'em up, got a sound, they played it and

I recorded it, basically,' confirms the deskman. 'And that was it – it was so old school it was untrue. And still, to this day, that's kinda how I do it. Sorting out what we're gonna do, how the song's gonna go, choruses and arrangements and whatnot, rehearsing it and then doing it. That eight weeks includes pre-production in the studio. The songs were pretty much there already, there wasn't much I had to change. Janick and Bruce had written them, and pretty quickly as well.'

The performances, as a result, are uniformly relaxed – and therefore rather excellent, not least from Dickinson. As the producer says, 'I think Bruce has done some of his best singing on *Tattooed Millionaire*. It's so confident, it's so upfront and it's so good, really. It's singing, it's not screeching. There are places where he needs to go for it, which he does – but it was proper singing and proper harmonies, the first time he'd really done any harmony work because there's not that much in Maiden.' Although we should remember that there was plenty of that kind of thing in Speed, Shots, Stuart Smith Projects, Jimmy Bain demos and Samson.

Bruce's other passion seeped into the recording sessions, however: 1989 was – after all – supposed to be his chance to take a year off from music, and so he'd take every opportunity to continue to refine his skills in other areas, to great effect. Bruce finished a creditable thirtieth in that year's UK foil fencing championship. 'When we were doing *Tattooed Millionaire*,' says Tsangarides, shaking his head, 'he'd be having his fencing lessons every other day. The coach would come in and we'd go and have a cup of tea while he fenced. In the studio! He is a real get-up-and-go character, he will not sit down for a minute. We had a great friendship at the time, as I recall, we were always at each other's houses, my kids used to call him Uncle Brucester, and all kinds of things. It was a lovely thing, a lovely time. I have great memories of it all.'

Of course, the track, 'Bring Your Daughter... to the Slaughter' was almost immediately snaffled up by a more-than-impressed Steve Harris when he heard it. Too good for a solo record! It had to be a Maiden track – and, to be fair, it sounds like one, even in its demo form. 'We did it as a one-off for the soundtrack, and that was that,' confirms Tsangarides. 'Then the album was something else. When Steve heard what we did for the soundtrack, he wanted to do [similar] for Iron Maiden.'

Smashing into action with the forceful 'Son of a Gun', *Tattooed Millionaire* puts down its marker as being a no-bullshit, balls-to-the-wall rocker. It's a track that re-treads one of Dickinson's favourite bonnet-bees, that of organised religion – and, in particular, certain hypocrites preaching love while concurrently planning destruction, death and double-cross. The solo from Gers wails, mirroring the gruff and vituperative delivery of the singer.

The next track – the title track of the album – is one of Bruce's most personal tracks to date. 'Tattooed Millionaire' is a monster of a pop/rock track directly attacking the LA-based hair metal acts that had so turned late 1980s metal into a competition of the bouffant – those acts that, while purporting to be rockers, would spend more time in front of the mirror, checking out how expensive they looked while their ex-beauty queens preened in their brand new Cadillac, dripping in jewellery and falseness. Its ultra-catchiness hides a very strong sentiment against the pedestal lifestyle that certain bands were chasing as their sole goal. As someone who'd always been surrounded by lads from the streets – and spent a lot of time paying his dues – it was a subject close to Bruce's heart.

'I'm not a millionaire,' he laughed, 'and I don't have any tattoos. The song is a specific reference to a lot of heavy metal, heavy rock bands who are coming out of the woodwork now that rock music is suddenly popular again... They're slapping on the make-up and the mascara, which is something I've never bothered about; there's another outrageous, androgynous-looking band every five minutes.

But where were they at the begging of the 1980s when bands like Iron Maiden were going around laying the foundations for all this?'

Bruce continued to muse on the motives behind these new acts, suggesting that perhaps there was a more prosaic – and financial – motivation behind that particular musical fad. 'It's an attempt by record companies to cash in on things, but I don't think kids are buying this stuff in vast quantities as they can smell a fake when it appears in their back yard.'

'Born in '58' continues the autobiographical tone – a real heartfelt, acoustic-led and restrained mid-paced, almost Springsteen-esque tale of his childhood, and the struggles and terrible messes created since then. Through his personal lyrics, Bruce shakes his head that the lessons of the past have hardly been learned. By contrast, the only real way to read anything more into 'Hell on Wheels' than a straightforward track about shagging is to – uh – shoehorn it in there. At a push, the choruses, talking about nobody waiting at the end of the line, and wondering what exactly is driving the protagonist, could be applied in retrospect to a deeper malaise, but it's tenuous at best. 'Gypsy Road' follows, a straightforward take on the rocker-as-itinerant-lover and the freedom of living by nobody else's rules but your own. The rather juvenile 'Dive! Dive! Dive!' follows – full of more of that *Viz* magazine-type double-entendre

Bruce was very fond of – over an insistently funky backbeat, Bruce clearly enjoying himself as he rasps out the lyrics with a cheeky gleefulness. The aforementioned 'All the Young Dudes' cover follows – Bruce doing a more-than-passable impression of David Bowie in his delivery. 'Lickin' the Gun' proves beyond doubt that this is no mere sub-Iron Maiden collection of out-takes, its funky approach and highly charged earthiness being a world away from *Seventh Son...*'s cerebral conceptuality.

More of the same follows in the frankly daft 'Zulu Lulu', which is one of the weaker bits of filler on a patchy-but-fun LP with the performances and spirit (plus some more great guitar playing) more often than not better than the material itself. 'No Lies' offers an anthemic, singalong feel to matters, and with that *Tattooed Millionaire* is complete. Not bad for two weeks' worth of writing!

As Bruce was to comment later to *MetalUK*, the album had done its job, which was to merely be itself without any pressure of expectation on it, although, of course, his profile would always attract certain amounts of interest. 'We had a great laugh and made a terrifically fun sounding record and unfortunately everybody took it seriously,' he sighed. 'Everybody was like, "Aha! The singer from Iron Maiden has made a new solo record and it sounds like this."' To which his response was that it was never something to be taken massively seriously, although he rates the title track, as well as 'Gypsy Road' and 'Born in '58' highly, while freely admitting that 'There is a lot of stuff on the record that I am thinking is generic but actually it is just as good as everybody else who is putting stuff out at the time.'

Bruce and Maiden were next involved in the Rock Aid Armenia project, which was a humanitarian single put together by rock musicians in aid of the victims of the previous year's devastating earthquake in that country. On 8 July 1989, a host of internationally famous rock stars gathered at Metropolis, Chiswick Studios in London to record Deep Purple's 'Smoke on the Water' for a charity single. Bruce lent his vocals alongside a stellar cast all doing their bit, including Bryan Adams, Ritchie Blackmore, Keith Emerson, Ian Gillan, Dave Gilmour, John Paul Jones, Tony Iommi and many others. The recording was filmed and the single duly reached Top 40 status, with an associated video – and subsequently an album, to which Maiden contributed the ubiquitous 'Run to the Hills'. How very long ago that release must have seemed! Seven years is a long time in rock 'n' roll. Maiden did, in fact, break their promise of a year off by gathering for the release party of the *Maiden England* video, which Steve had been working on for the first part of the year. Sanctuary and EMI provided a backdrop of union flags and people chomping on fish and chips while drinking bitter. It couldn't have been more English if it had started raining inside the venue. Still, the atmosphere was good and the band were starting to rev up into action.

Thus satiated, Bruce reconvened with the Iron Maiden boys at Steve Harris's music barn in early 1990 to get down to some serious writing for the business of pulling together the first Maiden album of the new decade. The intent this time was to strip down the histrionics and ambition of *Seventh Son…*, to bring back the feeling of the very early days; even unto *Killers* would they aim. As it turned out, the new sessions would see the first line-up change in Maiden for a long while. Although there had been persistent rumours for some time that it would be the vocalist who would jump ship – exacerbated by his solo venture

177

– it was actually guitarist mainstay Adrian Smith who parted company with the band. Having been fired up by the exploration of *Somewhere in Time* and subsequently *Seventh Son of a Seventh Son*, he was not overly enamoured by the back-to-basics intent of the new material. Smith had also been working on solo material, under the Adrian Smith And Project (ASAP) banner, and the taste of creative freedom that engendered far outweighed the lack of relative critical or commercial success of the project. After a decade with Maiden, and a good year off, Smith felt that the schedule for the new LP was too compressed and left the camp, as amicably as was possible. Bruce, as ever, had the answer, and it was staring the band in the face. One quick rehearsal later, and Janick Gers slotted into Iron Maiden like he'd always been a member. As an old compadre of Samson, Maiden and Gillan, he had the moves, the talent, the attitude and the enthusiasm to make it work – and it worked extremely well.

Sessions took place between January and April 1990, with Harris commenting to interviewer Henry Dumatray that it was 'a more aggressive side of Iron Maiden. I think some of our fans were disappointed in the musical orientation we had taken lately, so I think they'll be happy we're going back to a more aggressive and powerful style.' The new album, to be entitled *No Prayer for the Dying*, was originally going to be recorded at Battery Studios, but because the band were enjoying the rough-and-ready (but hugely adept) jam/rehearsal sessions at Harris's outhouse, the decision was made to hire out The Rolling Stones' mobile studio, and hammer out the tracks to tape in that very place.

Shorn of his most successful writing partner, Bruce turned to Steve as a creative buddy and the two blasters that begin *No*

Prayer… are so utterly early 1980s Maiden, it almost hurts. Bruce's new enthusiasm for the more simple, stripped-down and filthy straight-ahead rock aesthetic stretches – as it does throughout the album – to a much more raspy, smoky-throated rock delivery that even approaches Di'Anno territory on occasion. 'Tail Gunner' – which Bruce said had been 'inspired' by a pornographic film before becoming a straightforward war track – and 'Holy Smoke' – where that pesky character, Jimmy Reptile, is once more taken to task, are a pair of raucous rock tunes that make no bones about the fact that this is going to be an LP set firmly in the no-nonsense realm. As a statement of intent to move away from the ethereal meanderings of their previous LP, it could hardly be clearer.

Harris and Dickinson's other collaboration, the atmospheric 'Run Silent Run Deep' is one of the underrated moments of the project and its galloping basslines, piratical choruses and chugging guitars make it one of the tracks that probably could have benefited from a full-technicolour production. As it is, it feels like a demo – albeit a polished one – as much of the album does. The lyrics for this were apparently left over from some sketches that Bruce had in a notebook intended for use on the *Somewhere in Time* album. Bruce's eco-hypocrite-baiting track with Dave Murray, 'Public Enema Number One', is most effective for its twin-guitar harmony than any particular innovation, although its mix of bombast and sense of hopelessness are very much within the slightly paranoid feeling of the LP as a whole.

Prior to leaving Maiden, Adrian Smith had worked with Bruce on what became the AC/DC-esque 'Hooks in You', an update in the long-running 'Charlotte the Harlot' series. The lyrics, double-entendres all over the place, were inspired by Dickinson and his second wife, Paddy (they were married in May 1990, again at Hounslow), going to check out a possible house purchase, wherein they were surprised to find strange hooks attached to the bedroom ceiling, and the two speculated as to the probable sexual purposes they were designed for. It is a fun bit of rock silliness that could easily be at home on *Tattooed Millionaire*. Bruce and Adrian always did work well together. The album highlight, however, by an absolute country mile, is Bruce's 'Bring Your Daughter...' which, by virtue of not having been written specifically for Iron Maiden, stands alongside the greatest songs that the band have ever recorded before or since.

As soon as the Maiden LP was in the bag, Bruce set about pursuing another talent, taking advantage of an offer to appear in an episode of the television series *Paradise Club*. It was recorded on 7 and 8 June 1990. As a self-confessed ham – and, of course, with the weight of the Oundle Amateur Dramatics Club training bolstering him – he stretched himself to play a musician named Jake Skinner straining to find freedom from a dictatorial boss (in this case, a record label). Unhappy that he may, under the terms of a sponsorship deal, only drink one drink, Rock 'n' Cola, 'til the end of his tour, he walks out of the studio where he is meant to be recording. To be fair, Bruce's performance is as natural as could be expected, although his character is a guitarist rather than a vocalist. The track that was used for the performance was 'Wishing Well', a cover of the track by Free, which they would occasionally play on the *Millionaire* tour. The episode was aired on 6 November, entitled 'Rock 'n' Roll Roulette', and also featured Don Henderson and Leslie Grantham.

Above: Fuzzy-faced frontman scouring the pub crowd for people to verbally spar with, late 1977.

© *Steve Jones*.

Below: Samson, 1980.

© *Thunderstick*.

Above: Bruce and Chris Aylmer catching some sleep between tour dates in 1979.

© *Rob Grain/The Paul Samson Archive.*

Below: Samson during recording sessions for the *Head On* Album, 1980.

© *Rob Grain.*

Bruce and the band in the studio making good use of spare tape during the Shock Tactics sessions, January 1981. Fart sweets out of shot. © *Thunderstick.*

Above: The meeting of the newly-formed Samson Backstage Caravan Club was a great success.

© *Thunderstick*

Below: *Shock Tactics* studio sessions, January 1981.

© *Thunderstick*

Above: Robin Guy doing his best Animal from the Muppets impression with some cool dude singing his solo heart out, 2002. © *Stefan Reinholdsson*

Below: Outside Stockholm's Palladium venue, 25 September 1994, on the 'Balls to Picasso' tour. © *Mattias Reinholdsson, The Bruce Dickinson Wellbeing Network.*

Above: Iron Maiden performing at Download festival, 2007, as part of their
A Matter of the Beast Tour.

Below: Bruce, along with Ally McCoist, Captain Julian Todd and Walter Smith en
route to Israel with Rangers Football Club. © *Lynne Cameron/ Empire/Rangers FC.*

Bruce taking the fight to Download
Festival with Iron Maiden in 2013,
on the *Maiden Voyage* Tour.

© Karen Toftera, karentoftera.com

Iron Maiden's Renaissance man still shows no sign of slowing down. Long may
that continue.   © *Karen Toftera, karentoftera.com*

Immediately after these recordings, Bruce headed out on his first ever solo jaunt. Replacing the unavailable Del Rio with Dickie Fliszar, the band headed out merrily on a tour that debuted at Newcastle's Mayfair on 19 June 1990 – close to a hometown gig for North-East native, Hartlepool's Janick – and was completed in Los Angeles at the Foundation Forum on 14 September. As well as album tracks from *Tattooed Millionaire*, the band would encore with such classics as Deep Purple's 'Black Night' – and even, on occasion, Lindisfarne's 'Fog on the Tyne', later made infamous by Paul Gascoigne on his post-World Cuptears 'hit' single. The tour had been preceded by the release of *Tattooed Millionaire*, which was released on 8 May and peaked at a more-than-respectable No.14, being praised by the major music magazines, including *Kerrang!* That particular magazine opined that it was the kind of album that Deep Purple's Ian Gillan should be making – something that pleased Bruce immensely. The only blot on the landscape for the *Tattooed Millionaire* project was the concert recorded at Los Angeles' Town & Country Club on 14 August. The intent was to use the footage for a future video release. Unfortunately the audience – at a rock gig, no less – were banned from drinking, to make technical issues less problematic, leading to a rather less-than perfect atmosphere. The budget was very high, and the arena was crammed with huge camera cranes and flying jibs rather than the hand-held cameras Bruce had hoped there might be. The atmosphere was sterilised. Immediately after the concert, Bruce flashed to the van where the tapes of the concert were, and threw them into the river in disgust. Sanctuary officials later had to rescue them, and happily they weren't damaged to the point of no return. Bruce makes no secret of the fact that he is not a fan of these clips.

As ever with Bruce, he would not keep still for a second, rushing to join Iron Maiden for the *No Prayer on the Road* tour. 'Holy Smoke' had been released on 10 September, debuting at No.3, an excellent result for a band who many had been writing off for years. The Maiden fans, however, were always the vital component in their success. Shorn of radio play, major television coverage, and repeatedly condemned as less-than-credible, Iron Maiden shrugged it all off, got back on the road and worked their balls off with their usual determination. They were supported in the UK by an underrated act named Wolfsbane, whose singer Blaze Bayley warmed up the crowds neatly by being charismatic, aggressive and skilful. 'Wolfsbane was a live band and that's all we wanted to do,' Blaze says. 'We started touring by ourselves [in 1984] in a Transit van, selling tapes and T-shirts, unsigned. But when we got signed we spent money on a video that MTV wouldn't play – all that money, we could have spent on touring, which was a sore point with us. We had a good following in the UK, but never did our own headlining tour of Europe, which is what made a big difference to us. We played thirty-three sold-out shows in the UK with Maiden, who were doing for the last time all the small shows where they started. Theatres, all sold out.

'It was one of – if not *the* – best tours I ever did,' he admits. 'Supporting Maiden was very, very special. Every day sold out playing to hundreds, if not thousands, of people. It was really cool. Our name was on the tickets; we had a CD that came out during the tour, *All Hell's Breaking Loose Down at Little Kathy Wilson's Place*;

we were known by the magazines. We had this thirty-five-to-forty-minute set and were told to keep on time; we went out five minutes early if we could. The gigs were mostly full when we went on, not many people in the bar, and we did our best as four young ambitious musicians that believed in what we were doing. More than half the shows we did, we actually got an encore from the Maiden fans and that was really, really special. It made us think we could really get somewhere. Playing to three-and-a-half thousand people at Hammersmith Odeon was just incredible. There was proper catering cooking hot dinner, they had laundry people with them so if you asked them nicely you could get your trousers washed. As a young man it was everything I'd ever dreamed a tour could be.'

The idea was to be cheeky, get into people's faces, climb PA stacks and push things as far as possible, the vocalist says. 'Steve Harris said that it was great to have a band to push [them]. Nobody can blow Iron Maiden away, 'cause they've got this great catalogue of huge songs, but that was a great compliment to us. They had so much confidence they weren't small-minded about [where we went onstage] – they said just stay away from the drums and that's it. We videoed quite a bit of it.'

Things between Wolfsbane's singer and the Maiden gents were also going well offstage at this point, Blaze says. 'I remember being in Belfast, staying in the same hotel as Maiden and having a drink with the lads, and Steve Harris asked if I played football and invited me to be part of the Iron Maiden football team for the rest of the tour. Every Saturday we'd have a game of football with the staff from the theatre, or a local Sunday League team – it was fantastic, man. I absolutely loved it.' Of course, all things come to an end. Blaze says that the end of the tour, following that triumphant Hammersmith Odeon gig, was 'absolutely horrible'. 'To go home was just awful,' he confirmed. But there was still the memory of being onstage with Maiden to bring back a warm glow. 'I'd become friends with Bruce by that point,' Blaze remembers. 'Maiden used to do a really long 'Bring Your Daughter… to the Slaughter,' and he handed me the mic and let me sing a few choruses of it as lead vocal. I was actually singing vocals on stage with Iron Maiden! There's a great photo from that gig of both bands that *Kerrang!* or *Metal Hammer* did. It was a really special time: Nicko used to wear a Wolfsbane T-shirt onstage. It was fantastic.'

Bruce and Paddy (born Patrice Bowden in 1961) celebrated the arrival of their first son, Austin Matthew Bowden Dickinson, on 23 September 1990 at their house in White Swan. Tour-wise the travel arrangements at this stage were rather different to the usual tour bus-'n'-beer days, Bruce preferring to find his way between the British dates by train, indulging a passion that he had had since a child. He confessed, with his usual honest wit, to something that could be considered amongst certain circles as being a little – well – uncool. 'I love railway timetables,' he revealed, 'and I love travelling on trains! The British railway timetables are very disappointing these days as they have reduced the number of overnight trains and late-night trains, which are the ones I like to use. It's great on the Continent; get yourself a copy of Thomas Cook's Continental Timetable, get off at Calais, and the world is your oyster.' No wonder he and Paddy had gone on the Orient Express on their honeymoon.

After the tour wound its way through the UK, the album, *No Prayer for the Dying*, released on 1 October, went straight in at No.2;

another triumph in what was turning into rather a triumphant year for Maiden and their singer. That amazing return to basics for both Bruce and his main band had paid off in spades. It could only be topped off by one thing…

CHAPTER 15

NUMBER ONE

■ ■ ■ **A**nd that was the feeling when 'Bring Your Daughter… to the Slaughter' hit No.1 on 5 January as the first chart-topper of 1991, remaining there for two weeks despite not being playlisted on Radio 1 or enjoying a great deal of television support. It was a canny time to release a single: Maiden's fans had never been swayed by anything other than the music they loved so much, and while the rest of the record industry generally slows down after Christmas as the sales are naturally lower in the pop arena following the huge pre-Christmas splurge of marketing and jostling for that apparently important Christmas No.1, Maiden's fans would buy a single they loved no matter how or when it was released. Another measure both of the loyalty of the fans, and the consummate managerial skill of Rod Smallwood and Sanctuary Management in terms of excellent timing.

The tour rolled on through America, Japan and Europe that

year. It had been another gruelling spate on the road and, as was becoming the custom, the group took the rest of the year off from direct Maiden duty, before they would regroup just after the festive season for sessions for their next album. Bruce spent the time sketching out the plot to the follow-up to *The Adventures of Lord Iffy Boatrace*, which became a satire on organised religion, a thinly veiled attack on his old sparring partner Jimmy Reptile, a famous US TV evangelist – it was another novel full of shagging, sick laughs and slapstick, which if anything was possibly even funnier and more ridiculous than its predecessor had been. In the book's introduction, Bruce admits that it was written on night sleeper trains between various British cities, which were, 'some of the most productive sleepless nights I have ever spent; sitting alone with my Macintosh portable and a stack of cans of Director's bitter, I doodled and scribbled as the train clattered through the night.' He goes on to complain about the fate that the trains had suffered under successive governments in favour of the motorway.

Such strong sentiments and obviously politically adept intelligence must, of course, have helped immeasurably in the writing of a book that ranges from time-travelling sex maniacs to compulsive-eating sex-maniacs, mummified relatives, TV evangelists, coked-up rock managers, cult shenanigans, porn stars, incontinent secret-service agents and a plot by a Japanese businessman to turn America into the world's biggest golf course. It is as bizarre, and bizarrely moreish, as it sounds. A rubbernecking experience, with the *deus ex machina* being literally the hand of fate. Which is nice for everybody, to be honest. The Germans liked both novels, publishing translations in Deutschland during 1996 to good response. In a later interview, Bruce was to refer to the experiences with some fondness, but felt a certain sense of trepidation as to the possibility of taking on another such project. He reflected on the mixed reception that the books had received to a *Moshville* reporter. 'Everybody that bought them seems to think they were very funny,' he noted. 'It was only the tossers who write for the music magazines that went all snotty on them. Frankly, some of the literary magazines, some of the regular newspapers and Radio Four gave them great reviews.'

As for the writing process itself, it was no deep secret as to the way it all worked, according to literature's latest newcomer. 'I know how writers do it,' he rightly noted. 'I spoke to some and they say you basically get a typewriter and bash away for eleven hours a day and you've got a novel. I wrote the second one more like that. I was told I *had* to write a sequel and it was really difficult. I just couldn't get the pace.' Bruce did work on a prequel to the *Iffy…* series but the process simply wasn't as enjoyable. 'I got about sixty pages into a third one,' he said, 'and just thought it was rubbish and ripped it all up. It was Lord Iffy's schooldays. I didn't think it was funny. Maybe I'll have to revisit it sometime.'

Caught up in the Maiden rollercoaster once more, the next project was to begin in January, 1992 with writing and recording sessions at Steve Harris's house – which was now home to a high-spec studio, in contrast to the set-up for *No Prayer for the Dying*. It made sense for the band to decamp there and work on the sequel to the next phase in their career. The back-to-basics albums of the early 1980s had, of course, produced the stunning trilogy of *Number of the Beast, Piece of Mind* and *Powerslave*; perhaps *No Prayer…* would kick off another productive period of technical, creative and explorative musicality for the band. The differences between 1982 and 1992, however, were marked; while in the former year, Iron Maiden had been at the forefront of the New Wave of British Heavy Metal, a decade later they were something of the old guard, holding onto concepts that were dear to their hearts. Metal had come so far during the 1980s that it had once more fragmented into niches, genres and sub-genres. Maiden and Harris's wish to keep things as close and true to their ideals – their street-smarts – as possible, was something of an anachronism when set in context of the younger tattooed millionaires that now posed and preened in the rock world. A reaction against these false rock gods was therefore inevitable.

But while in 1982 it had been a very British coup, borne on the ideals (and by some of the musicians) hailing from punk rock, by the early 1990s those same ideals were causing a raft of street-punks to rise across the pond – and it was called grunge. Seattle in particular was the epicentre of what became a movement that would capture the imagination of a new generation. Nirvana's Kurt Cobain became a kind of reluctant avatar for the disenfranchised. And while the punk and NWOBHM movements had been largely led by genuine street kids, grunge was a repackaging of rebellion for the MTV generation. On the face of it, Iron Maiden were a group clinging solidly to an older generation's set of values. And admirable though those ideals might be, an older generation's values are the only thing that teenagers truly have to rebel against.

The album that became *Fear of the Dark* also had the spectre of Harris's recent split from his wife hanging over it. It is, altogether, one of the darkest albums in Maiden's oeuvre. Harris's own tracks seem full of paranoia and imagined demons; for Bruce's part, some of the themes he explores in his offerings seem – on occasion –

inextricably linked with his own growing restlessness, albeit multi-layered and wrapped up in allegory. Janick's presence in the group had given Bruce an extra gear for the latter Maiden album, as only a new member and an old mate can do, and indeed, the two would contribute heavily to the new LP.

Their first collaboration is album opener, 'Be Quick or Be Dead', clocking in and out in sharp time, with Bruce spitting out lyrics that could on one level be about organised religion and the manipulation of the followers thereof, or, indeed, at any kind of authority figure pulling the strings and demanding that people jump into line.

Bruce and Janick's second contribution is the moody-but-bluesy, and rather 1970s-style 'Fear is the Key', which has elements of Jethro Tull prog writ strong through it. Lyrically, it is an exceedingly pointed attack on double standards – a song wrapped up in smothering lyrics about being outnumbered, fighting battles vainly, remembering old times when the nights were hot, bodies were hot and the passion, and possibilities were endless. It's also, very clearly, about AIDS, as Bruce remarked to Henri Dumatrey. 'Sex had become a synonym for "fear". When we were writing the songs, we heard about Freddie Mercury's death… in the States nobody really cared about AIDS until Magic Johnson announced publicly that he was HIV positive. As long as the virus was confined to homosexuals or drug addicts, nobody gave a shit. It's only when celebrities started to die that the masses began to feel concerned.' 'Wasting Love', a second collaboration with Gers, is another downbeat track, this time dealing with the groupie phenomenon and the emptiness of casual one-night stands. Bruce's days of being involved with that world were long gone; now happily married and a father, it was anathema to him. It's also tempting to take the lines about the empty days, the lonely years and the desperation on the part of the song's protagonist to finally be honest and resolve them another way entirely. It's a cry in the wilderness, a shout at an empty sky, an emptiness inside. Whichever way you want to read it, it's damned bleak stuff.

In the absence of Adrian Smith, Bruce and Dave Murray collaborated on two tracks for the *Fear of the Dark* album: 'Chains of Misery' – based around a shadowy character preying on the unwary – and 'Judas Be My Guide', which revisits the theme of searching for answers, or being guided by voices who may not be reliable. It is an LP that is relentlessly downbeat and though the band are more technically together than on its predecessor, the darkness that underpins it makes it a very, very difficult album to listen to. 'There's a break between *Fear of the Dark* and the old Maiden albums,' explained Bruce. 'I really believe it will make a huge impact; we're going straight into the 1990s this time. But the Iron Maiden style remains, we didn't compromise, we didn't renounce... we took some of the energy that's currently in the world and transposed it into our music. When [people] listen to it, I hope they say, "We thought the last Metallica [album] was good, but check *this out*!"'

As had become the norm, the first single was one that Bruce had been involved with, and his and Gers' snappy LP opener, 'Be Quick or Be Dead' slammed in at No.2 on its release on 13 April 1992. The album itself debuted at No.1, on 11 May. It was a double celebration for Bruce, coming three days after Paddy gave birth to their second son, Griffin Michael Bowden Dickinson, back in Hounslow.

The subsequent supporting tour saw Maiden playing to massive audiences across the Americas, pausing to play a huge gig in Rio's Maracanã on their way back to the UK to headline Donington for the second time on 22 August, a gig that went out live on BBC radio, and was subsequently released as the stunningly titled *Live At Donington August 22nd 1992*. Nervous though the band were, the crowd of 72,500 was ecstatic, Maiden – and Bruce – played a blinder, and things went without a hitch. Adrian Smith even appeared onstage for the encore, slinking his way through the standard 'Running Free' to a roaring reception. Bruce had also found time to contribute to a cover of Alice Cooper's '(I Want To Be) Elected', a charity single for Comic Relief, in which he appeared with comedians Rowan Atkinson and Angus Deayton, which reached No.9 on 9 April 1992.

The *Fear of the Dark Tour* then moved on to Australasia and Japan, where part one of the two-staged world jaunt was completed, on 4 November 1992. Dark themes, but a band who had absorbed the skilful, playful Gers into their line-up with hardly a stumble. It would, then, be a good and relaxing Christmas break for all those involved with Maiden. Well, most of them, at least: Bruce took a call from the record company that had released *Tattooed Millionaire*, asking him if he might like to build on the relative success of the first LP with some more solo material. Bruce being Bruce – and never one to stand still – he immediately agreed.

Chris Tsangarides was lined up to record some demos once more for the project. A sensible choice, as Tsangarides recalls. 'When … *Millionaire* came out, we had a whole lot of hit singles off it as well, which was a bonus. I suppose that's the way the best things are done – there's no real end to it, you just do it, and somebody likes it, and they buy it in droves, thank God, and there you go. Because of our good experiences of that first record, we decided to make another one. So he found a band, basically a pre-set band called Skin, and he went into rehearsals with them on these songs he'd written. Now, I'm not sure who wrote what, or if any of the band came up with whatever, but a whole load of material was done, and we went in and did the backing tracks. Then Bruce had to go, he was still with Maiden and they were playing, and in-between the odd day here and there he came in and we did a couple of days of rough vocals on the thing.' The project, however, was pretty much stillborn, the tracks remaining rough demos. Tsangarides is to this day slightly baffled by what happened next. 'I don't know if it was him, or what happened,' he continues, 'but that was about as far as we got. And to me it was very, very strange because I tend to establish myself with somebody and we carry on to do two or three records, and then it might be time to move on and it's all fine and dandy, you can appreciate that. But it takes a record to learn each other and so on and so forth, you know.' The material was a little different from the classic-sounding ...*Millionaire* sessions, however, with an edgier, heftier sound to proceedings. 'It was a bit heavier, Janick wasn't there. And I think possibly a load of the tunes should have been for Maiden, maybe,' the producer says.

Bruce was having huge doubts about his future over the period of Christmas 1992, having come to a few conclusions about his status and context within Maiden. 'The intention behind that changed after the first couple of records for me,' he explained. 'Because it became obvious that Maiden worked to a timetable. A '[timetable] that wasn't absolute but it had to be stuck to: "Now you'll write for six weeks, now you'll make a record for three months, now you're rehearsing for two weeks, now you'll tour for eight months." It was organised like that and that seemed to suit the style of writing of the band. Maiden was not the kind of band which I would term "experimental". In the early days they were doing stuff that was very different, but it didn't stay that different, it didn't continue the process. It pretty much developed into a formula.'

And that was never going to satisfy Paul Bruce Dickinson. It was becoming clear that for him to move on, he would have to take the decisions for himself – be they good or bad. This quest for personal development – he'd begun taking flying lessons in 1990 and in 1992 had finished twenty-second in the UK foil fencing championship – permeates everything that makes him an artist of constant surprise and excellence. It is, as much as anything else, ingrained in his personality. The two strong characters in Maiden were beginning to find that their creative paths were taking very different directions. 'It's just the way [Steve] is, you know. He knows pretty much what he wants and I think he tends to exclude a lot of options,' Bruce reflected. 'He's never taken a drug in his life, he doesn't smoke, he never smoked dope, he's never taken acid or anything that would alter his possibilities. He very rarely gets drunk even, because he likes to stay in control and I think that's the fundamental difference between me and him. Sometimes you have to be in control of things and there are times when you need to be out of control.'

But for someone as well-read and ambitious as Bruce Dickinson – who had a library many academics could only dream of, and a penchant for alchemy and the altered imaginative states of creativity and magic – that was anathema. 'That's sometimes when the best ideas happen – when you just take a big leap into the unknown and you don't know what's gonna happen,' he observed. 'That can be very creative and it can be absolute shit but some of the best and the most exciting pieces of music have been created out there on the edge of destruction. But people have different interpretations of that and, fundamentally, to me, "being on the edge" means being on the edge of actually destroying the creativity. Not being on the edge by playing fast, technically, but to try stuff that's so out there at a gig that the whole show might fall flat on its face or it might be completely brilliant.

"I saw my position in the band as being the one to try and take Steve's ideas, reinvent them and fuck around with it as much as I could, or as much as he allowed… when we got to *Seventh Son of a Seventh Son*, I was quite optimistic about that album. I think it was the last really good record the band made and it was a record where everybody was really trying hard to come up with directions, but it was so slow developing that record and it took such a long time to record it and it was so *terribly* expensive. But it was a pretty good record and there were several ways the band could have gone at that point – but as it turned out, the next one *No Prayer for the Dying* was a huge backward step, I thought. The idea was to do something low-key and not particularly complex, to do something that was the opposite to *Seventh Son*… – something that was very street, very happening and something that was gonna sound good. The fact is that it sounded terrible and everybody kind of acknowledges it now.

'We all collaborated with it and we all had a great time making it because we were out in the middle of a field making a record in a barn on a twenty-year-old mobile truck. But basically the [ex-]Rolling Stones mobile [that we used] was a piece of crap! It's exactly the same as when Deep Purple recorded *Machine Head* on it. And the only reason they recorded *Machine Head* on it was that their real studio had burnt down! It wasn't because it was such great sounding equipment, and it certainly sounded much better twenty years ago. They didn't even have a pair of monitors in it that were suitable for mixing on so they got in a pair of small monitors – and I believe they mixed the album on the Rolling Stones mobile as well which, I think, is completely crazy. Martin Birch suggested that we'd do the album in a proper studio at the very beginning but everybody was like, "No, no, no, this'll be really cool." And Martin did the best he could.'

… As is the job of any producer worth his salt. Martin Birch, being one of the greatest producers of all time, would have understood that one of the key issues is not necessarily producing a box of tricks to make everything sound magnificent, and pushing the band into a sterile white THX-type studio to attain pristinely-tracked music, but to keep the client happy and relaxed in order that they perform to the best of their abilities. And though Birch had semi-retired but for the Maiden albums, the quality of the mobile truck was not ideal.

'Steve, at that point, started getting very interested in the idea of himself being a producer,' explained Bruce, 'and he was already editing Iron Maiden's concert videos… Then we did *Fear of the Dark,* and I took Nicko aside and said, "You heard this band called Dream Theater?" I had some demos of theirs and I played [our] album to him and I played some of their demos and I said, "Listen to these, these are 24-track demos, no samples, no nothing, no machines, listen to this band." And then I said, "Now listen to *No Prayer for the Dying*; this is our album, and these are their *demos*. It blows Iron Maiden's sound into next week and it shouldn't." *Fear of the Dark*, then, was recorded in Steve's studio because he wanted it to be. I think it was the first album where we were attempting to recapture something in the past. In many ways, I think that we were looking backwards to other albums that we've done in the past while other bands are looking forward to something new. And that was the last studio album I made. Shortly afterwards I just woke up to the end part of the twentieth century and went, "Shit, I'd better try and do something different."' And so he revisited the Tsangarides tapes, and asked his manager Rod Smallwood for an opinion. Smallwood's reply was along the lines of advising Bruce that if he were to want to do something different from Iron Maiden, musically these tapes were perhaps not what he was looking for. Then Bruce dropped his bombshell: he was going to pursue whatever it was that was driving him to look for new adventures.

And he would be leaving Iron Maiden to do it.

CHAPTER 16

EXPLORING
AND EXPANDING

The second half of the …*Fear* dates – known as the *Real Live Tour* – were played with the intention of recording and releasing two live albums, one of 'classic Maiden' and one of newer material. Before the shows started, Bruce – with his decision to leave already made – took himself off to Los Angeles to try and extract some new material. Chris Tsangarides was a little befuddled by Dickinson's change of heart. 'I got a call into [the management office],' remembers the producer, 'who basically told me that my services were no longer needed because the record company had decided they needed to explore more with the vocals… I remember feeling very befuddled and thinking, "Well, we really haven't done any vocals, what's going on, what the hell?" Really at the time I thought, "What's happened here, what have I done?" You know, you look and think, "What's the matter with me?" But quite frankly, it was nothing to do with me, to be honest. I think that's when he sort of decided that he didn't want to be in Iron Maiden. I think that's kind of what really was behind it, when you look back with hindsight… I mean, I was paid for it, but it was just very strange.'

The fact remained that for Bruce to leave Iron Maiden was a huge deal. Conversely, leaving Maiden to do something that sounded similar to that band was pointless. So, in early 1993, Bruce flew to LA to seek out Keith Olsen, another absolutely legendary producer who had worked with the likes of Fleetwood Mac, the Grateful Dead and Sammy Hagar. 'He had just left the band,' remembers Olsen, 'and I think that exacerbated the problems because he didn't want to do anything that reminded anybody of the band. The early 1990s were also a time of experimentation, with one particular record setting the scene for many rock and hard rock artists. So with it being 1991, with Peter Gabriel coming out with "Shock the Monkey" that didn't even have a single cymbal on it anywhere, not even a hi-hat, [that was a very influential approach]. Everybody wanted to be Peter Gabriel back then, everybody. And I think that he had that influence also. Instead of wanting to be Maiden he wanted to "shock the monkey". So everything was changing. Stuff was changing in front of our eyes. Sounds were starting to change, you know, Nirvana was there, the grunge sound was just starting to attack everywhere, Pearl Jam had just been released. It was a very confusing time for an artist. Especially an artist from a very, very popular, world-renowned rock band. For the lead singer to kind of go off on his own, to leave that very happening band and go try to do something different [was unprecedented]. It was all troubling him, he saw the end of Maiden, because of the change in music.'

What Bruce brought to Olsen was a clutch of ideas, but as the

Skin/Tsangarides material had been dismissed as not hitting the mark, there was no band to work with. So the singer and his new deskman set about discussing how to approach the new project. As the producer remembers, Bruce was adamant that he moved away from the Iron Maiden approach as far as was possible – and to experiment with new studio possibilities. 'Groups like Dream Theater and people like that at the time were using technology a little bit better than Maiden were. Maiden had kind of hit a rut I think, they were just kind of doing the same thing over and over,' agrees Olsen. 'And that's the thing with Bruce, we were saying, "We'll take a shot, we'll see if it works but let's at least give it a go" and that's kind of what he was trying to do. As a shot to see if it worked and to see if he could be a little more theatrical and broaden his musical scope a little bit. That's where it made sense. It was interesting in the way that we put it together and tried to be as unique and creative as we could because, God only knows, we had Bruce's name. Because if someone was going to pull it off, maybe it could have been Bruce Dickinson. So that's kind of the wrap of what we did.'

Stripped of a band, Bruce's intent was to push the boundaries further than ever before: to work with sequenced drums and backing tracks rather than hit on a band vibe, and to construct painstaking keyboard lines and percussion completely in a digital realm. In a contemporary context, this is as commonplace as auto-tuning the drunken bassist's backing vocals – but in 1992–3, it was absolutely at the cutting edge of studio and sonic technology. 'He wanted to do something really radically different,' confirms Olsen, 'and we did. He wanted to have it programmed instead of played, he didn't want to have any metal in it at all. So I went, "Oh, that's unique."

He basically wanted me to construct and programme kind of beats around what [he had written]. We worked with Jimmy Creighton, as a programmer. Because he was taking about being more "Euro" in the programming. Kind of euro-programmed. "Prock" I call it, you know, pop-rock? So you know, euro-programmed, non-German-but-sells-in-Germany Prock.

'He wanted to be a hundred and eighty degrees away from Maiden. So because of that we tried this stuff that he wanted to do. And all that I can say is that we tried. It was unique. It had some merit to it. But it's not what he does best. And the songs were not a strong as they should have been. For me it was unnerving, the lack of direction and trying to be something that he's not. Bruce is a great hard rock artist and he's got to be a hard rock artist. That's why he's been successful all these years.

'Technologically,' Olsen argues, 'we were trying to do something ahead of its time, trying to do something kind of the way they make records today, back then. You sit down with a programmer and you try to put together something with an approximate feel, and the right length, and this, that and the other. And you make a copy of those files and you go off to a guitar player who's great, who puts on a bunch of stuff; you take your hard drive underneath your arm and you fly to Austin, where they have really great drummers that won't kill you with their price. Then you put drums and percussion on. Then you fly back to LA and you do vocals, background vocals and mix. Tim Pierce did play guitar on it. And then we had a percussionist come in and do some work on it. And that's kind of the way it's done today, you're going from project studio to project studio till finally a [real] studio to mix it. And that's kind of what we did. We did all that stuff in that little studio of Jimmy Creighton's, then we went over to Goodnight LA to do vocals and mix. And it was different, it was unique, it was okay.' Keith Olsen knows what it takes to make a hit; this is the man who, after all, is responsible for The Scorpions' 'Winds of Change'. Although the radical approach had satisfied the side of Bruce that was desperate to experiment and move from the Maiden blueprint, the sessions themselves had yielded only very modest amounts of useable material for his second solo album.

But in early 1993, it did not ring true for Bruce. Even as he was recording with Olsen in Los Angeles, Rod Smallwood was telling the rest of the Maiden camp of Bruce's decision to leave. Bruce had said that he was at the mercy of the rest of the group: should they want him to leave immediately, then that's what he would do, but he did not want to let the band down either, and in the end he was to play the scheduled concerts during 1993. It was, in retrospect, something that was no good for anybody involved. The gigs were nearly all sold out, and it was intended that Bruce's last tour was something of a final farewell to the fans who had been so instrumental in the success of Maiden in the Dickinson heyday. But tensions were inevitable: the general feeling among many observers was that Bruce was, at best, inconsistent during his final gigs with Maiden, and by the time the tour finale came about, it was a relief to all concerned.

Inevitably, under the pressure of touring life, and when tiredness begins to take its toll, people can snap and come out with some things that appear stronger or harsher in the cold light of day than they were necessarily meant at the time. Add this to it being 2 a.m., post-gig in Bremen, having had a drink and being asked for the umpteenth time about Bruce's imminent departure, it's understandable that eventually harsh words might be said. So it was with drummer Nicko McBrain, who in a notorious April 1993 interview with *Kerrang!*, said that Bruce was "going his way, we're going ours – fuck 'im, let's get a new singer. That's it – cut and dried." When the journalist asked if Bruce had 'shit on Iron Maiden' by leaving, the response from an obviously tired drummer was immediate and vituperative. "Course he has! He's said, "Fuck you, I'm off." If that ain't shitting on you, then what the fuck is?' McBrain went on to criticise Bruce's recent Los Angeles jaunts, and speculated that perhaps pressure had come from other influences goading him to leave Maiden's 'bunch of has-beens behind' in favour of a solo career. But the drummer was also defiant about the future, raging that rather than the current tour being *Bruce's Farewell*, it was still the *Fear of the Dark* tour, no matter who was screaming up front. He likened Maiden to, 'the phoenix rising; we will rise again, as a stronger and more positive bird'. Strong stuff, heartfelt at the time no doubt, but also exacerbated by a mixture of alcohol, the demands of touring and a pervading tiredness. Bruce was relatively philosophical and later told an interviewer from the French magazine, *Hard Rock* that, 'the journalist spent three days... trying to dig some dirt. And he couldn't. In the end he got Nicko a few drinks and, after about five hours, he finally got three sentences out that made that bloke's day. I didn't mind, I've known Nicko for too long.'

Bruce was philosophical about matters in that same *Kerrang!* feature, commenting that completing the tour was, 'easier than the other way of leaving Maiden... [sitting] there, gnashing my teeth and dumping it on the band after the tour's over. This way, it's out in the open, and all I see in the audience is people smiling.' He went on to comment that generally the fans had been understanding, and although *Fear of the Dark* could have been better, it was still his favourite LP since *Powerslave* some seven years earlier. Downplaying any reports of friction within the camp, Bruce comes across as if indulging in the archetypal break-up conversation: 'It's not you, it's me… I need to change and find myself.' The remarkably adult attitude to matters – bearing in mind that the band still needed to tour together – was continued by Steve Harris, who took the old 'this band is bigger than any one member, and if anybody's not into it 110% then it's not gonna work out' line, while also expressing his surprise that Bruce felt he could not pursue parallel careers both in and out of Maiden. An uneasy peace, but it all was during a dark period of the bass player's life in general, and Harris was to comment in *Kerrang!* that it had come 'at a time when I was at a bit of a low ebb anyway. But you have to pick yourself up and steam back in… Bruce quitting knocked me for six, and I thought maybe the rest of 'em would be looking to me to be a leader. For a week or so I didn't feel like that, but now I feel stronger as time goes on.' Stronger indeed: there is very little under the heavens, or for that matter below the earth, that is powerful enough a force to knock Steve Harris's vision off course. And once the *Fear of the Dark* tour finally came to a close, Maiden were to begin the search for another new lead singer with renewed vigour and self-belief.

That last 'gig' was a particularly crass affair, a televised piece of silliness on 29 August 1993 alongside magician Simon Drake, during which a member of the audience was 'killed': Dave Murray had his arms 'sawn off '. Finally, Bruce himself was put inside, fittingly, an Iron Maiden torture device and summarily 'killed'. Completely over-the-top, possibly ill-judged, but certainly final.

The show was recorded at London's Pinewood Studios and broadcast on pay-per-view television, subsequently to be released under the moniker *Raising Hell*.

Afterwards, the various members of Maiden – arms restored – and one newly-ex-vocalist, sidled off to their respective homes – and that, as they say, was that. The Worksop chap was no longer Iron Maiden's singer. He was, once more, Paul Bruce Dickinson, itinerant musician, fencer, pilot and bon viveur, and he was looking for the next challenge. He was bored of the cycle of long tours revisiting the same set-list and similar performance; the inside of a tour bus no longer held any appeal for him. Musically speaking, he admitted that the recent albums he was listening to were Alice in Chains' *Dirt* – but also, surprisingly, *The Soul Cages* by Sting, an LP he praised to *Ravin' Pestos* for being, 'beautiful and consciously naïve… it describes a multidimensional universe quite well and with a lot of honesty'. He went as far as to label larger rock concerts as boring and overly controlled, and admitted that he was occasionally prone to attending rave parties – which, to him, were reminiscent in spirit and freedom to the concerts he had grown up with in the 1970s. 'That's where you can find drugs, girls and the freedom to react the way you really want… in rock, the artist on stage has all the rights, he's the boss for the night, the audience has no prerogative and just waits passively for the show to end. In rave parties, each individual can participate. It's no longer just a circus show for the crowd, people are part of it.'

John McCoy, who'd been a factor in the music scene since the 1970s, postulates that in part, the split was possibly down to the differing backgrounds of the musicians. 'My impression was that Bruce was just trying desperately to fit in,' he says, 'as he was in the

Samson camp. The Samson camp was kind of an on–going comedy show, and the Maiden camp was like rock and football and football and rock. I think he was just trying to fit in really, to be one of the guys, but unfortunately that's never gonna happen because of background and education and he's just from a different world. But it's strange in bands because people come from all kinds of different lives and backgrounds, but it doesn't really matter, if what they contribute to the band works then you put up with their sort of [differences] in personal life, or you try to.' It can work, and work well – as it had in the case of the Gillan touring band of the very early 1980s – but, conversely, sometimes the constant flux of having to create a viable working relationship can get exhausting, and rather stifling after a decade together.

'I didn't have any clue [that Bruce would leave Maiden] during the tour we did,' Blaze Bayley says. 'Nor that there were any problems. They were an established band, they all travelled separately to gigs as they had family, wives and kids, somewhere to be, something to do. That didn't seem unusual at all to me, although later on I found out a lot more about what was going on and that not everybody was happy. I was very surprised when he announced he was going to go and that his last show would be a magic show.'

'He just outgrew it,' offers Tony Platt, who also gives a rather interesting insight into the perceived insularity often inherent in the Maiden camp. 'I saw him a couple of times after he had joined Maiden, I happened to be in Germany and somebody phoned me up – they were doing a warm-up gig in Hamburg or Cologne. And I was working in a studio just outside Cologne; I pitched up, Bruce had organised passes and it was really great to see him and meet his wife for the first time, it was really nice but there was definitely a frosty atmosphere from the rest of them. Nicko was the drummer and I had a huge history with Nicko because of working with him in Trust. We were great mates, Nicko and I; he used to come down to our house in Sussex and we'd spend the weekend. That was even stranger in that circumstance. The Maiden camp was very much a closed-rank thing. So you could potentially think he'd outgrown all that… And, of course, he'd got other things to do; other fish to fry as they say.'

Indeed he did, not least on the material he had been trying to pull together outside the often restrictive confines of the Maiden Machine. For Bruce's part, the experience of the stuttering solo recording sessions to date had been a valuable – but expensive – one. Dipping his toe into the water of something so *extraordinarily* radical – creatively speaking, and in terms of his career to date – had been of great interest, but ultimately of little use to his immediate plans.

'I took Myke Gray over,' recalled Bruce to *Book of Hours*, 'who did the original guitars on the first album but I didn't use him on all of it. I used some session guys over there in the States and I used the keyboard player and the bass player from Saga to do a lot of programming. The recording was basically put together electronically, written on computers, keyboards and shit and I then got human beings in to replace that. It was an interesting experience and I learned an awful lot about what I *didn't want* to do out of that record.'

However, what he had achieved, if nothing else, by virtue of indulging in those LA-based Olsen sessions, was meet a character whose talent, approach, humour and production ideas not only matched his own, but surprised and often bemused him. That character is Roy Ramirez, who had been around and about the So-Cal rock scene since the late 1980s, playing with the likes of Warrior and Royal Flush before renaming himself Roy Z and forming his own band, Tribe of Gypsies, in 1991. 'I grew up in the valley in a place called Pacoima, explained Ramirez to *Hard Rock*. 'It was a very, very bad part of town. It's famous 'cause of [cult comedy film stars] Cheech and Chong, a lot of shootings. A lot of gang activity. Lots of friends of mine are either in jail or dead. People that I grew up with. But it's a beautiful part of my life, 'cause we were happy! I did not know that I was poor. I come from a very traditional family, very family orientated. We still see each other all the time. Very close knit. I am proud of who I am and what I do and where I am from.'

Roy Z was also an accomplished producer and engineer, with a real feel for how sounds go together. When he and Bruce met in Los Angeles – courtesy of Shay Baby, who had been Keith Olsen's engineer on the ill-fated second shot at the new album sessions – the two musicians got on famously, both personally and on a creative level. 'He played me his band, the Tribe of Gypsies,' continued Bruce. 'And I just listened to his band and said, "Fuck – what am I doing fucking around with computers and all this LA crap?" And he was really into writing some songs with me, so I said, "OK, let's do that."' Roy's fearless approach was in part down to his upbringing, although he felt the meeting was, 'surreal and wonderful. It was pure destiny. The scary part was that he was so enthusiastic about my music. It vindicated what I was doing, for me. Trying to do heavy metal in the past never got me to meet these kinds of guys – or I would meet them and they would not think about working with me. Then here I am doing this, what you could call traditional-type music; and then you get noticed! I thought it was so strange."

The original intent was to collaborate with Z on three or four new tracks, band-based, to complement the six songs Dickinson had accumulated through the Olsen sessions. But despite the fact that Bruce had dipped into his own coffers to fund the recordings, he came to the conclusion that it would be a fudge, and something of a betrayal of his ideals, were he not to scrap *everything* on the second album so far, in favour of starting again in cahoots with Roy Z and his merry band of musicians. It would be a case of 'third time lucky': the Tribe were a stunningly proficient bunch, and Bruce had found a solo band – and a collaborator – with whom he could work extremely well. Bruce and Roy began to write together, and in short order had come up with a collection of songs that at last matched the vocalist's vision for what his second album should be. Roy would play him material, he'd scream along – to the point of almost crashing on the freeway more than once – and the pair came up with a raft of material that they began to lay to tape, with Shay Baby at the controls, at Metropolis Studios in London. Shay Baby had been enthusiastic about the possibilities of utilising African and Spanish rhythms alongside the Gypsies' skilful, but streetwise, approach, and was well aware of the talent of Roy Z as a guitarist and creative force.

When the call came to produce the Metropolis sessions, Shay Baby and the band were somewhat disturbed by an occasionally odd ambience in the facility, which was one of The Who's hang-outs and was said to be visited by the ghost of Keith Moon. 'Weird things were happening,' said the producer, laughing, to *Sunset Strip*.

'Mic stands were moving; we would tune the drums, and we'd come in the next day and all the drums were out of tune.' They even found a weird, gooey substance on the kit one day; even from beyond the grave, Moon was playing the prankster – settings would be changed on the studio desk and there were several occasions in which takes had to be redone when mysterious drop-outs appeared on the tape.

The sessions were notable for a real willingness to try different sounds and equipment out, as Baby recalls. 'We used 1950s Fender guitars, vintage Gretsch guitars... and even hunted down a Hendrix amp... we used some of Brian May's amps. So we got to put Roy's stuff through the amps Brian used with Queen.' Bruce had finally managed to negotiate through a very difficult creative period in his life; while there was a certain amount of sniping in the media between himself and his old bandmates, he'd got on with it and – eventually – recorded his second solo album, which was to be called *Balls to Picasso*.

The album opens with a sense of foreboding on the atmospheric, sinister, 'Cyclops' – one of the first tracks that Dickinson and Ramirez had written together. Its blend of doomy-funk, metallic bass and robotic samples is offset by a sinister, *sotto-voce* vocal from Bruce that speaks of secrets, lies and falseness. As the texture thickens into a passionate chorus it becomes pretty uncompromising stuff and although it's one of the heftiest tracks on the LP as a whole, it's as far from the Maiden days as 'Run to the Hills' was from 'Vice Versa' – and miles away from the knockabout daft romps that permeated *Tattooed Millionaire*. This is serious stuff, as evidenced on the Latin-tinged percussion and scales of 'Hell No', another set of lyrics about belonging, and starting afresh on his own terms. It doesn't take a huge leap of faith to extrapolate what that's all about. Roy Z gets an opportunity to show what he can do as a guitarist on the expansive anti-war track, 'Gods of War' with an evocative and squealing solo.

There are more digs at politicians and double standards, two pet themes of Bruce's, on the growling menace of '1000 Points of Light', before it kicks into one of the greatest tracks of Bruce's solo career – which on the LP cover is credited to B. Dickinson/Roy Z/A. Dickinson. If you were wondering who the mysterious A. Dickinson might be, it is an artist making their lyrical debut. Step forward Austin Dickinson, Bruce and Paddy's second son, who inspired the track with one of those phrases that only children – with their mix of unfettered imagination and open-eyed naivety – could come up with. '"Laughing in the Hiding Bush" is about my youngest son, Austin, playing with his cousins. He said, "Look, Daddy, I'm laughing in the hiding bush." I thought it sounded cool, so I wrote it down and Roy came up with a cool riff. It made me think of all of these fucked-up things kids think of. It makes me think of what we teach our kids,' Bruce told *Sunset Strip*.

Bryan May's amplifiers must have come in handy on the soulful, introspective 'Change of Heart', which recalls Rush in their more pensive moments and discusses lost days and strength of love. 'Shoot all the Clowns', by contrast, is an insistent Aerosmith pastiche that had its genesis in a particularly, peculiarly record company-type moment when an album – *Aerosmith Rocks* – was slipped underneath Bruce's hotel room door by a Mercury Records gofer, with a note to the effect of 'the album's cool, but can we please have a track that sounds like this?' (while Bruce was in discussions with that label to seal a deal in the USA). Three days later, Bruce and Roy had dashed one off – nonsense though it is – and despite the obviously superior musicianship, it is a marked contrast to the rest of the album. That said, it is notable for Bruce Dickinson rapping on record for the first time, which is a mark of how open to new ideas he was by this time. Regardless of record company meddling, the cautionary tale of 'Fire' brings the album back to form, followed up with another track featuring Dickinson rapping, the chuggy, funktastic 'Sacred Cowboys' – a tightly controlled exploration that, musically, sums the album up entirely, and again features some rather insightful lyrics. Bruce sings that there aren't any Indians to kill any more, they're not on the hill – harking back not only to his own work but also perhaps talking of having faced down the enemy one by one, and now looking for a new challenge. There are similar nods and cues throughout his solo work.

The album ends with the only song Bruce is credited as having written alone: 'Tears of the Dragon' – the only track also to have survived through all three ...*Balls* attempts, and the only one to have retained Dickie Filszar's original drum part. It is an evocative piece, with more lyrics about escaping from an oppressive past into an uncertain future. It's Bruce as an artist at his most vulnerable, and in sentiment, arrangement and delivery, it's as poignant a statement of regret – and hope – as he had ever allowed himself to be associated with. This brave, soft-rock, epic-feeling song rams home, via a beautifully delivered and occasionally understated vocal, exactly what his motivations for leaving Maiden and pursuing solo ideals were, and rounds off an album that is sometimes pertinent and pointed, but also – '... Clowns' aside – an honest offering.

Balls to Picasso was released on 6 June 1994 – by which time Bruce and Paddy had welcomed Kia Michele to the tribe, born on

10 May that year. The venerable *Kerrang!* awarded the album three stars, and though they felt it was a little patchy, they praised its occasionally 'magical' moments. Generally, however, the response was muted from a press who were either obsessed with grunge, or simply didn't understand the point of the project. On his own website, Bruce later said the he felt were talked into making a softer album and should have produced it differently. Unluckily, after three short months, Bruce's contract with Mercury Records was terminated, along with that of several other artists, as that organisation had to cut its roster due to financial difficulties. And touring was out too; the Tribe of Gypsies were unavailable, busying themselves with their day jobs – being a damned fine band and rockin' the free world. Although the initial intent had been to rip it up together, circumstances dictated that the Gypsies' career had to remain (rightly) at the forefront of their minds. After all, they'd only been 'borrowed' for the project in the first place.

As for Bruce, he was now becoming an accomplished pilot, clocking up the air miles during 1994, as well as finding some time to collaborate with the band Godspeed on a cover of 'Sabbath Bloody Sabbath' for the tribute to the Sabs, *Nativity in Black*, which also featured a raft of artists that included Biohazard, Megadeth, Therapy?, Corrosion of Conformity, Ugly Kid Joe and 1000 Homo DJs. Despite the relatively modest impact of *Balls to Picasso*, it was still a refreshed Bruce Dickinson who, after finally having got the second LP recorded, had conquered some of the questions he was asking himself.

The Maiden boys were busy, too, auditioning hundreds of hopeful singers looking to fill Bruce's considerable shoes. There were inevitably reports and rumours that there was to be a reunion with Paul Di'Anno. He categorically states that this was never on the cards. 'I was never approached. Not in a million years and to be honest I wouldn't do it for a million pounds,' he told the author. 'Once that door's closed, it's closed. At the time it was best for me to move on and my head was nowhere near where I am nowadays [in 2016]. I am a hell of a lot more sensible. I think that would have been totally wrong for Iron Maiden, getting me back in the band. No, no, no. Me and Steve know how to rub each other up the wrong way, that's for sure.' So it was back to trawling through tapes, CDs and videos for 'Arry's Army.

One particular vocalist had previous history with Maiden, and immediately stood out: Blaze Bayley. 'I auditioned like everybody else but had the advantage that Steve had already seen me live onstage as had the rest of the band,' he says, 'And I'd given them all copies of the CD, so they knew what I was like on record. But I never thought I'd really be successful because my voice was so different to Bruce. I can sing a lot of the melodies and things that he does but I'm just not the type of singer that sings way up [in the high register] and makes it sound convincing the way Bruce does. My voice has always been in the middle registers because of the [music] that I've been a fan of. I knew the set – it was ten of the songs that were always in there: "Number of the Beast", "Wratchchild", "Heaven Can Wait". I went along having learned them the best I could. I knew all the drum parts, where the solos were, the guitar melodies, the vocal melodies perfectly and I thought, "For an hour, I am the lead singer with Iron Maiden." I couldn't do any more and just tried to relax and enjoy being with a band where the sound in rehearsal was fantastic. A small backline, a cut-down kit, but you could hear everything perfectly. Standing in the same room with Dave Murray and having that Iron Maiden sound in the rehearsal room was just mind-blowing. I don't know how to describe it: hairs come up on the back of your neck when you hear those classic solos and melody parts.

'I got a call back and they asked me to do some singing in the studio. They asked Doogie White as well to that, plus another couple of people. And a day before Christmas Eve I got the call to say, "Well, you're in." I really wanted it but I didn't think I'd get it by any stretch of the imagination, so I bought myself a crate of Guinness and that was my Christmas. Then I had to buy an answerphone, so I didn't miss any messages. This was before cell phones and text messages, email was just starting. You had to be available all the time.'

Iron Maiden's latest singer was in place. Meanwhile, having put creative, physical and temporal distance between himself and his old band, a rejuvenated Bruce Dickinson set about looking for a new set of musical collaborators for the next phase of his career.

CHAPTER 17

ANOTHER
NEW BAND

The new project was to be a little different. Having had such a difficult and long gestation, the second solo album had brought one thing home to Bruce in spades: a solo album is all very well, but being part of a *band* has many upsides. The experience working with the Gypsies had reminded the vocalist of the inter-band dynamics that could work wonders with creativity. Having been out of Maiden for nearly a year, officially at least, Bruce was also on a quest to find his place in music and clarify his cultural context.

Bruce recalled that some seven years previously, while out for a pint of Ruddles Bitter near his home, he'd been very impressed by a young guitarist who happened to be rocking it up with his band, Gun, down the boozer that night. Alex Dickson was his name and the pair began to write and jam together. The next thing was to try and put together a touring band, as the Tribe were busy wowing record executives with their own material. Specifically, he needed a bassist and drummer. Following a recommendation from old mate Myke Gray, Bruce set about tracking down Atom Seed bassist Chris Dale.

'[Atom Seed] did quite well touring the UK and Europe,' Chris Dale told me. 'We had a deal with London Records, but it all went bottoms up, as many bands do. After that I did a few more projects and was looking around for a new band to commit to. I auditioned for Thunder (whoops, don't think I meant to say that), then I read in *Kerrang!* that Bruce was looking for a band. I was working with a very talented young Italian drummer at the time called Alessandro (Alex) Elena, so I asked if he wanted to do it too. He was, like me, a Maiden fan, so we sent in the demo of our latest band together. I also knew a couple of the guys from Skin, who were also on Sanctuary Management, and Janick Gers, so I asked them to recommend me to Bruce. We got called up to go to a meeting with Rod Smallwood first, then a first audition.'

Elena recalls the time well, and looks back on it with a lot of affection, having previously worked with Dale in the band Machine. 'Oh man, that's a silly story. I was in London, obviously. I had pretty much just arrived from Italy and it was funny because I didn't quite speak English. And so Chris and I went and it was a pretty funny audition, I must say. It was amazing to meet Bruce because when I was a kid I was like a major Iron Maiden fan, I used to go and see them play and stuff, I like all of their records. But then when I turned fifteen or sixteen it all died. I was like "Oh, *fuck Iron Maiden*, now I wanna listen to something else!" You know. Meeting him was a trip, he was super-cool, man. He like helped us unload the gear from the car and, you know, he was super-friendly. We started playing, you know, we played a couple of songs from *Balls to Picasso*.'

In fact, guitarist Alex Dickson, Alex Elena and Chris Dale clicked immediately, both on a personal and musical level, to the point where the three continued to bring the funk long after the 'official' audition was over. 'Bruce went out,' says Elena, with a laugh, 'and me Alex and Chris kind of kept playing for probably a couple of hours, from Chili Peppers songs to Kiss covers, anything. Alex and I clicked immediately, and again he's still one of my best friends, and he's a sick guitar player, he's fucking *crazy*. And he kind of always wanted to get into funk, and funk was always my thing, so we kind of clicked on that. And I remember Bruce asked Alex, "Should we get these guys?" and Alex was like "*Fuck YEAH, man!*" So we got the gig. It was all quite exciting. The first new material we heard was *Balls to Picasso*. That was already recorded and Bruce needed a live band to go on tour with it. I was pleasantly surprised that he was making a brave move and doing something quite different from Maiden. I love Maiden, but a change does everyone a bit of good doesn't it? I just wanted to join a good rock band, go on tour and play bass a lot. The fact that this band had Bruce Dickinson singing for it was a bit of a bonus!

'So after the audition we ended up going to Maidenhead,' continues Alex Elena. 'There was an airfield where Bruce used to keep his plane. An airfield for me was a *trip*. Imagine, man, I was eighteen years old, literally just arrived from Italy – which compared to the UK is like a small village, you know. I don't quite understand what's going on around me because I don't speak English that well, and I'm kind of like thrown into this. And at the time I was *completely* broke. I was living in Kennington in some housing project, and next thing you know I have a limousine that comes to pick me up to take me to *Top of the Pops*, I was like "Okay, what's going on here?" you know. And that's kind of how I got into it. It was trippy, man. And it was kind of bizarre because I got so much media attention back home, I was on like the front cover of the national newspaper, "What's going on here?" And obviously my parents were super-happy because my dad is also a drummer and my mum is an artist, so they always kind of supported me doing my thing.'

Bruce also had another impact on the twenty-year-old Italian drummer's life, as he happily acknowledges. 'It was kind of like a life-changing experience. I was really lucky, because at the time Jamiroquai wanted me in their band. But Bruce is a really cool, grounded, wise person, he's a good friend. And for me at the time – man – I could have gone either way. I could have gone down the route of rock 'n' roll, drugs, fucking mayhem, bullshit, you know, fake people. But he kind of trained me in a way, you know. He kind of took a liking to me.

'Like, at first I lived in his house, he's got a couple of houses in Chiswick and said, "Alex, you know, come and live with me, I'll rent you one of my rooms and you can live there." So for a while we used to hang out a lot. I used to go to his place at night-time and drink endless amounts of vodka. He's got a freezer full of vodka man, from all over the world! And I remember leaving his place *completely* drunk, not knowing, like I couldn't even walk home and home was like four blocks away man, it was ridiculous! He's been, at least for me, he's been a bit of a mentor. You know at the time he taught me a lot of really, really good things I must say; he was one of the people who first taught me to speak English. He was always very patient with me and I would ask him like, when I was learning I wasn't the guy who would just always say, "Yes" to things I didn't understand. I would be like, "Hey man, what does that mean? How do you use that word?" And because he speaks incredibly good English, very proper, and he is a great writer as well, I got the best out of it, you know, I had a pretty good fucking teacher right there.'

Band duly sorted, Bruce and the boys spent the rest of 1994 playing what was, effectively, the *Balls to Picasso* tour throughout Europe and America, ripping up a series of small clubs with a tight band, and playing far smaller venues than you'd associate Bruce Dickinson with in his Iron Maiden days.

'The States was really crazy,' says Chris Dale, with a laugh. 'We were supporting Jackyl across the Mid-Western states. Remember Jackyl? They had a song called, "She Loves My Cock", which was a subtle little ditty they performed most nights. They also fired shotguns and played with a real chainsaw, sawing up chairs and stuff. They had a bucking bronco type thing, which they'd get girls from the audience to have a go on, all this onstage during the gig. They were full-on, good-time Southern boys – nice guys, actually, but kind of scary to be around for a lad like me from a small town in Wales! Outside in the audience and the streets, things were more mad, with strippers dancing to Kiss, cab drivers trying to sell coke at gunpoint and chalk outlines on the ground to show you where their last customers had been. Looking back, I'm amazed we survived – the food was good, though. When we did the US leg of the *Balls to Picasso* tour Bruce flew us in a little seven-seater twin prop plane all over the States. He might be a wild metal frontman, but when he's in the pilot's seat he's a proper pro.

'We flew to Dallas, I believe it was,' says Elena, chuckling, 'and we rented a plane there. He had a co-pilot, just because of us in the back, but we basically flew for months straight, man. We had the crew travelling on the bus and we basically flew from place to place. And we went through storms and, you name it. But the guy is a monster of a pilot man, you never feel scared, it was amazing.'

'Europe was a bit calmer, at least more familiar,' Chris Dale explains, 'Alex Elena was, of course, Italian, and we'd all been on European tours before with other bands, so it wasn't so alien to us. We had a lot of fun here, I seem to remember, we were headlining clubs and it was very cool to meet all the fans and have a few strange beers.'

Alex Elena also threw himself into it, and remembers the European dates as being both exciting and, occasionally, a little surprising – and the experience of watching a true master at work was something that made a huge impression on the drummer at the start of his career. 'Playing live was a trip, man,' he gushes. 'It was really a trip at first, because the guy has got *total* control over the crowd. We spent six weeks touring Germany, we played every fucking venue in Germany – man, it was ridiculous. And Germany is not a great place to play, because the food is crap, the chicks don't look that good and German people don't quite have a sense of humour, so it's kind of a weird combination. A lot of history, you know, but besides that it's very, very exciting. The funny thing about Germans, man, is that people come to your show and they don't clap their hands. They are really still. But Bruce has got this thing where he can literally get people going, even when people don't want to go anywhere, he's just got this energy.'

Bruce used that energy to great effect as the tour wound through the Continent, both on and offstage, as Chris Dale remembers. 'It was great fun, we used to jam around a bit, occasionally throw in a different song in the encores, and generally have musical fun onstage. For me, although I'd toured Europe before, it was my first time in the US, South America and later Japan – they were all great experiences. We'd all have our little jobs on tour. My job was to check if the beer was up to standard in the dressing room. If the promoter had given us Fosters or something, it was my job to get some proper beer in. Bruce trusted me there. At some of the German venues it was amazing to go into their cellars, see what they'd got and pick out *a case of this… and two of that please!*'

Before too long, however, the tour was on its way back to England. 'The UK tour was great fun,' remembers Dale. 'It was quite a small club tour – by Bruce's standards. They were mostly venues I'd played before in previous bands, but this time it was all sold out and the crowds went crazy. After just coming back from touring the States and Europe it was nice to see familiar faces in the crowd.' That UK tour included a raucous date at The Marquee Club, which was recorded for posterity. 'I remember there were a couple of mistakes I'd made during the Marquee gig,' recalls Chris Dale. 'It was a crazy gig with stage diving and everything going on, I'd had a couple of beers and mistakes do get made. We discussed whether to fix them or not later. But when we listened back to it all, I didn't think they mattered much, so I said I'd rather leave them in there and keep the vibe live and real. Isn't that what live albums are about?' Those recordings ended up being released as *Alive at the Marquee*, which was the 'bonus' album released as a double CD with *Alive in Studio A* (which itself was intended, originally, to be broadcast live to US radio). Essentially, it is an extended radio session that shows off how the group had come together during the 1994 tours.

It was one of many plans that were flying around at the time, says Dale. 'There were loads of ideas going around all the time from management, record companies and Bruce. It was quite exciting – not all the ideas happened, of course, but it was good that there were loads of them. Radio broadcasts, live albums, tours of Eastern Europe, camcorders for everyone to make video diaries, B-sides written by the daft bassist, living in LA for a bit, Frisbees with the band name on… all these ideas were bandied about. The more stupid ones worked better, we found, hence I wrote some B-sides and we got the Frisbees made up! It was a day or two after we'd finished up our tour at The Marquee. So we just played the live set as we had on the tour, the only difference being we set up in a studio rather than onstage. The studio was Metropolis studios in Chiswick, where we'd previously recorded some B-sides for 'Shoot all the Clowns'. I think most of the original *Balls to Picasso* was done there too. We recorded this live stuff in Room A, hence the title. The vibe was good, it was just like a gig, except not in a concert venue.'

Notably, the performances on *Alive in Studio A* take the blueprint of the Tribe of Gypsies, but morph the songs via the skills of the new musicians performing the material – something that Dale feels is inevitable. 'When bands tour for a while, the songs start to change and evolve a bit,' he says. 'In this case more so, because we weren't the band that had played on the original versions of these songs from *Balls to Picasso* and *Tattooed Millionaire*, so we took them and played them in our own style. We jammed around and improvised a bit with songs too. Alex Dickson particularly improvised new solos every night on tour; most of them were incredible. Bruce fully encouraged this. He's a big Deep Purple fan and liked the way they jammed for hours back in the 1970s. While we weren't quite going down that avenue, it was a similar vibe.'

The idea behind *Alive in Studio A/Alive at the Marquee* was to counteract the growing trade in unofficial releases of live gigs, often recorded badly and therefore giving something of a false view of the band. 'I think part of the idea was to beat the bootleggers at their own job,' agrees Chris Dale. 'There had already been a bootleg out of the Milan show on that tour. Inevitably, bootlegs do come out and die-hard fans will buy them all. I can't blame them, I've got loads of Kiss bootlegs. I think Bruce has done a good thing by releasing a live album or live video on almost every solo tour he's done. The fans can then get hold of a live recording of the tour they saw and at least they know they won't get ripped off. A lot of bootlegs are expensive, have awful sound quality and poor packaging. This double CD was priced as one CD, it was recorded well and had loads of cool photos inside from the tour. A lot of those photos were from my personal collection when I was snapping away with an Instamatic. I used to take loads of photos on tour, and most of the fully clothed ones ended up on that CD cover.'

Both the *Alive* albums are fizzing with energy, but, crucially, also have a superior sonic quality. The fans were not short-changed, although on the 27 February 1995 release of the double CD, *Kerrang!* rather uncharitably asked whether people really wanted to spend their '1,299 pennies' on it. *RAW* magazine, however, saw it for what it was and enthused about its spirit, moody, clinical precision and splendid performances, awarding it four stars.

ANOTHER NEW BAND

The months together on the road had brought the band even closer together, both as people and as musicians, and when a rather odd call came from *Kerrang!*, the group jumped at it — of course, they'd love to play the gig that was on offer. The only small problem was that it was in war-torn Bosnia. It was a gig for a local rock society, on behalf of the United Nations. Metallica turned it down; Motörhead pulled out; Bruce and the boys decided to go for it.

Chris Dale remembers it very well. 'Sanctuary, the management, got a call from a British UN officer asking if Bruce would play in Sarajevo. Bruce is always up for an adventure, so he said yes. At the time, December 1994, the war was still on but had dropped from the headlines, so we assumed it had probably all quietened down over there. As had happened before, we were wrong. We flew into Split in Croatia and were met by the United Nations at the airport. They said, "Thanks very much for coming but things have got a bit worse here recently and we can't guarantee your safety so we advise you to get back on the next plane home." Which was a bit disappointing. Bruce, meanwhile, had met some guys from a charity who regularly drove trucks into Sarajevo despite it being under siege at the time. They said we could go along with them if we wanted a lift.' In for a penny, in for a pound, the band decided to press on with their planned gig. After all the preamble, they'd not come this far to turn back at the first hurdle; it would become clear, however, that this was no ordinary drive to a gig.

'So later that night, we got into the back of a couple of brightly painted trucks and drive overnight towards Sarajevo,' continues the bass player. 'Straight away it became obvious that this wasn't just a little trip through normal countryside. There were shell holes around, some roads were destroyed, there were military roadblocks.

But the really odd thing was there was no one else on the roads, and very few signs of life anywhere. It was mostly just dark. No houses with lights on, most of the electricity was down. One of the few signs of life was hearing sporadic gunfire throughout the night. We were told it was mostly fired up in the air by drunks, but that didn't reassure us too much. We only stopped once or twice on the journey, and never saw anyone except for soldiers at the roadblocks. When we did stop we were warned to stay in the middle of the road, even to have a piss. You didn't know who might be in the hedges or if the side of the road was mined. It had suddenly become quite serious.'

The group pressed on through the war zone, toward their destination, which by now had taken on rather a more serious tone than the 'adventure' that had enticed the band in the first place, Dale explains. 'We arrived on the outskirts of Sarajevo just as dawn was breaking. At a Bosnian army checkpoint, we switched from the charity truck into a UN armoured personnel carrier. We were warned to keep our heads down, as snipers were common around here. Going into Sarajevo, we saw most of the buildings had bullet holes, some were riddled with them, some had a whole wall missing. There was a bullet hole in the wall next to my bunk in the UN barracks when we got there. I found that a bit disconcerting. There was a discarded tank here and there, some houses had smoke billowing out of them – people were cooking inside on open fires. And this was the amazing thing: life went on for the people of Sarajevo. They'd lost the roof off their house, had no electricity or gas, no shops or money to buy things anyway, they were cut off from the world, their brother and sisters were all dead, their sons were conscripted and at the front line and yet they carried on with life. When we met people from Sarajevo, they were mostly quite cheery, very generous with the very few things they had and [they] just had tremendous spirit. That affected me most.

'You know back here in Britain and the West, we're always complaining about everything – the weather, day-to-day life, the price of things, getting home from work late, not having the latest DVD… over there they had nothing, it was all taken from them. And yet they smiled. The gig we played became a very minor part of the trip in a sense. It was a good gig and the audience were very, very appreciative, but the major parts of the trip that stuck in my mind were a visit we made to an orphanage (for which I cannot describe the emotions in words) and conversations with locals where they told me things that were so horrific, and yet day-to-day life and death for them. Then we left Sarajevo via Serbian army checkpoints, a Sea King helicopter and Hercules transporter plane into Britain in the middle of pre-Christmas consumerism and overindulgence. We were all still a bit shocked and stunned by what we'd seen. I think it made a deep impression on us all. As far as I know, no other foreign bands played in Sarajevo during the siege.'

The band returned to the UK for a quick Christmas break, having bonded deeper than many bands do over a ten-year career. The group duly toddled off to South America, where the single 'Tattooed Millionaire' had been a huge hit for Bruce, and where the audiences had always been enthusiastic for the singer's work within and without Maiden. 'The audiences in South America are the craziest in the world, second to none,' confirms Chris Dale. 'They scream the loudest at gigs and all through the gig, they don't stop. They camped outside hotels all night, tried to climb over high fencing to get in to the gigs. There were riot police called out in Chile at the gig. It was all quite crazy – but then, when we met the fans, they were the nicest people in the world, really open and welcoming.'

Dave Pybus, perhaps best known as Cradle of Filth's bass player, recalls the UK dates that he played with his band, Dreambreed, who were supporting during April 1994 having only just released their debut record; by now Bruce was guesting on the *Radio 1 Rock Show* as a DJ, where he first spun Dreambreed's disc. Subsequently, as Pybus reports, matters took something of an unexpected turn. 'Bruce played it a few times on the show,' he told me, 'which was a great buzz for us. Then, totally out of the blue, I had just gotten up with a terrible hangover and was having breakfast when the phones goes and it's Bruce on the line! He asks me how things are and would the band like to go on tour with them around the UK for a few gigs. I was like, "Erm… sure, sounds cool to me." I was in a bit of a daze. So he said, "Great!" and told me his manager would give me a call later to arrange things. Rod Smallwood was from Huddersfield, which was like five miles from my town, Heckmondwike, so that went down well with him. It totally didn't sink in for a few hours. I mean, there I was eating cornflakes at my mum's at eleven in the morning, and Bruce had just called me to ask if we'd go on tour… surreal. The word got round pretty quick, 'cos our label was good at networking. We were all over the moon to even have one show, never mind a whole tour with Bruce! We were very excited.

'For the size of my band, the venues were bigger than we'd ever played or hoped to play on our first release,' continues Pybus. 'I mean, on average we were playing to five or six hundred a night. Most of the audiences were into what we were doing, very receptive and respectful that Bruce had asked us. It was great. We were three bands and three crew sleeping in a Transit van with our gear. It was great, looking back. Some great memories, like a lads' camping trip, but with lots of people to play to every night! [Bruce was] quiet, but fun. He'd pass by and tell a joke or two, ask how things were and if we needed anything we just had to ask his crew. All cool. But we never really saw much of him, as he'd fly to each show and the rest of the band would go their own way, train or whatever, so we'd see more of them.'

Pybus got a chance to chat to Chris Dale and the others a little more than he did with Bruce, who was often engaged elsewhere. He recalls the tour with great fondness, no doubt because on more than one occasion his band hit such a chord at one particular gig that their free alcohol quotient was doubled. 'Obviously going round the UK in a van has its moments,' continues the bass player. 'We were sleeping on the beach in Weston-super-Mare, and a police-woman knocks on the van door at 6 a.m. simply to warn us the tide was coming in! We used to drink Special Brew back then just to get to sleep – so some memories are lost, as you can imagine. One of the best buzzes for the band was in London. The venue promoter thought we were so good he paid us double! And in Nottingham a local record label wanted to take us out but we asked for a crate of lager instead so we could get to sleep later. I sometimes reminisce with the guys about it even today.' He remembers that there were often calls for tracks from Bruce's old band, which he was still firmly distancing himself from. 'Obviously everyone was like, "Shouldn't you be singing Maiden songs?" But I guess it's down to the person at the end of the day, if they want to follow something else, that's their business, right?'

And, so, by mid-1995, it was clear that this wasn't merely a Bruce Dickinson solo project any longer. This was a band, of which Bruce was merely one member alongside three compadres, and the band were to begin recording some new material of their own.

They even had a name: Skunkworks.

CHAPTER 18

SKUNKWORKS

Although the band were as tight as you could possibly get, the fact remained that – certain B-sides aside – they were still by and large performing the *Balls...* material – which, of course, had been written by Bruce and Roy Z. That was soon to be rectified, and in order to facilitate a contemporary sound as well as stretch the boundaries, Bruce brought in a rather surprising producer to the project.

That man's name is Jack Endino, whose stock during the mid-1990s was of the highest order, having been at the helm for albums by most of the major movers and players in the worldwide phenomenon of the grunge era, including Soundgarden (one of Bruce's favourites), Mudhoney and a huge number of the bands coming out of the incredibly influential Sub Pop label in Seattle, including the band who had blasted their way to the front of the new movement and were capturing the imagination of teenagers all over the world: a small outfit named Nirvana. 'I produced the first album of a Kilkenny band called Kerbdog,' Endino explained to the author, 'who were managed by Sanctuary. Bruce heard the album and liked it. The following year, he just called me up, at my home in Seattle, out of the blue. He explained his whole solo situation, and how he wanted to make a modern-sounding hard rock record that didn't necessarily sound like what he'd done before. He seemed to know a lot about what I'd been up to in Seattle.'

From the outset, Bruce was keen to get away from the concept that this was just the latest folly by the ex-singer in Iron Maiden – the obvious comparison being David Bowie and his Tin Machine project. Bruce, at this stage, was driven strongly by the part of him that was trying to cast off his baggage and be recognised merely for his work. The band would be named after something that Bruce was increasingly obsessed with: flying history, as he explained to Henrik Johansson of *Book of Hours*. '*Skunk Works* is the name of the design bureau of Lockheed Aviation company that make very secret and advanced aircraft,' he explained. 'Planes that can't be seen on radar, and the Blackbird, which is the world's fastest and highest-flying aeroplane. They designed the U-2, America's first jet-fighter back at the end of the Second World War, the F-104 Starfighter, all kinds of really very revolutionary jet planes. Skunk Works is their nickname, which became the semi-official title. We changed it from being two words to just one word.'

'Bruce was adamant that it was a *band*,' Endino told me. 'He told me he would have preferred to just call the band Skunkworks and not had his name on the album cover. He didn't treat it like a solo album. He went out of his way *not* to seem like he was calling all the shots, and to treat the other guys respectfully, but at the end of the day, you still knew he had the final say on things. So the power relationship was a little strange, and maybe a little bit artificial. The other guys knew they were working with a heavyweight who was almost twice their age, but Bruce really tried not to act like one too much. Maybe he should have. But they were good players and Bruce respected that. And I respected the fact that Bruce acted a *lot* less like a "rock star" than some Seattle people I've known!'

'We did about six weeks worth of pre-production in Fulham,' recalls Alessandro Elena. 'We used to rehearse upstairs from this old pub called The Kings Head. It was run by a bunch of Irish people from Belfast. Honest to God, it was like one giant room with two fireplaces and two gigantic windows. And Robert Plant and Jimmy Page were there rehearsing before we got in there! It was just like a gigantic room with a PA, you had to bring your own gear, but the vibe was amazing. We did a lot of pre-production there with Jack Endino and again, for me, it was amazing working with him man, the stuff I learned is priceless. And he is like one of the *mellowest* cats. He would come out for dinner, I'd cook for him and we'd sit down and listen to music. At the time, Alex Dickson was also living with me. We were both renting one of Bruce Dickinson's multi-pads in Chiswick. So it was me and Alex, drinking ourselves stupid at the time, it was so much fun. And you know Jack would come over and discuss songs and arrangements and stuff.'

Chris Dale recalls how the tracks would come together. 'Alex Dickson recorded a load of instrumental demos, which he gave to the rest of us. Me and the two Alexes would jam them about a bit, while Bruce came up with vocal ideas. We went through maybe thirty songs like this and picked the best. He's good fun to work with. He works hard and plays hard. He has a good work ethic, but once the work's done, it's time for a pint!' Quite right too. Music-wise, the producer had also been well-primed for the tracks. 'It was pretty much what he had led me to expect,' recalled Endino. 'In fact, I think I agreed to do [the project] before I even heard anything. At their request, I was actually present much of the time while they were writing the songs. The only songs I had a hand in writing were "Innerspace", which was a riff me and Alex Dickson came up with together, and two of the B-sides: "Americans' and the 'Italian Drummer' sketch. They were just silly songs I'd written for fun. I'd written a bunch of tunes like that. They weren't intended for Skunkworks, but Bruce heard them, laughed a lot and said we should try recording them. As I'd written the music and lyrics, I was kind of directing Bruce how to sing them – that was fun: here's me telling one of the best metal vocalists in the world how I think he should sing a song!'

The recording sessions took part at Great Linford Manor, a studio in an impressive amount of grounds, and a very comfortable environment in which to work. 'It's in Milton Keynes,' explains Elena. 'It's like a castle from the [seventeenth century]. And that was an amazing learning experience, because we were all together. I mean, Bruce was hardly there, but us as a band and Jack were there every day. We would sleep there. And we would literally listen to music all day and dissect it and learn from it. It was incredible. We learned more during that process than anything I can think of. When you bond with a band like that and they all want to grow as musicians – man, that was amazing. And we were getting paid to learn, that's like the most amazing gift. So anything I did in the past during those days was like, "This is my only chance to do this and learn as much as I can so I can have a career on my own" as a drummer and now as a producer. So it was brilliant.'

'Cool old manor house,' offers Endino. 'Very big, though, with a tiny control room. Nice gear, and there was excellent cooking for us while we were there. Pete Winkleman, who ran the studio, was a funny guy. There was a canal nearby with a walking path that was obviously an old railroad bed or something. I walked it all the way from Milton Keynes to Newport Pagnell a few times – quite a distance. Being able to exercise like that in the mornings was very good for my head. It was a pleasant environment, a lot like Rockfield [Studio, in South Wales]. Bruce seemed pretty sharp, open-minded and also a nice guy; in fact he's six months younger than me, so it turned out we had a lot in common as far as the 1970s records we grew up with. He has broad music taste. Recording in the UK is always a good time, there's some great studios. And I liked the idea of trying to make a 1990s hard rock record with Bruce. If I could work with Soundgarden and Nirvana, why not Bruce? Why the hell not? He was done with Maiden, he could do whatever he wanted, so I was intrigued. Working with great singers is a pleasure.'

As for the Skunkworks band, Jack Endino loved the vibes coming back from the youthful musicians. 'Musically, it was excellent,' he continues. 'There was a chemistry. But they were young, so it was hard to get them to stay focused sometimes! Bruce and I are, of course, total workaholics. But those guys would break into Kiss tunes at every opportunity! The music and the whole creative process was pretty collaborative. Alex, Alessandro and Chris would come up with riffs, or demo them on a four-track. Bruce would pick the ones he liked, and we would all get together in a rehearsal room and just start throwing ideas around. The melodies and lyrics are all Bruce; the music was largely from the band, though with Bruce pushing in particular directions. I sat in the corner taking notes, noting the tempos they were playing at, making comments like, "Why don't you try playing that part four times instead of eight?" or, "What if we went back to that other riff after the solo section, and then into the verse?" I tried to be a catalyst and keep things moving along.'

The sessions were also a good opportunity for Bruce to continue his full-paced lifestyle, and according to Elena, the singer was never still. He recalls a certain early morning with a lot of affection. 'I've got this image in my mind that I think I'll never forget. We were doing the record out in Milton Keynes in that old castle thing and in front of it we had this gigantic park, man, I mean it was so fucking beautiful. And I woke up early in the morning, [the rest of us] used to smoke a lot of everything at the time, as the band, and drink a lot. So I woke up at six in the morning, I think I was still drunk and stoned from the night before, [and] went for a piss. And as I was pissing, I looked out of the window [and] there was Bruce Dickinson dressed in his white fencing, you know, suit, whatever it's called, practising in the park, man. Literally, it was kind of like, "Am I hallucinating here?" The way he was moving and the discipline and just the technique I guess, that he's got was amazing, flawless, great man. And, you know, he tried teaching me a couple of times. But with him, he's so fucking crazy and he will stab you and it's really hard to stab people with those fencing things, but it hurts. I tried a couple of times and I was like, "Dude, you know what? I need to practise by myself first before you can stab me fourteen times," fucking *ridiculous*, man! Sometimes we would tour Europe and he would organise fencing events and so he wouldn't turn up for soundcheck because he was killing somebody somewhere else with his fucking sword, you know! But it was cool and I liked that about him, man, that he had all these crazy hobbies.'

There was also the matter of refining the songs in the studio, and Endino made sure that the band would stretch themselves out as much as was possible. 'There was one funny moment,' he remembers. 'After weeks of watching them painstakingly putting together all these heavy mid-tempo songs, I suddenly realized that what this band was lacking was, simply, plain old bashing rock and roll. There was not a trace of punk rock in this band. Or irony. Coming from such a bunch of wise guys and comedians, the songs were all so damn *serious* and earnest. In Seattle, I well knew, hard rock and metal and punk had kind of blurred together – that was how grunge came about.

'So one day I just got fed up, and I challenged them to write a fast song right on the spot with just *three* chords, NO MORE, and a guitar solo with almost no notes in it! It was like an exercise. *Could they do it?* That's how the B-side "God's Not Coming Back" came about – to my eternal delight, especially with Bruce's lyrics. They welcomed [my input into the arrangement of the tunes]. You see, it was a brand-new band, and they were just starting to write together as a band, throwing ideas around. Arranging is one of my strong points; I tried to make sure the songs and riffs didn't get too clichéd or repetitive, and also, since I had thirty years of rock history in my head, it was easy for me to see if anything was unwittingly plagiarizing something earlier.

'So the Skunkworks songs all sound fairly original. It's pretty hard to be original in guitar-based hard rock these days, since so many have gone before us, but I think we did a good job of creating something with its own strong identity. I also kept pushing Bruce to try new things, both with his voice and his lyrics. "There will be no dungeons and dragons on this record!" was our motto. Bruce has a very keen sense of humour about his past, and about heavy metal in general. We had many a good laugh. The concept of "wheels and rainbows" became another running in-joke. Perhaps you had to be there!'

The material is strong throughout a record that stands and falls on its members. Bruce having brought the players together had created an unit of some force, but he was still suffering from the fact that he was such a recognisable character. Unfortunately, the record company refused to allow the album to be released without his name on the front, thus negating the point of the project somewhat.

'The idea was to have [a band] all the while, but we never really got the timing right to get things together,' Bruce told *Moshville*. 'So the first opportunity I got to do something sensible with a bunch of people, you know, we got *Skunkworks*. And it's *shitloads* better than anything else we've done. Loads better. It's really fresh, it's really new. It's nothing like the old stuff. From the next album, it's just going to be Skunkworks. There's just no point in persisting with this "Bruce Dickinson" nonsense. So what you're seeing now is the last vestiges of it. Promoters somehow cling onto this thing. You know, Bruce Dickinson – ex-Iron Maiden – and people will turn up. People aren't turning up for the *real* Iron Maiden, never mind *ex*-Iron Maiden!'

The contrast with the Maiden camp was marked. Blaze Bayley's tenure as frontman had been delayed while he recovered from a serious motorcycle accident. He gives an insight into the writing process for the new Maiden album at the time, *The X Factor*. 'I went to Janick's house with my folder of [lyrical] ideas; he messed around with a few riffs and melodies. We had a couple of things that really gelled, and started working with Steve. [In Maiden] it doesn't matter who comes up with the songs. It just has to be absolutely fantastic. Steve said he really didn't give a fuck who [wrote it], but it had to be absolutely great. I had six songs on *The X Factor*. It was very tough in the studio; difficult in the style that Iron Maiden recorded. It was so different to the style I normally recorded. You were on your own in a room; normally I'd record from the control room, working very closely with the engineer and producer, but it wasn't that way in Iron Maiden. We were still in the days of tape; the advent of hard drive recording saves so much time and you don't waste your voice. If you are concentrating on a certain shape in your voice, and you have to wait for the tape to rewind [it's not ideal] but with digital you can just go straight to that particular part to put a particular inflection, darker or brighter. It's much easier to create that picture when you are recording digitally.

'It took over a year from the start of the writing [through to the finished product.] It was a very different album: dark, more progressive musically. We thought we had something of very good quality. I often got blamed for slowing the recording down [due to the accident] but it wasn't really anything to do with that. I could still stand up and sing even if I was in plaster. There were lots of technical issues.' To this day, Blaze and his solo band play tracks from *The X Factor* live, particularly the ones that Maiden have never performed onstage. Twenty years after the event, he explains that his voice has matured into the material: 'The songs are really emotional. Back in the day I did my best, but with the voice I've got now it tells the story better. I can bring the songs to life in the way I couldn't [at that time.]' He has also re-recorded several tracks with the Dutch acoustic act Nylon Maiden over the years.

As to the fans' reaction to him as the latest singer in Iron Maiden, Blaze is circumspect and has a typically thoughtful analogy to illustrate. 'It's like losing your girlfriend,' he muses. 'You haven't got any problems but you weren't engaged and it's like she's walked out on you. Whoever that new person is in your life, or whatever your new circumstances are, it's never going to be quite the same and you're going to miss that old girlfriend. That's the closest I can say. People really missed Bruce. I have met people since who have said, "When I heard it was you that had joined [Maiden] I was really looking forward to it." But there are quite a few people that looked at the past through rose-coloured glasses, or ears, and didn't for some reason [read] the interviews Bruce gave about his past and his legacy that were really mean-spirited and horrible. People seemed to just forget that; they didn't want to hear it. You know, your girlfriend's left you, you are miserable and she's called you a smelly bastard. That was a real problem.

'We were making *The X Factor* and Steve was almost in tears one time reading something that Bruce had said. Not that Steve took it personally but that Maiden is so precious to him and here was Bruce slagging it off as if it had meant nothing. All those years they'd worked, the thing that they'd created, the barriers they'd broken, the things that they'd done. It was like it didn't mean anything; like it was a bit of a fake. And that really, really hurt Steve. That was tough for him. I think Bruce was going through some emotional difficulties at the time. It was a massive adjustment [in his career.] I do not bear him any ill will whatsoever. He's always been the nicest person to me; he's always given me his support knowing that it was a very difficult job to do [succeeding Bruce in Maiden]. I am one of his greatest admirers. Bruce was going through a lot there and I don't think he realised what he was saying, didn't think it through.

'I remember being on tour and thinking, how could Bruce leave this? Sold-out gig, people singing the songs, the most loyal, wonderful fans you could get. How could you leave that? It didn't make any sense to me, as a young man coming into a dream job. I couldn't imagine – as tough as it gets sometimes, and you have to make many personal sacrifices to continue to do that at high ability – how anybody could leave. It's like being in the first team at Manchester United, if you're from Manchester, and have played there since a boy. It was fairly uncomfortable when we were making *The X Factor*, but we started the tour and I had a very positive reaction from most of the fans. I'd been a fan of Maiden, watching them on the *Number of the Beast* tour and many others. I knew why I liked Iron Maiden and I knew the British fans knew I respected the legacy of the band. I tried to sing and phrase the songs well and a lot more precisely. I took much less liberty with the songs and treated them with respect, trying to get them as right as I could. Get the old songs closer to *Piece of Mind* or *Number of the Beast* performing.

'They liked the new album in France; in Sweden, Maiden were the biggest they'd ever been with me in the band and people really seemed to like it. In Sweden and Finland *The X Factor* is still one of the most popular Maiden albums because it's so different. It seemed to appeal to those long, dark days [in Scandinavia.] Italians really struggled to understand it but now I'm more popular in Italy than I've ever been.' Blaze feels that people are now looking at the back catalogue without the context of Bruce's departure, and reappraising the work with new ears. 'Many people didn't want to show they liked it, [at the time], but now it makes sense [to them] when it didn't at the time. I think that's just because when Iron Maiden chose the new singer they decided to have a big change, not just replace the voice for another voice. So they got a different voice and I think it was a bold thing to do. You couldn't expect Paul [Di'Anno] to sing the Bruce songs, just as Bruce struggles with a couple of the songs from my era that just don't suit him at all. He is a brilliant singer and does [most of them] brilliantly. We each have our own eras, our own strengths and weaknesses.'

Bruce Dickinson, out of the Maiden firing line and pursuing a different tack, had achieved his aim according to his producer. 'We succeeded in what we set out to do,' said Endino. 'But it didn't really do much for his career, or for mine. People who know me but never heard it, imagine it must be a typical metal record, and wonder why I would do it. And some of Bruce's hardcore fans were upset that it didn't sound more like Maiden, though there were a smattering of people who totally *got it* and seemed kind of amazed. Other than that, I think I would have mixed the vocals a little louder!' Endino recalls it being a little more difficult than other records had been to make, with perhaps a slight lack of focus among the group as a whole. And although the songs on the album rock along merrily, the process itself had become exhausting. Away from Bruce, those extended jam sessions between the Skunkworks band had produced a real hunger for the three younger players to form a funkier band, playing the dafter songs of Dale's, eventually under the moniker Sack Trick. Although they were focused on the job in hand, it began to become clear that perhaps their destiny and Bruce's lay down different paths.

'I think Bruce might have gone even heavier, in a kind of Sabbath-y direction, if he could,' says the producer. 'But the band wouldn't go there. With hindsight, it's easy to say now that Skunkworks was essentially Sack Trick impersonating a metal band! Their hearts did [lie] elsewhere, and about halfway through the project, I realized this; that was when I knew in my heart it would not be a long-term band for Bruce. It did not come about organically: the guys were picked, or hired, or invited by Bruce to "become a band". It was like a grand experiment; everyone participated willingly in it, and the results were good, although years later when talking to Bruce I compared it with trying to animate a sort of Frankenstein's monster, built from dissimilar parts. We agreed, however, that the monster did actually come alive and even sit up and look around a bit. But it was a pretty hard record to make. I had to apply relentless willpower and total focus for almost four months. Even thinking about it now, I feel tired. Records should not have to be forced into existence like that. But some of those songs are pretty good, regardless of how hard it was to make the record. "Space Race", "Strange Death", "Meltdown", they're *killer*. I still *like* the record.'

Alessandro Elena, the baby of the band, agrees that although it was a great deal of fun – and he had learnt an enormous amount from the process – the future did not look great for Skunkworks as an on-going concern. 'The *Skunkworks* album is a pretty cool record. We, as a band at the time, were listening to Soundgarden, we were really into the Chili Peppers and *majorly* into Jane's Addiction. And if you listen to the record now, you will find bits and pieces from those bands everywhere. Or if you check any of the live stuff, it was a crossover, literally, between the Chili Peppers and Jane's Addiction.' He feels, however, that Bruce could have taken things a little further even than the huge steps the singer had taken to destroy his past, and speculates as to whether there may have been pressure from other angles – still – to create 'hit singles'. Whatever the reality of it, things could not carry on for long in their present form.

The band, however, did embark on another tour during 1996, including a stint as special guests to Helloween, putting in the hard yards on the road backing up the release of *Skunkworks* in the time-honoured manner, with the increasingly masterful pilot Bruce again flying his group from gig to gig. The album was released on 26 February 1996, and although it barely scraped the Top 40, the music magazines were much-enamoured of this new swerve in the increasingly winding path of Bruce Dickinson's career. *Metal Hammer* felt it was a 'tour de force of modern metal' and *Kerrang!*'s legendary British Metal expert Malcolm Dome gave it four stars, opining that Bruce had successfully harnessed the skills learnt over the previous decade-and-a-half near the top of his profession, while also releasing an album with the vigour to appeal also to the grunge generation.

Sadly, despite ripping it up on tour, the band's days were limited, and this time it was down to that age-old concept/ excuse of 'musical differences'. 'I think he wanted to challenge himself musically,' says Chris Dale. 'Before he left Maiden he'd never rapped on a track, never done acoustic songs, I think he just wanted to try something new and see what happened with it. He'd tried doing something different and I think really enjoyed it. But to be honest, the fans weren't enjoying it that much. It was kind of a love/hate thing. Some people loved it – some absolutely *hated* it. I remember one fan in Spain told me, "Bruce is a traitor to heavy metal," which made me laugh at the time – but these people take their metal very seriously and, well, they should. I think the *Skunkworks* era was like a holiday from metal for Bruce. At the end of the day, Bruce is a metal singer, he loves metal and that's what he's best suited to doing.

'I don't think any of us regret doing the *Skunkworks* album, but it was a one-off. I think of it in Kiss terms – I think of most things in Kiss terms – as being like *The Elder*. I'm glad Kiss made *The Elder* – but I'm glad they went back to *Creatures of the Night* afterwards. And if I could choose just one Kiss album to have played on, it would be *The Elder*. So of all Bruce's albums, I'm proud to have played on his most different and the one that causes most controversy amongst fans. If you don't try something, you'll never know. Maybe we could have done it a bit more commercial, maybe we could have had a more metal single or video… nah, we did what we wanted to do with no outside pressures to conform to standard and that's the best anyone can do. People say it was a commercial failure in that it sold less than Bruce's other albums, but Bruce's least-selling album is still a lot more than many bands sell!'

Alex Elena feels that the experience was something that money could not buy, despite the group splitting after their 1996 tour. 'That's how I started my career professionally, pretty much,' he offers. 'He opened the doors to me becoming a professional musician.

Because if you don't do it professionally, you will never learn how to do it correctly, you know? You can be the best drummer in the world, but if you don't go on tour for three years straight and if you don't record in proper studios with proper producers, you'll never learn. You'll never know the gap between people that make it and people that don't make it. Like, "Why didn't I make it?" Because it's obvious that *you weren't good enough*: that's always my answer. Obviously, there is always bad luck that always plays its part with some musicians. But everyone you see out there doing stuff is [doing so] because they deserve it or because they're good at doing it. Whether you like it or not, they are good at doing something.'

Bruce made his debut on the musical game show *Never Mind the Buzzcocks* on 12 November, managing to deal with the innuendo of Richard Fairbrass of the band Right Said Fred as well as the aggressive sarcasm of host Mark Lamarr. In an interview around the same time, with *Book of Hours*, he was to explain how the band decided to call it a day. In mid-1996, there had been talk of a second Skunkworks album, but, 'the direction that, particularly the guitarist was going in, was like east and I was going west. I wanted to do a much heavier album. I was quite prepared to call it *Skunkworks* and carry on with the idea – but the stuff that was coming through from them was really so far removed from hard rock music, so I was like, "This is not gonna work." Skunkworks was kind of a Tin Machine[-type] project, basically, and you commit yourself to that as long as you can and as soon as it became obvious that it wasn't working, you just have to abandon it and start again. I think we had a situation where I think the guys weren't as committed to the idea of Skunkworks as a band as I was, you know. Otherwise, when I suggested that we cancel the whole thing they would have gone that, "Oh no, What a shame", you know, but everybody went, "Oh, okay." Just like that!'

It was time to find out what Bruce Dickinson could do again. As 1997 dawned, despite the relative disappointment of Skunkworks' reception (and the pride in the achievement), two individuals were to return to the creative sphere of the Worksop chap. One a relatively new collaborator, and one a very old friend. Things were about to be flipped on their head once more.

CHAPTER 19

ACCIDENT
OF BIRTH

While *Skunkworks* had been somewhat of a catharsis for Bruce, a project that released the urge to pursue his craft in an entirely different direction, the response had been – at best – lukewarm. In truth, for Bruce to be able to shake off his fame and recede into the confines of an unknown band to begin an assault from ground level once more was unfeasible and unlikely. Working with such a high-profile producer as Endino, in any case, was bound to attract attention. And although the LP remains an underrated and excellent set of tracks, it had neither made a mark among the grunge generation nor entirely satisfied those fans who had stuck with Bruce from the Maiden days. Sales were respectable, although anything would feel a failure when put up against the multi-million-selling albums of his past. With the Skunkworks band effectively going off to do their own thing, Bruce was left once more pondering his place in the world of music. Was anyone really still interested in what he had to offer? Or was he to be unjustly written off as yesterday's man? The questions were maddening and circular; had anything really changed for him since he'd left the Maiden camp? Sure, he'd pursued his imagination and developed many projects outside music. But at root, music was still a passion. And in the aftermath of *Skunkworks*, where was there left to go?

'I was devastated by the *Skunkworks* thing,' Bruce told journalist Henrik Johansson. 'I was on the verge of saying, "This business is so fucked, I just don't care any more," you know. *Skunkworks* was a record which I tore myself apart to make and nobody seemed to give a shit. I don't think anybody in the management really understood what was going on either, because otherwise we wouldn't have been touring with Helloween. They were totally the wrong band for Skunkworks to tour with.' However, he also saw the inherent value in his expeditions into different sonic valleys, not least because it was like, 'a bucket of cold water for a lot of people, 'cause it was like, "What is he doing?"' In particular, Bruce remarked that he rather enjoyed the fact that [the album] was hated by the hardcore Maiden fans and those with the narrow-minded attitude that he should do only one particular style of music. 'I took great pleasure in that,' he continued. 'They were feeling something other than this kind of numbness that you get when you get the same old shit day after day after day.' Avoiding that restrictive routine was one of the things that motivated Bruce to leave Maiden in the first place and pursue his own path. Otherwise, he felt, the danger was that he would, 'Sleepwalk through tour, album, tour and just keep on going and suddenly realise that I would be forty-nine years old. Hey, pension in ten years' time. Another tour, another album, another tour, another album, get the Grecian 2000 down, another tour... I used to wake up getting night sweats about it going "AARGHHH!! You might as well be dead."' Interesting words – told to *Club 5619* – for sure.

A combination of record label problems once more meant that the LP was almost bound to become a lost cult classic as soon as it hit the streets. Bad luck? Bad timing? Or a combination of more factors? Regardless, as the vocalist approached his late thirties, a crossroads was presenting itself. Kicking these concepts around in his head, and wondering where to head next, Bruce's world was to change once more when he took a call from Roy Z, who was enthusing about some new riffs he had been playing with. What Roy played him suddenly made a huge amount of sense. It was, unashamedly, balls-out metal. And though Bruce had some initial reservations that it was re-treading old ground, the thought of doing a metal album again appealed both to his musical instincts as well as his well-developed sense of mischief. If metal was by now the last thing that people expected from him – after all of his well-publicised pronouncements that he was done with a certain genre, and after all of his avowed aims to explode preconceptions – if he was expected *not* to come up with a hard-driving, heavy metal set of songs, then perhaps that was *exactly what he should do*.

Going into sessions along with Roy Z, things started to click into place, as Bruce told interviewer Matthias Reinholdsson. 'So there I was, boom, in Los Angeles, on my own, it's kind of sunny and I thought, "Let's see what happens." So I went in and we came out with "Accident of Birth" and I was like, "That sounds great." And then it was like a big light went on in my head: "I can do this, I know exactly what to do on this record, *exactly*. I don't know any of the songs yet but I know I can write them." It was almost a huge relief that I was going to do something that I knew exactly what to do… I just wanted to make an album that fucking rocked and I guess that makes me sort of some kind of weirdo because nobody's making an album like that.' There was also a certain sense of fatalism about the project, a determination to see things through to their natural conclusion and *que sera, sera*. 'Then I thought, "If this fails this will be the last album I ever make," and I thought, "I don't give a shit. If this is gonna be the last album I ever do, I'm gonna do the best straight heavy metal album I ever made in my life."' And so Roy Z and Bruce sat down together and began to write a set of songs that took metal as their starting point and, melding the genre with the possibilities of the studio, ripped the paint off the walls. That was also achieved by virtue of the addition of another musician to the mix, a shock to many, but a well-received bit of news: Adrian Smith would be adding his guitar skill to the project.

Smith had been relatively quiet since his own step back from Maiden almost a decade earlier, working on his own solo material and putting together a new act of his own – Psycho Motel – who by 1997 were on the verge of releasing their second album. The material was rooted in classic influences like Hendrix, melded with a more modern approach engendered by the group's other members, who brought a contemporary touch of Alice in Chains and Soundgarden to the mix. Psycho Motel was a lot of fun, and musically satisfying, but the temptation to work on a true metal LP was strong for Smith, and he agreed to put down some guitars to the Z/Dickinson material, and renew his long-standing and successful writing collaboration with Bruce. Needless to say, Smith was reasonably easily persuaded to stay on for the tour, too.

'When we were in Maiden, we always talked about maybe doing a joint album outside of the band,' said Smith to *Club 5619*. 'So, I heard he was going to get in touch with me and he did. He got an idea for this next album and called me up, he'd already written some songs with Roy, I had a couple of ideas that I thought might suit and we wrote two or three songs and that was it.' The album that became *Accident of Birth* was bound to have Maiden-esque elements, not least due to the metallic approach and Smith's guitar contributions. However, it would be churlish to pigeonhole the LP as such. Bruce's vocals are hugely controlled, as fluid as any Smith guitar line, and as gravelly as any heavy Z riff, but only when the material warrants it. His development as a singer during the solo years is perhaps often left unsaid, but having explored many different styles since leaving the Maiden camp, and with the passing of time, there's a richness of character in a timbral sense on *Accident of Birth* that allows for even more expression. If *Shock Tactics* had been the album where, in the words of Tony Platt, Bruce stopped shouting and started singing, *Accident of Birth* is where he added consummate classical technique and maturity to his still-incredible vocal range. There is not a moment on the album where Bruce is not in control, despite some very demanding melody lines and interval jumps that would test lesser vocalists beyond their capabilities. It is, in many ways, the best set of vocal performances of his career.

Lyrically, also, *Accident of Birth* is much more conceptual than the sometimes brutally honest personal nature of its predecessors. There is passion here, but more often than not it's couched in allegory and imagery. Bruce always was a good storyteller, after all. He returned to the source material of an old friend – Mr Aleister

Crowley – for the epic 'Man of Sorrows', which – in concept at least – was a track he'd been playing with for nearly five years. The lyrics outline neatly the quest for answers and alternatives that also was, in part, based on Crowley's childhood sketched out for a movie treatment entitled *The Chemical Wedding*, which Dickinson had also been toying with for a while. 'The Magician' also referred to Crowley, but *Accident of Birth* is far from a concept album. The themes and tales, although they share a certain aesthetic, are wide-ranging and each track stands on its own merits. The title track, Bruce revealed to *Club 5619*, is both self-aware in terms of its references to freedom and homecoming, as well as, 'about a family from Hell. Except they're in Hell and one of them has accidentally been born, and they want him back and he doesn't want to go. For all the same reasons that you wouldn't want to go back to your family if they're a pain in the arse.'

He said that although every song was bound to have an element of a personal theme behind it, it was more about the interesting stories he wanted to tell. 'I had to construct quite an elaborate storyline and then maybe only tell half of it in the lyrics. I had to do that just for my own benefit to show that I could, you know, daydream properly. There's not a single thing on this record which is not rooted in imagination in some way, with the exception of maybe "Man of Sorrows". All the other songs were written in the space of five weeks,' he told *Book of Hours*. Notably, also, the cover art was provided by long-term Iron Maiden cover artist, Derek Riggs – who, similarly, had not worked with that group since the early 1990s. The cover was a Mister Punch-esque character jumping out malevolently from the belly of his parent, and again the themes of rebirth and mischief are writ strong therein. The character is even named Edison – no prizes for guessing the reference there.

On its release, on 12 May 1997, *Kerrang!* awarded the album three stars, reviewer Liam Shiels remarking that it was something of a return to type for Dickinson, who was saying, 'hello again to preposterously overwrought vocals, [and] great big hooligan riffs'. The reviewer went on to note that it was an album that Maiden fans would snap up after being, 'sent reeling by the dour, plodding *X Factor* blunder'. Tracks that attracted particular praise included 'Darkside of Aquarius' – which the reviewer felt echoed 'Revelations' – and the Smith/Dickinson collaborations, 'Road to Hell' and 'Welcome to the Pit'. Dave Ling, meanwhile, writing in *Metal Hammer*, praised the set's 'thrilling vibe' and awarded it four out of five. Referring to Bruce's intent to play Maiden songs on tour, the legendary journalist ended with the words, 'Bet Harry's worried!'

After a quick week of acoustic and in-store appearances to push the LP, Bruce's full band embarked on a tour that scooted round Europe before hitting America once more, beginning at the Mastetrax Festival in Madrid on 5 July and culminating with the group's concert at Springfield, no less, on 4 October. Whether Otto and Bart were at the gig is unverified, of course. Of that American tour, Smith commented in his *Club 5619* interview that it was real ground-level stuff, and that as the band, 'moved across the states it seems that the audiences have been getting bigger. In the 1980s, with Maiden, you had video, MTV and all that kind of media stuff and loads and loads of rock stations. Now we're doing it the hard way, going across doing the clubs, it's getting around by word of mouth and it's kind of paying off.' And although the crowds were more like five hundred than fifty thousand, he felt refreshed and challenged by the experience, enjoying standing there, in the moment, soloing and watching Bruce work the crowd once more. By the time the group joined Lynyrd Skynyrd as special guests for their European tour, they'd managed to build their profile to the extent that audiences were now touching around a thousand. Bruce himself was pleased with the reaction, citing the sense of excitement and anticipation there seemed to be for the album and the return to his metal roots.

The band continued to gig all the way through to 22 November 1997, after several dates in South America hooking up in Brazil, Chile and Argentina with the Monsters of Rock Festival. There was no doubt about it: Bruce was back, and the addition of Smith to an already great band of Roy Z, Eddie Castillas and Dave Ingaharam made them a unit of some force.

So it turned out that Bruce's reservations had been unfounded. Far from being the last album he would make, *Accident...* had returned fire to his belly, and received critical acclaim that had been previously (and perhaps unfairly) absent from his solo work. Given that Bruce had also found the time to duet with opera singer Montserrat Caballé on a recording of 'Bohemian Rhapsody', complete with a forty-eight piece choir, direct the video for 'Inertia' (his second as a director after the previous year's 'Back from the Edge'), as well as keep his hand in with radio work and television appearances, 1997 had been some year for the singer. But the following twelve months were to be *astonishing*.

It all started in February, when Bruce teamed up with DJs Tommy Vance and Krusher Joule to serve up rock on air throughout the month on Manchester's All Rock Radio. It was well-known that Bruce was a talker, but often putting a microphone in front of someone in a radio context dries up their verbosity, but an increasingly confident Dickinson was becoming audibly more and more comfortable as a DJ.

It was clear that a follow-up album to *Accident of Birth* was not only advisable but inevitable, and to that end Bruce, Adrian and Roy began to get their heads and riffs together for some more metal madness. This time, remarkably the results were to be even heftier than *Accident of Birth*. Bruce and Roy had been sketching out ideas for a while before the singer found himself, as is his wont, wandering into a second-hand bookshop to browse for some idea-pie to feed his hungry brain with lyrical and thematic ideas. And what he stumbled across meshed in perfectly with the idea of alchemy that he'd already been formulating from the original clutch of songs that had begun to shape up for the new album, which he'd already decided to entitle *The Chemical Wedding,* as he explained to *Hard Radio*. 'This thing caught my eye, which was an encyclopaedia in art history of alchemy, a big thick book with loads of great pictures in it, ranging from early pictures of alchemical engravings, right up to H R Giger and stuff like that. And what's linking them all together is that they all have an alchemical thread to them. And Blake features very heavily in this book, both his paintings and his poetry.'

Bruce had hit upon the central theme around which the whole concept could be hung: the English artist, philosopher and visionary William Blake was an outsider in his time, but author of some of the most remarkable social commentaries and esoteric literature of the period. Blake's world was one in which the boundaries of internal and external consciousness were blurred, where demons and angels could co-exist with the physical plane, and heaven, hell, madness and love often meant the same thing. The theme of alchemy, of transformation of base materials into wonderful and magical substances and experiences, was as close to William Blake as it was to Aleister Crowley's delvings into the darkness, or the poet Arthur Rimbaud's cross-sensory destructiveness, and had huge parallels with any esoteric medium that demanded sensory interaction. Music being the ultra-powerful transporting force it is, made Blake a perfect inspiration for a set of tracks as uncompromising as they are intriguing. Blake had, of course, written the poem 'Jerusalem' – for many, England's unofficial national anthem, as well as a hymn that proud Englishman Bruce had sung many times in his Oundle days. Now, in his fortieth year, he revisited it for the basis of the track of the same name on the LP. One of Bruce's heroes – and, by now, one of his mates – Arthur Brown also appears on the LP, reciting sections of Blake's poetry, something that pleased Bruce immensely. If it is, in one sense, a high-concept album; in another, it is one of the most immediate, straightforward and downright *brutal* records Dickinson was ever to put his name to.

One reason for that – in addition to the very heavy riffing and themes that often touch on the dark arts – is a particular guitar set-up that the group perfected during the recording sessions in California. They called it the 'Molossian Guitar', after the huge, two-hundred-pound dog. 'We took the D string off a bass guitar,' Bruce told *Terrorizer*, 'and put that as the E string on a normal guitar and started with that, tuning the other strings in proportion. This guitar was just a fucking monster!' Not least for Roy Z and Adrian Smith, who were charged with playing the beast. The sound was an enormously bassy, taking the concept of detuning guitars to the nth degree.

In the same interview, Bruce expanded on his affinity with William Blake, feeling that there were many parallels, particularly with Blake's single-mindedness and willingness to tear deep into his own soul to pull out the art that lay therein. And the LP reflects that: the press went absolutely bonkers over it on its release. Ian Glasper of *Terrorizer* rated it full marks, commenting that when it came to doling out the album to the journalists in that office, 'almost all of us regular contributors, be us Hardcore hooligans or Metal maniacs, were scrambling to review it.' He was much enamoured by the 'vicious grit of the guitars' and the 'heaving menace of the chorus' in the track 'Trumpets of Jericho'.

The title track itself struck him as 'more typical Dickinson territory, with a soaring vocal hook carrying the chorus's mighty riff sailing up into the tempestuous skies, destined for the halls of Metal greatness with all the languid doomed majesty of the bottom-bound Titanic'. He concluded by referring to Bruce as 'the cheeky jester who pulled the rug from under the throne of the cursed Hype King'. Liam Sheils, of *Kerrang!*, found 'King in Crimson' and 'Killing Floor' akin to bulls charging around 'in search of china shops, all bottom-end groove and duelling guitar dust-ups' before comparing those tracks to a 'down-tuned Thin Lizzy'. The reviewer referenced Dio-era Black Sabbath, and Led Zeppelin, in the album's more epic moments including 'Trumpets of Jericho' and 'The Alchemist' before commenting that, although to make an LP like this was resolutely unfashionable, it supplied 'enough piledrivers to send you reeling'. It was given four Ks, a very good result indeed. Meanwhile, Dave Ling at *Metal Hammer* gave the LP eight out of ten, finding it a meaty and powerful offering from his old acquaintance, and one that saw Dickinson out to claim, 'the unwanted middle-ground between the heaviosity [sic] of Fear Factory and Pantera and the more accessible end of progressive rock'. Ling name-checked 'The Book of Thel' for its precision – an indication that Bruce was on his way to claiming exactly that.

By all accounts, then, the album was a triumph – a masterful concept delivered exceptionally well via some exemplary performances of great songwriting and Roy Z's excellent production skills. *The Chemical Wedding* was also notable for being released on a new label – Air Raid – which was Bruce's freshest project. After many years of dealing with the excruciating politics of record labels, and being pressured by time and money to hit ridiculous deadlines and – if Keith Olsen is to be believed – create radio-friendly tracks, the vocalist had taken matters into his own hands and set up, with a little help from Sanctuary Management, his own independent label. It was, mainly, a vehicle for Bruce's own work, being wary as he was of the financial and time pressures of signing unknown bands and trying to help them through to the next phase of their development, although he did express a wish to sign up those cheeky chaps, Sack Trick.

The previous six years or so had certainly taught Bruce a great deal about the overheads inherent in marketing records and, of course, the lessons of the Samson days were still with the singer – when management and labels seemed to be falling by the wayside one by one, and everything that could have gone wrong went *horribly* wrong. So much so, in fact, that he planned to re-release the four Samson albums on Air Raid during the next year, partly to reappraise his past, and partially, perhaps, to try and generate some income for his former bandmates from any sales that might be forthcoming. The band were, in fact, still active, more or less.

'Over the years, Paul, Chris and Barry [Thunderstick] would occasionally get together,' explains Rob Grain, tour manager of Samson and member of that band's inner circle. 'They would book a rehearsal room for two or three days and just go in and play. It never transpired to a full-on reformation at first, but because 1998 was like twenty years of the NWOBHM, they thought they'd do a few more rehearsals in case anyone wanted to put on any shows to celebrate it. Suddenly out of the blue, Paul got a phone call from Bruce, who said that basically he'd heard through the grapevine that the three of them had been rehearsing, and were they thinking of doing anything – or was it just for fun? But if they were gonna do anything he hoped that they would involve him. So everyone thought, "Great, we can probably do something here. Have a bit of success and maybe at last earn some money, get the back catalogue sorted out."'

'Paul and I had been out to America,' Thunderstick told me, 'and done a couple of gigs out in the States, which kinda prompted it. We said, "Fuck this, let's go back to England and write some material." And we wrote what I consider to be some great, mature, adult Samson material, it really was. And this is what we sent to Bruce. He said, "Yeah, great, let's do this." His solo career was doing really great, he had no need to come back to us but he just wanted to do it as an old pals thing and just another challenge for him. The comeback from it was, "Yeah I'm interested [in a reunion]" and we had [a concert in] Japan in the offing, and it was all kind of the fact that, "Bruce Dickinson on board, that'll be great!" But we ended up doing Japan as a three-piece, playing stuff from all those three Samson albums. Bruce was really interested and saying, "I'm thinking we should get together and do this anniversary thing," even though his solo stuff was successful at the time.'

Bruce felt that at best it would be a temporary reunion, however, saying that he had plans for a follow-up record to *The Chemical Wedding*, which would be recorded in 1999 but released in 2000.

More imminent, however, than all the talk of reunions with old bands, was the tour schedule for the latest LP, and the band. set out on that familiar trek round the world to promote their stunningly received latest release. Blackshine were the support act on the European leg of their tour, which weaved its way through Scandinavia during October 1998. But the tour did not get off to the most auspicious of starts, as Joakim Stabel, the Swedish band's guitarist recalls. 'The first venue we were supposed to play at was *way* too small,' he said with a chuckle, when I asked him about those days. 'It was like a strip club or something, there was some major trouble there, and the stage was like big enough for the drum kit or something and we were definitely not going to play, if there was to be a concert at all. But somebody must've made a lot of phone calls to the right people because they fixed [things so] that we played in a bigger venue, more suitable for it. Which was really great, sold out as all the gigs were, great. Bruce and Adrian, we felt very shy meeting them because they were like these major people to us, as we are huge Maiden fans, we felt we weren't like worthy or something so they must've thought we were really strange! Actually they were the ones that started saying hello to us and everything, because we didn't want to get in the way and so on!'

The gigs were at venues holding anything between five hundred and a thousand people, which didn't faze Bruce and the band in the slightest, according to Stabel. 'I can tell you one thing, he gave one hundred per cent no matter, I don't think he cares if it's like a hundred people or ten people or ten fucking thousand people – he gives one hundred per cent anyway. It's really amazing to see that kind of professional at work [...] The audiences, yeah they liked us, but when Bruce and the guys came, it just went crazy every night. It was *amazing*. They played "Powerslave" and I think "Flight of Icarus" as well and, let me see, "2 Minutes to Midnight".'

Although Roy Z was unable to tour due to other commitments, his place was taken by Richard 'The Guru' Carrette, the band's guitar technician. He'd had to learn the set in a very short space of time after Bruce had contracted a virus ten days before the tour started and was therefore too unwell to rehearse fully during this period, but The Guru nevertheless rose to the challenge, held up his end manfully, and played a blinder to boot. Elsewhere, Bruce and Roy ran through The Scorpions' track 'The Zoo', for an *Extreme Wrestling* CD, and similarly 'Trumpets of Jericho' appeared on the soundtrack to the movie, *Bride of Chucky*, the album released on 6 October.

The year 1998 wound up, then, with Bruce and the boys ripping it up with the heaviest LP he'd created outside Iron Maiden. Inroads had also been made into reuniting with one of his previous bands, and the singer's stock was at its highest point creatively for many years. It wouldn't hurt at all were he to hook up with some old mates and play those classics one more time, surely?

CHAPTER 20

SHOCKING
THE WORLD

When 1999 began, Bruce's schedule swiftly started to fill up. First, a contribution to an Alice Cooper tribute LP by himself and Adrian was released in January (they played on a cover of 'Black Widow', alongside Bob Kulick, Tony Franklin, Tommy Aldridge and David Glen Eisley). There was to be a tour of Brazil in April with his solo band, with those gigs recorded for a planned live album. Recording sessions would then take place, and a new Bruce Dickinson solo album would be added to the Air Raid release roster, which would also include the repackaging of *Survivors, Head On, Shock Tactics* and *Live at Reading '81*, the live BBC set that had been originally put out by Repertoire in 1990. Following a swift drink for the pesky millennium, activities would then begin in earnest in 2000 with more of the same. The future looked bright.

While the calls continued from the Samson camp, things were

taking rather an unexpected turn. Rob Grain remembers it well. 'Bruce was in the States with his own band, and [mentioned that in] April 1999 there was a festival in New Jersey, a Heavy Metal festival. Paul took a call from Bruce, who said, "Look, I'm compering this show, how about I get Samson on the show, we'll bill it that you'll do it as a three-piece, but actually on the night we'll do it as a four-piece." And he asked if they had crew and all that, and it got to the point where Paul was phoning me to get a crew together to do it. They were rehearsing, they'd sorted the set out and Bruce was asking them to send him the set so he could learn the songs. It got to early 1999 and it all went quiet.'

Blaze Bayley looks back on the situation with an experienced and philosophical eye. He explains that Maiden had pressures of their own in those years. '*Virtual XI* [released in 1998] wasn't too bad as a process; we had a bit of time off and when we came to writing we had loads of ideas. More ideas than we had time to record, and they were really good quality. *The X Factor* was a gruelling tour. Dave Murray turned to me and told me it was the toughest tour he'd ever done. And he'd done bloody *World Slavery*! It was winter everywhere we went! We were in the US, there was snowfall when we played in New York, really bad everywhere. We got down to Florida where it was all sunny and nice but we didn't have a day off! We had to drive back up north. We played in Brazil and it was raining all the time. The *Virtual XI* tour had more festivals, so it was a lot less intense. We played Monsters of Rock in São Paolo, seventy thousand people in a massive stadium. It was the biggest thing I'd ever done, I was bricking it, man. A massive stage set, everything, it was great. But as it was coming to an end I was getting a funny vibe. I thought, "Well everybody's tired, it's been a difficult tour."'

Blaze had been plagued by allergies, too, and was suffering much as Bruce had some years earlier. 'You are working at your highest point; the most stress that you can put on your voice and just about keep it, all the time. Because of the travel, the sleep, the disjointed thing. It's like people that work shifts always have health problems and I was on antibiotics for the whole tour. There had been a horrible sore throat going through the crew and they can't cancel the gig. I just had to battle on. But this one time I got allergies on top of everything else and that was it. I sung the gig, and *bang*! That was [my voice] gone. The monitors weren't very good that gig, it was a very small one in Phoenix. I absolutely loved it and went over the top. I couldn't get my voice back. I just couldn't recover it. And I used to take steroids like anything. I was sneezing and everything. It was just one of those rare occasions that will happen with any athlete or anyone on the edge. You are always at the breaking point. You know, Bruce has had to cancel quite a few shows during his career, Paul Di'Anno the same. It's just a thing, man. When you're a guitarist you've got all your wires. When you're a vocalist, you've got your body. That is the thing: your body is your instrument and when that goes wrong there is nothing you can do except complete rest. If I lose my voice on tour, that's it. The only thing that can get it back is steroids and rest. You have to rest and be silent and that's the only way to do it.

'I don't like cancelling shows. Dee Snider didn't cancel a show once and it completely changed his voice. He sang with a sore throat, with the flu, because he didn't want to let the fans down, and he was never the same. Luckily, he changed it and the songs they wrote after he got blown out were their biggest songs. I'm from Sunday football [to continue the analogy] and suddenly you get this chance to step up and you do everything you can. It is a lot to adapt to. On that tour my singing had improved and I thought I was doing really well.'

It was a rare occasion in Blaze's life and career that he had been unable to fight back and hold on to his voice, but there was a huge change about to take place. 'We finished that tour just before Christmas,' he recalls, 'and then in January they phoned me to go to a meeting. I thought it was about plans for the [next] US tour, but they gave me the sack. And that was it. It is the shittest time you can probably have, when you get the sack from any job, unless you absolutely hate it. I loved what I did. I absolutely loved it. I never tried to build up my own fan base, I never tried to get any TV work on the back of it, I never tried to become a celebrity. Because all I ever wanted to do was be a singer with a heavy metal band and tour the world, and there I was doing it. I never wanted to be anything else or do anything else. I never thought there would be an "after Iron Maiden". I thought I would be there, writing and getting better and doing albums, working with Steve, Janick and Dave and just really creating the next phase of Iron Maiden. Almost – although not as big as this – like post-Peter Green Fleetwood Mac or like Deep Purple. I thought we were going to be creating the third wave of Iron Maiden. The hardest of the hardcore fans would gradually go, "Actually these songs are really good. Actually they have got loads of energy. This is really happening, these guys are really committed to what they are doing and this music is really good." I thought that was what it was gonna be but I was, as I have been many times before in my life, deluding myself.'

He had no inkling who might be taking over the Maiden job. '[I'd heard] not one thing. I never used the internet, never bothered with email. I used to phone people up,' Blaze remembers. 'I never bothered what anybody said on the internet. Then after they sacked me I looked at it and I was shocked what people were saying about me on the forums and that. It was horrible, a horrible day.'

There had been omens, too. 'When I was on my way to the office, the car in front of me had a registration that said *666*. A big flash car. And when I had my motorcycle accident, the odometer read *666*. I never stayed in a room that could be [added up to make] 666 on tour. So in a way I felt it was like "The Curse of Eddie". Almost like a supernatural darkness had come between me and the rest of the guys. A poison, and that was it.

'In reality, it was a business decision. When I joined Iron Maiden, EMI started selling off pressing plants and outsource pressing all the albums. They started doing partnerships with Virgin in different territories and stuff like that. The writing was on the wall there that CD sales were going to go down. Metallica were fighting Napster. That income that bands like Maiden were used to was evaporating slowly. As Deep Purple and Black Sabbath did their reunions the pressure came, from EMI I think, that, "Oh we need to get some interest in this band." And the only real way to do that was a reunion [with Bruce]. Maiden do it with a twist, don't they? They got Adrian back as well, and kept Janick too. It wouldn't be just a reunion, they would do something musically unusual as well.

'I never had any animosity towards them. I got paid well. I just didn't want to be out but if you've gotta go, you've gotta go. One of the things I said at the meeting when it became obvious it was over for me, was, "Is Bruce coming back?" and nobody could look me in the eye. Rod said, "Yes." And I thought, "Well, OK. There's no point talking any more. I wish you the very best. I will never badmouth this band the way Bruce did and I wish you all the best."' A classy exit from a singer and musician who has kept his dignity by and large over the years about the situation. 'I've had the odd drunken moment when I've been emotional, but generally speaking in the press I've never said anything bad about the guys,' he says. 'To be honest, they deserve what they have got because they have worked their arses off to get it. They have made a lot of personal sacrifice to get where they are and to stay at that level, the top level. They have worked their whole lives to get there and the world is a better place for having Iron Maiden in it.'

Another former Maiden vocalist, Paul Di'Anno, has toured extensively with Blaze Bayley over the years. 'I really like [him] and I thought he got a raw deal there to be honest with you,' he says, in typically honest mode. 'There are quite a few Blaze Maiden fans. But it was never quite right; fair play to go for it, to be honest with you. But he deserved much better than that. He's not as operatic [as Bruce Dickinson]. It's a shame. It's not Blaze's fault. I love him to death and I've got a lot of time for the guy. He's a good man.'

History, however, will record that in March 1999, it was announced that Bruce Dickinson was to rejoin Iron Maiden full time. Tony Newton is well placed to give his view on the situation, having played footy with Steve Harris for many years before Harry found out his tough-tackling teammate was also a musician; subsequently, Newton's lot – Dirty Deeds – toured with Bruce – on the *Accident of Birth* tour, and also Blaze-era Iron Maiden. 'The great thing with Maiden,' says the Londoner, 'is that everything's behind closed doors. If they've got problems or whatever, you never seem to know about it. They somehow really keep it in-house.' Newton also feels that the time was absolutely right for the heavyweights to come together once more, having laid some ghosts to rest. 'Bruce probably got [his keenness to experiment] out of his system,' he continues. 'He'd probably be the first to admit it didn't all work out how he probably would've hoped but the bottom line is he's got it out of his system, and I'm sure they all missed playing in the big places.'

Di'Anno says that Maiden's sound simply works with Bruce Dickinson. 'It also spawned a million imitations as well. Some of those bands, like Helloween, sounded like a second-rate Iron Maiden. Even in the early days, bands like Queensryche sounded a bit like that, a bit like Bruce. His voice fitted them songs and that was it, it was perfect. It's one of those things. It seemed to be the style and has never gone away. When I'm on tour a lot of bands sound like bleedin' third-rate Iron Maiden. It does your head in.'

'To be honest with you,' confirms Newton, 'I never saw it coming, I *never* expected Bruce and Steve to get back together, it shocked even me. I remember Steve telling me when we went to play tennis one day that Bruce is coming back, but part of it is that Adrian's coming back as well, and I said, "Is Janick gonna go, then?" And he said, "'No way, no!" And in actual fact Jan, when he heard, he phoned Steve up and said, "Look, I'll step down, Steve." And Steve wasn't having none of it, he said, "No, you ain't going nowhere, I want us all in there." But that's what they're like, they're very loyal, what with the management and a lot of the crew have been around, from almost day one, you know, It's like family, the whole thing – and that's why it's remained so strong. It really done

269

'em a favour, being apart, it really did. Bruce's solo material is stuff he would never have been able to do in Maiden, you know. Steve's off the wall sometimes on arrangements and this and that, but he's also very focused... on certain other things that he'd never have happening in the band. Like, he'd never de-tune and play a song that wasn't in concert pitch, you know what I mean, he'd *never* do that, I know him. Like, just 'cause everyone else is going drop-tuning, he wouldn't go down that road. Bruce obviously has experimented with all that stuff and whether he's got it out of his system or not, I dunno, I'm sure he'll do [another solo album].'

'It was the best move they could make,' says producer Chris Tsangarides. 'I was surprised that they'd got what they had got. It didn't surprise me that they went back because that's what the fans wanted. Maiden sales went down and all the rest of it, so they needed to get the band back – and I thought it was great that they got Adrian as well, and kept Janick and them all in the band.'

NWOBHM guru and author John Tucker, agrees with Tsangarides' overview of what happened. 'I guess they needed each other,' he says. 'Yes, Bruce was writing good songs and making a living, but [he was] never gonna be bigger than that. And like a lot of these bands, people wanted to see them back together. I could never understand why people would flock to see Thin Lizzy but not Phil Lynott's Grand Slam. The same songs, by the same guy – but played with a different band. He had his die-hard fans but a lot of people just wanted to see Bruce Dickinson fronting Iron Maiden. And their popularity had gone down; Blaze is not [the same] frontman and they'd gone to playing Odeon-sized venues, two-and-a-half thousand. It's quite respectable, but you're back doing one day in each, like you were in 1983. And now look at it:

Earls Court, NEC, Download. I can appreciate why, in their forties, they wouldn't want to go back to thirty-four-date treks of the UK. In the early 1980s, the Gillan and Iron Maiden tours stretched on forever; there must come a point when you think, "Let's do a couple of really big gigs and go for it."'

'I don't blame Steve for it, he knows what he wants,' says Thunderstick. 'He's made millions from it and he's got a world-class band there who have the back-up behind them. They really have – great. You wouldn't have thought a band like that would have held that longevity and been able to achieve what they've achieved.' However, Samson's long-discussed reunion was one of the first things to fall by the wayside in the Maiden melee. As Rob Grain puts it, 'Suddenly you picked up the papers and it was "Bruce rejoins Iron Maiden".'

Bruce, however, was still thinking of his Air Raid Records project, rolling out plans to release a compilation of his solo material, and rarities left in the vaults (the planned album was called *Catacombs* and was due for release in 2000), as well as re-release the *Metal For Muthas* compilations. He had not forgotten his Samson compadres, either, and pressed ahead with plans to re release those four albums. 'There's still quite a bit of money ending up to get paid off,' Henrik Johannson was told, 'because we invested quite heavily in the records to buy them off of the record company, which was going bankrupt. Rob Grain, speaking in 2007, was philosophical about things, telling me that, 'The Air Raid releases didn't sound very good. They weren't mastered very well and there were mistakes on the covers, they spelt the name wrong on one of them, [down the spine of *Survivors* the band's name was mis-spelt as] 'Samsom'. Paul later got in touch and said to Sanctuary,

"If you're going to do them, let's at least do them properly." So he then had a bit of input when [Sanctuary] reissued them properly in 2001, Paul supplied the pictures and stuff, and licensed some additional tracks, but that was basically because at the time there was a Samson reformation going on and it all helped.'

Rob Grain, as tour manager and close friend of Paul Samson, feels that there has been a misunderstanding, or missed communication over the years, that has led to some perhaps unnecessary bad feeling between old friends. 'Having spoken to Bruce recently,' he now says. 'I think that he probably thought that he was helping his old mates out by releasing the Air Raid things, and is probably unaware that nobody was getting paid from them [as they are still unrecouped].' Thunderstick still feels let down, sadly, and opines that press interviews over the years have concentrated more on the extra fuel that the band would indulge in, rather than the music that Samson produced. 'I get people on MySpace telling me they have these albums and they're from the most bizarre places!' Nicky Moore subsequently rejoined Samson for a series of dates, bringing the reunion to some kind of conclusion, at least, but tragically Paul Samson was to lose a battle with cancer, and he passed away on 9 August 2002.

April 1999 saw the very final dates of *The Chemical Wedding* tour, which was also to be the final set of Bruce's solo dates for the foreseeable future. The gigs were held in Brazil – home to some of Maiden and Bruce's most fervent fans – and in the immediate aftermath of the shock announcement of his and Adrian's return to the Maiden fold, the concerts were hugely well received by crowds of around seven thousand each night. The accompanying live album, *Scream For Me Brazil*, is simply Bruce at his bombastic,

metallic best, running through the heavier moments of the latter
two albums – no 'Fog on the Tyne' nonsense to be found here,
or even 'Tattooed Millionaire' for that matter. It is a wonderful,
gnarly, full-on fire-bastard metal performance, and an absolutely
excellent live album by anyone's standards. *All Music Guide* agreed,
thinking it an LP full of 'consistent, inspired performances' on its 2
November release.

By that time, of course, Bruce was full-on into pre-production
for the first Iron Maiden album with which he'd been involved
for almost eight years. Maiden had been bedding themselves in
with – by their standards – a short tour between July and October
1999, playing a set of classics to coincide with the release of their
new compilation, *Ed Hunter*, which also featured a computer game
based on the antics of their mascot. Bruce flew the band from gig
to gig, although there was a rather scary moment when one of
their engines apparently packed up on them over Greenland (it
was later discovered to be a false alarm caused by a loose wire).
It wouldn't have done reluctant flyer Steve Harris a lot of good
nerves-wise, although his singer's calm mastery of the aircraft was
beginning to change 'Arry's mind as to the pleasures of air travel.
In general, the tour served both to reintroduce Bruce and Adrian
to the fold, as well as whip up anticipation for the forthcoming
original material as the new millennium beckoned.

CHAPTER 21

BRAVE
NEW WORLD

Reue ning to the fold meant largely returning to the set-up of old: rehearse, write and release an album, and subsequently tour the hell out of it, have a break, and do the whole thing over again. The contrast, however, to the early 1990s, was that Bruce's multitude of other interests and activities were as important to him as was the musical aspect. It was now a matter of time management rather than prioritising one over the other, which – along with his perceived view of a slip in recording and even quality control standards – had been instrumental in his leaving Maiden in the first place.

Brave New World was one of the most eagerly anticipated albums of all time, as far as metal was concerned. The questions were hanging in the air: would Steve and Bruce get on musically and personally? How could the group accommodate three lead guitarists? And, most of all, what would the album be like, sonically? The last question was answered in no uncertain terms: it would sound, simply, like classic Iron Maiden, at their imaginative, and occasionally very dark, best. *Brave New World* is more *Seventh Son...* than *Beast*, of course, with the six-piece band allowing themselves to stretch out on some tracks that refine and expand the Maiden blueprint to a very contemporary level, with the returning singer putting in a sterling and confident performance on top. Less heavy than Bruce's latter two solo efforts, the LP nonetheless faces down the weight of the band's own past and looks to the future with assurance.

Bruce's writing on the album is classic Maiden. His album opener, 'The Wicker Man' (not to be confused with a song of the same title he'd written a number of years earlier), stomps in with an insistent guitar riff and Steve's busy bass before exploding into the melodic choruses that uplift and soar with an essence of a new rise. Appropriately so – this collaboration with Smith and Harris locks in as if the three had never been apart. It was released as a single on 8 May 2000 and reached No.9 in the UK.

The second track on the LP is a collaboration between Bruce, Steve and Janick (who was at the time sharing a house with Bruce and his clan). The expansive 'Ghost of the Navigator' peals on for almost seven minutes as Bruce indulges himself in a tale that takes in a sea journey as a metaphor for life, fears, aspirations and the fundamental wonder as to what might happen when the journey is completed. Fairly involved stuff, of course, but hey – there's a great solo in the middle to help speed things along.

The title track, written by Bruce, Steve and Dave Murray, is a prog-tinged effort that recalls the themes of Aldous Huxley's book of the same name, which speculated on a dystopian future. It takes an image of a dying swan as its central tenet to hang round a rather relentlessly dark and broody number that is essentially the flip side of the previous track. Bruce's final writing credit on the album is the second single to be taken from the LP, 'Out of the Silent Planet', released on 23 October and reaching No.20 in the UK charts. Again, it clocks in at over six minutes, the theme this time being based on the film *Forbidden Planet*, the 1956 B-movie… which was based loosely on Shakespeare's play *The Tempest*… from which Huxley had extrapolated the title of the book… that became the Maiden album! It is a fun, gallopy Maiden track that pulls and pushes itself through typically complex changes of tempo and rhythm, retaining a live feel that, more than anything else on the album, sounds like a band *enjoying themselves*. If there were any further clues needed as to the fact that the air had been cleared, Harris's album closer 'The Thin Line Between Love and Hate', with its lyrics of respect for the right of each man to take their own road in life, is one of the bassist's most strident efforts.

Dean Karr directed the evocative video for 'The Wicker Man', telling the author that he had admired the original 1973 film, featuring Christopher Lee and Britt Ekland (we all admired her contributions to it, in truth). He said that inspiration, allied to Maiden's first single back together, gave him the opportunity to put something amazing together. 'I put my own twist on the film,' he said, 'working closely with Bruce more than anyone else. We hung out all week prior to the shoot, looking at wardrobe and having tea. In the end, we [made] the film current, featuring my green 1970 Dodge Challenger, which Eddie claims in the end of the video, and a bevy of beautiful women, who flank the actual Wicker Man – which was the biggest thing I've ever constructed in my career! The only problem, explained the acclaimed director, was the weather, which was so heavy it cost half the day. 'It rained so hard in Los Angeles,' he says with a laugh, 'that when the band jumped out of their motor home, they sunk in mud up to their knees.' That same bad weather meant that Karr – a perfectionist – still feels he and Maiden missed some important shots, 'but I just can't fight Mother Nature!

'I had wanted to do the aisle-way of Pyro balloons gag for years,' he continues. 'And I thought of no better band to do it with than Iron Maiden. I had each of those giant weather balloons, inspired by the TV show *The Prisoner,* electronically connected to live detonators, to blow once the man ran past it – it's a miracle they all went off in perfect sequence!' He commented that everyone got along 'famously' and that he was personally extremely pleased to see Adrian back in the band 'where he belongs', as well as the return of Bruce.

The *Brave New World* tour began in earnest on 2 June 2000 – on the back of the album hitting the UK charts, reaching No.7 after its release on 25 May 2000. As ever with Maiden, it was humungous in ambition, and although this time around there were more rest days built in, the touring behemoth nevertheless kept raging until 19 January 2001, at Rio – a concert that was recorded by cameras and a huge sound rig. It was part of the Rock In Rio festival and the crowd of 250,000 was treated to a set full of old and new classics. The recordings were subsequently released as a live album and DVD. 'It sounds really, really strong,' said Bruce to *Hard Radio.* 'It was the last show of the *Brave New World* tour, it was in front of a quarter of a million people, it was broadcast live on TV to over 100 million people... it was a great place to do a live DVD and CD!

So, that is why we decided to do the recording in Rio, and since it was only one show, we knew we had to do it right so there was a lot of pressure on stage, knowing we've only got one shot at this.'

Dean Karr recalls the huge logistical pressures that were involved in facilitating the project successfully, recalling that he and his crew had travelled with Maiden's crew through Mexico City, Argentina, Chile and Brazil for what he terms 'The Big One'. 'We edited footage from the other countries into the Rio gig,' he explains. 'Those other locations were covered with four or five cameras each night, whilst Rio was covered with eighteen [...] In Chile, we fastened the cameras onto the tips of the guitars and locked onto Bruce's shoulders to create that cool, lockdown effect. It bummed out the crowd but it was necessary to create something fresh for this DVD.' Fresher than the band's clothes, at least; for continuity, they were required to wear the same wardrobe. 'My favourite memory,' concludes the talented photographer and movie maker, 'was rolling in above the crowd in a helicopter, feeling the excitement below. There were multiple choppers and I had Steve Harris, Bruce Dickinson and Jimmy Page in mine – pretty cool stuff. I had goosebumps bigger than Lemmy's warts!' There was another very memorable moment, Karr recalls, although it was more than a little unsavoury. 'I saw a partially decomposed skull roll up to my foot whilst I was on the stairs below Dave Murray, filming,' he says, chuckling. 'I reached down and picked up the skull – which had been thrown onstage by a fan. I was sure it was fake – until I stuck my finger into the spine hole in the back and held it up to Bruce, suggesting he took it from me and sang like *Hamlet*.

'While the once-occupied head of someone's was next to my face, I noticed a horrible reek coming from within the inner cavity and quickly threw the head onstage, cleaning my stinky finger off as good as I possibly could! I have worked in graveyards for many years and I never had an experience that gross! Later in the DVD, when the band is winding down, you can see Janick and Dave hold the skull – and quickly get rid of it! It had some crazy voodoo painting on it, and leather strings tied to the cheekbones. Obviously some maniac fan had dug it up to make an offering to his favourite band – and, hey, it made the DVD – I would have given the dead man credit if I'd known his name!'

For Bruce, 2001 was also a year where his involvement ended in a rather daft film that was all about eighteenth-century zombies, postponed from a 1999 project that was supposed to have been brought to fruition by a Swedish company, and due to star Dean Cain. After original filming sessions – in the beautiful city of Prague – were postponed that year, the project, as often happens, had fallen down the list of priorities and was subsequently canned. He had, however, found a spare day to fly across to Holland to lend his vocals to the title track of Dutch curio Ayreon's album *Universal Migrator 2: Flight of the Migrator*. The artist was ecstatic to finally get Bruce on to the album, he told *DPRP*. 'I was a fan already of Samson, Dickinson's pre-Maiden band,' he gushed. 'Production is very bare, but the vocals, at that time by someone unknown, mysteriously called "Bruce, Bruce" are very strong. So you understand, that when he agreed upon participating, I was shouting and jumping in the room. But then distress started. How to get this man into my studio? This has cost me ten thousand phone calls and in the meantime he travelled all over the world. When I reached him in Paris, where they were recording the new Iron Maiden album, he said, "Call me in two weeks." But after five times of, "Call me in two weeks," I thought, "Forget it," and I recorded two alternative versions with Damian Wilson and Lana Lane. So the last time he called, saying, "In two weeks," I said:

"No, it's now or never, no more delays." And he replied, "Okay, I'll come over next Sunday."

'When he arrived at the airport, he carried his home with him in a bag, 'cause he has to live abroad for tax reasons for a year. In the car I played him this song and he really got into it. So, he went directly into the studio, recording three takes. And that was so difficult, because I'm not gonna say, "That's awful." I was already impressed when he opened his mouth. But it really was incredible, superb. That night we spent here in the attic, listening to each others' demos and he was really relaxed. And the next morning we had a nice breakfast together and I brought him back to the airport again. A great experience and a wonderful performance.'

By mid-2001, Air Raid Records had run its course, and Bruce accepted an offer from Sanctuary to buy his half of the project. Running a label truly is a full-time job if it is to be done successfully, and time was at a premium for the Worksop singer, as he prepared to release his own *Best of Bruce Dickinson*, a two-CD retrospective of the pick of the solo years, with an added cornucopia of out-takes and extra tracks that were originally intended to be part of the *Catacombs* album. The second CD is a set of acoustic tracks, alternative versions of classics (including the original recording of 'Bring Your Daughter…') and some surprising material, including a ten-minute audio explanation and overview of all the songs included on the release. It is a splendid insight into the development of the artist, not least the inclusion of 'Dracula' – which was, of course, the first track Bruce had ever put down to tape. Disc one launches manfully through the solo years, and although there will always be some debate among fans as to which tracks are and are not included herein, the subsequent 2005 Sanctuary reissues of his solo albums all included enough extra tracks and outtakes to satisfy even the most geeky completist. With Roy Z busy producing solo material by Judas Priest's Rob Halford, and with plans to begin work on a new Maiden LP during 2002, Bruce commented that he was unlikely to be looking to work on any new material of his own for quite some time.

Still bubbling under in 2001 was the idea for the film based on Aleister Crowley's life, to be entitled *The Chemical Wedding*. Things had moved on by this time to the extent that the script was in the hands of Messiah Pictures, the company owned by Monty Python's Terry Jones, who were seeking funding for a number of projects, of which Bruce's movie was one.

Other projects for him that year included co-writing the track 'We Are One' for an album by rock band Warrior. Bruce had bumbled into a studio session that band were undertaking, while visiting Roy Z at his studio. He had some spare lyrics that he thought would fit the track the group were laying down; Warrior decided they fit neatly and so a collaboration was born. Easy as that! Another collaboration that was much-mooted was a three-way vocalist shindig along with Rob Halford and Queensryche's Geoff Tate, after Bruce had joined Halford onstage the previous year to duet on 'The One You Love to Hate', which subsequently appeared on Halford's solo album *Resurrection*. The original plan was to take the blueprint of the famous Carreras, Domingo and Pavarotti collaboration, *The Three Tenors*, albeit renamed *The Three Tremors* – a name soon changed to *The Unholy Trinity* and then simply, *Trinity*. Although the project was an intriguing one for all concerned, sadly the respective schedules of the protagonists meant that it quickly became a non-starter. Bruce and Roy had written three songs before realising that with the talent involved, it was hardly the case of merely swapping the lead vocal lines around, chorus by chorus. 'That would be a crap way to do it,' Bruce told *Book of Hours*. 'But it's a bloody difficult thing to do, to try to make a song with three different voices to get the full benefit out of it. And it takes longer than three weeks, and we didn't have longer than that to do it, so I canned it in the end. It's a great idea, everybody loves the idea; we had marketing people salivating about the idea of the Trinity project.'

On 5 November 2001, Bruce jetted over to Stockholm to pick up an award voted for by the listeners of radio station *Rockklassiker 106.7* naming him 'Greatest Heavy Metal Singer of All Time'. All rather nice, and another one to add to the growing collection as another decade kicked into action with all going peachy for Bruce and all associated with Iron Maiden.

CHAPTER 22

FLYING METAL

It was while bringing together Maiden members past and present to offer their thoughts for the retrospective historical DVD *Iron Maiden: The Early Years* that the band found out that, tragically, ex-drummer Clive Burr – joker and occasional freelance hellraiser for the band in the early 1980s – had been diagnosed with the muscle-wasting disease multiple sclerosis. And although 2002 had been designated a year off for the group following Rock in Rio, they immediately set up the Clive Burr MS Trust Fund to help their mate and his family as much as possible. The band not only performed at three sell-out concerts at Brixton Academy (19–21 March 2002) but also auctioned off memorabilia and re-released 'Run to the Hills' with two previously unreleased live tracks. *Clive Aid*, as it has become known, had not only raised money, but also awareness for the debilitating illness, for which there is no known cure.

Bruce himself continued his activities outside Maiden by snagging himself a regular DJ spot on the BBC's new flagship digital radio station, 6 Music. The station was launched on 11 March 2002, with Bruce presenting – of course – the weekly rock show, which he would continue to enjoy – touring permitting, of course – for eight years. The radio station's site described Bruce as 'the face of British heavy metal… truly a member of the international metal élite'. In a short Q&A for the site, Bruce confessed that he wished he had written the song 'My Way', made famous by Frank Sinatra (and infamous by Sid Vicious).

Mike Hanson, a producer at 6 Music, analysed Bruce's presentation style for this book. 'The most obvious skill [for a radio presenter] is being able to string a sentence together,' he began. 'You'd be amazed by how many can't – even the articulate ones. People who are personable, or are good interviewees, are not necessarily good presenters. It's a different mindset to initiate a conversation or read a link. And it's hard for some who are used to getting instant reaction from an audience to speak into a vacuum. Bruce was quite good at doing that. He's a natural storyteller. What Bruce brought was a big personality (obvs), a real knowledge of the music (especially classic rock – he knows his Deep Purple, etc). He had in-house producers, then, later, an independent company did it. When I did produce him, I found him easy-going and pretty easy to work with. You need them to be able to follow direction, which he did. The nightmare with Bruce was just getting time with him – he's such a busy boy, nailing him down on a agreed time was like nailing jelly to a wall. And even you did agree a time, often that would change at the last minute, or he'd be horribly late. We referred to it as being on "Bruce time".'

Metal expert, renowned author and top-line journalist Joel McIver recalls being invited on to Bruce's show to discuss one of his many highly successful books about music. 'It was surreal to sit opposite Bruce at the BBC and hear him saying things like, "What an amazing career you've had." I felt like a complete fraud, although I admit that such a level of validation was enormously rewarding. But don't worry, I went home afterwards and had to change some nappies, so my ego was soon restored to normal levels. [He is] excellent. He is a master of the relaxed, one-on-one conversation, which to me is key to any interview, radio or otherwise.'

The year 2002 also saw a raft of Maiden reissues and repackages, but also the intriguing use of one of the band's tracks. '2 Minutes to Midnight' was selected as part of the soundtrack for the Playstation game *Grand Theft Auto: Vice City*, as part of the 'virtual radio station' V-Rock, putting Maiden in the company of Quiet Riot, Twisted Sister, Loverboy and Ozzy Ozbourne.

The band's relative inactivity during 2002 enabled Bruce – itchy feet as ever – to set about arranging a return visit to Europe, this time with a solo band, which was mostly those crazy Sack Trick boys, although the drummer this time was to be Robin Guy, who had ended up sharing a house with Chris Dale and joining Sack Trick.

'We did a gig at the Kingston Peel,' recalls Robin. 'Bruce came down with Janick, we rocked out and did our thing and then at the end of the show, I'm packing down my drums in various states of undress and all that jazz, and Chris comes up to me, he'd be talking to Bruce in the corner or whatever, and says "Just to let you know, Bruce wants to do some European festival headlines, and he wants you to play drums [for him]" and I was like, "Fuck off mate, that's not even funny, don't joke with me," you know, 'cause that's a matter of the *heart*. Maiden changed my life when I was thirteen, you know, when this one big band basically changes your life, whether it's The Beatles, or Michael Jackson or whatever – and mine was Iron Maiden, the *Killers* record in France on a French [school] exchange. So for me, I literally took it as a joke, but Chris looked me in the eye and said, "No, no, Rob, I'm serious" and at that point my jaw hit the floor and I went 'You fuckin' what, mate?" and he goes, "Yeah, you know he wants me to play bass, you to play drums and he wants Alex Dickson to play guitar, and we'll find another guitarist," which [eventually turned out to be] a good friend who'd also played in Sack Trick, Pete Friesen, who was the Almighty guitarist and also Alice Cooper guitarist.

'Because Chris and me were in the same house it was fairly easy. Chris would be like, "I've spoken to Bruce, we might be doing 'Children of the Damned', and I'd run off and check it all out and a coupla days later he'd say, "Bruce has changed his mind, he wants to do 'Flight of Icarus'… 'No, he wants to do… whatever," and it was just brilliant. It was great: I knew all the Maiden songs anyway, but when you actually have to really knuckle down and learn them, there are some really specific little bits and obviously with Nicko's drumming there are pushes going on every second, so I really had to lock myself in and work out what he's doing on the bass drum. I'd sit in my car actually with really rubbish stereo speakers, absolutely like cardboard pieces of crap, the kind of ones that are moulded in the dashboard already. Really, really shit, but it was fantastic 'cause every time the kick drum went, they'd go "bbuphhurphhhp", so I'd turn it up really loud, and I'd just get Nicko's kick pattern coming through. Especially on *Live After Death*.'

It was to prove a surreal experience for Robin, however, although one he wouldn't swap for the world. 'I was talking to someone about seeing Maiden at Donington on the *Seventh Son of a Seventh Son Tour* and it was like Donington's biggest attendance when Maiden headlined. You know, we're all very proud of that as Maiden fans, and just thinking, what if I went back and tapped myself on the shoulder, and went "It's alright kid, see that singer up there, you'll be playing 'The Prisoner' to forty thousand people." That's just too huge to comprehend, and when you do it it's just amazing but you can never really comprehend it, you just get on and do it, and it becomes quite normal. Which sounds a very strange statement to say, but I remember checking myself, actually *checking* myself, as I was onstage for Sweden Rocks, [on 8 June 2002, which was] the first gig, thinking, "Well, how am I feeling?", trying to do the old out-of-body conversation with myself. I remember drumming away, and going "There are fifteen thousand Swedes out there, we're headlining, and Motörhead, my other favourite band, were on before us!" and no one really follows Motörhead, do they?'

Aside from the *Chemical Wedding* tour, Robin and Bruce had actually met a few years before, in the drummer's home village of Chiddingly. "I was sixteen or seventeen, in my little local pub down in a tiny, tiny village,' Guy laughs. 'It was about a week before they played Donington, and I remember being fairly drunk coming back from the toilet and my mate was pointing at this bloke with long hair, and my initial thoughts were, "Who's this short-arsed hippy in my way?" And I looked at my mate, and his face looks like he's just seen *The Ring* or whatever, you know he's like freaking out pointing, mouthing something and I'm like looking at him, and I go round the back of this bloke with long hair and my jaw hit the floor as well, 'cause it was Bruce Dickinson, and you don't expect to see Bruce in your pub. It turns out, about ten miles away, he's got a fencing buddy and he was having a few drinks down there. And, of course, I was just like, in my drunken voice, "B–Bruce! Bruce!" And he was a consummate pro, totally cool, and had a little chat, and he obviously didn't want to draw in massive attention [although] I was sort of flailing around spilling beer at him, but you know, he signed a little tiny scrap of paper for me, which I dare say I've still got. He said to me, which is hilarious, "I bet you're thinking, why isn't he taller than that?" And it was exactly true, 'cause I was! All sort of big rock stars seem to be tiny.

'So when we were rehearsing for these festival headlines, I mentioned all this to Bruce. I said, "What, don't you remember meeting me Bruce? You know, the first time you met me?" And we had a good old giggle about that. It was quite funny. Doing those festival dates was just a phenomenal experience. But also it did all roll into place. I'm surrounded by my best mates, we're playing rocking metal, having a whale of a time doing it. It's all fairly simple. Chris would just be like, jump on this plane, you know, we all travel Ryan Air, and got there and set up the show, and all my drums would arrive from Pearl and I'd unpack them, and an hour before show time Bruce would jump out of his plane and go, "Alright chaps, everything alright?" and we'd be like, "Yeah, it's brilliant, Bruce!"'

Bruce had reached the limit of the size of aeroplanes that he could afford to fly on a private licence, and during 2002 had been studying hard for his commercial pilot's licence, which he attained, subsequently being taken on as a first officer for the charter airline company Astraeus – which caused some mirth on occasion, as Robin Guy recounts. 'The hilarious thing about the gigs we did, was he'd got himself a job being a professional pilot and he actually had to go and ask his boss for time off so that he could do these shows. Which I thought was marvellous. Can you imagine that? "Hello, yes, it's Bruce Dickinson here, singer of the biggest metal band in the world, can you spare me a few days? I've got some gigs, you see..." We'd be rehearsing, we'd sort of get there at eleven or ten or whatever, and in would stroll Bruce at one o' clock going, "Sorry I'm a bit late" and we'd all be like, "We've been here for ages, we've been working hard" and try and rub it in, and he'd go, "Sorry I'm late, I had a pilot's exam in a flight simulator at seven in the morning at Gatwick" and we'd just be like "Fuckin' hell, we'll shut up then, shall we!"

'We played Greece and had finished this gig so I, like, cracked open a beer, and offered one to Bruce, who said, "No, no, no, I've got the flight at six in the morning, I'm flying to Afghanistan," or something. You know, some big commercial flight. And I was just like, "Jesus, for God's sake have a drink and take some drugs, will ya!" Do what's expected of you. It's really amazing. I don't know how anyone does it.'

Robin was to be very grateful for Bruce's constant aversion to sitting still, and the singer's love for the fast pace of life was to prove vital on one occasion. At the time, Robin's main project was with his band Rachel Stamp, whose schedule he was very careful to check before taking on the Bruce gig. Seeing no problems, he signed up for the Dickinson solo tour – until the very eve of matters. 'The worst fuckin' thing in the world happened. Right nearing the time, after we'd done a few rehearsals with Bruce, the Rachel Stamp camp phoned up and said we've got a gig, and it clashed with when we were going to be playing Graspop in Belgium. And Rachel Stamp were booked to headline a smallish festival in Essex called the Thurrock Music Festival (TMF).

'And you know, I just shat a brick. I was just like, "Fuckin' hell, I'm done for, what am I gonna do?" Then, on closer inspection, I realised okay, Rachel Stamp were headlining so a guesstimation [was] we're probably going to be onstage about ten o'clock at night. And as luck would have it, the only one European festival that Bruce Dickinson and clan didn't headline was Graspop – we were on just after Rob Halford, and before Dream Theater and Machine Head; Slayer were headlining. I managed to work out our stage time was five o'clock until six o'clock in Belgium – an hour ahead of the UK, so I figure that gives me five hours to do a James Bond and get from Belgium to Essex. I contacted airlines and there were no flights or they were booked up, and I was beginning to sort of crumble.

'Then I thought, "Hold on, Bruce is a pilot," and this is before I'd played any shows with Bruce, so it still could be a bit like, "Who are you causing problems, fuck off! I'll get someone else." So I phoned up Bruce at his home, and I got through to one of Bruce's kids and I said, "It's Robin, I'm doing the drums for the tour" and he knew I was in Rachel Stamp – we had a video on the TV at the time. And he said, "Are you the guy that's spinning all your sticks and all that?" and I thought, "This is really good news, the kid digs me!" you know what I mean. And I went, "Yeah, yeah, that's right, man." And he was like, "Cool, man."'

So Dickinson Jr went to fetch Daddy, during which time Robin Guy freely admits he was, 'shitting myself, I could literally hear the steps of Bruce approaching and I just said, "Bruce, Robin here, I'm doing the drums, got a little bit of a problem. I'm supposed to be in Essex with Rachel Stamp later on and I was just wondering if you'd possibly consider flying me and you in to Belgium, doing the gig and flying me back?" and I just sort of paused thinking, you know, that's it, he's just gonna go, "Fuck off!"'

He did not: Bruce asked where the Stamps' gig was – and immediately started concocting a typically Dickinsonian plan. 'I could hear him flicking through some atlas – "Oh yes, there's a little one in dur-dur-dur Thurrocksville," or wherever he said. And he went, "Oh, we could probably land in the field," and I'm thinking, "Fuck, he's considering this." And then he goes, "We could go one better. I've got a friend who's got some medieval bombers. Why don't we do it in a bomber?" and I'm going "Fu… fu… fu… " you know, 'cause I was expecting him to just boot me out of the camp immediately, let alone go *Why don't we do it in a bomber*. And I'm thinking, "We'll be on the cover of all the mags!" So I said, "That'll be very nice if you don't mind organising that." So he said "I love a challenge. I'll get back to you on that."'

As it turned out, the bomber idea didn't come to fruition – but impressively Bruce, Sanctuary and the management pulled some major strings regardless for this mini-adventure. 'There was a little minivan waiting by the side of the stage in Belgium at Graspop – we literally finished with "Powerslave", big old ending and walked off the stage. Me and Bruce grabbed our little kit bags and we're still in our sweaty shorts and all that, and Bruce signs a couple of autographs and I sign a couple and Bruce turns around and goes, "Come on, get in the van!" A swift hour's drive to Brussels airport, with both artists getting changed in the van, ended up with Bruce and Robin boarding a scheduled flight together.

'This is a little last insight into the great man,' says a beaming

Guy. 'Bruce had some first-class flight ticket and I was in the old *Knees Up Mother Brown* section and he changed his ticket just so he could come and sit and we could chat and all that and hang out and what have you on the flight back. I was like. "Fucking hell, who do you think would do that?" He actually changed it from first class to come and sit with me. I turned around to thank Bruce, "Oh, cheers mate, really cool of you to help me out doing all this…" and he's going, "Just get in the fucking car, go, you've got a gig to do!" and there was a Sanctuary laid-on company car, chauffeur driven, leather seats, bloody fast car in a James Bond style, and I got in.'

His phone was red-hot with calls from Rachel Stamp members enquiring as to where he was – which was, obviously, always 'just round the corner. We pulled up and drove straight through security, right past the crowd [who] of course are stretching to see Rachel Stamp on stage – there was no time for me to go backstage so I just bolted over the crash barrier, jumped onstage, I'd managed to get a mate to set my kit up you know, the crowd sort of recognised me and go "Whoa! Great! Rachel Stamp!" and I just checked the kit really, a man on a mission, and went back to the side of the stage where the rest of the guys… [three of] their faces were chewing wasps. And I thought, "There's nothing I can possibly say at this point, I'll just go 'Let's rock!'" I walked on and nailed it for an hour and then just passed out.

'It was fuckin' one for the books. I've done a kind of Phil Collins, playing in two different countries in the same day, and I arrived two minutes before our show. So we did it, and technically, I wasn't late.'

CHAPTER 23

DANCE
OF DEATH

The second 'comeback' album, 2003's *Dance of Death*, is a huge step up from its predecessor, both in terms of production and also with the space allotted for each of the members to shine. While *Brave New World* had been an excellent stab at the occasionally epic expanded possibilities of a three-guitar line-up, its successor is a beautifully arranged prog-tinted beast of classic metal storytelling. Sonically, it is streets ahead of anything that Maiden had put together through their career – even including *Seventh Son…*'s widescreen approach – and, twenty-one years after *Number of the Beast* caused such a massive stir among all lovers of the distorted guitar and the esoteric lyric, all elements of Maiden's outlook had finally come of age.

Bruce's first writing credit is another collaboration with Harris and Murray, the tight and melodic 'Rainmaker', which offers a smoothness of songwriting that underpins the lyrical wordplay (injecting thoughts of Travis Bickle from *Taxi Driver*) and wanting the rain to come, to seal cracks in the protagonist's relationship with… well, with whatever or whoever you choose to make of it, really. It could refer to another person, missed opportunities, regrets or hope. Again, on the face of it, the song seems straightforward but it raises more questions than answers.

'Montségur' – written by Janick, Bruce and 'Arry – is one of Bruce's typical historical tales, this time telling the story of the Cathars, a Christian sect who believed in vegetarianism. They felt killing animals for food was cannibalism, as each human soul was reincarnated as an animal. The Cathars' view was that rather than being one, omnipotent God, the vengeful Old Testament Lord was a separate being from the New Testament's benign Father. Denounced by the Catholic Church as heretics, the Cathars were subsequently hunted down and killed or set free after confirming themselves in the Catholic faith. The song' serious source material is perhaps framed a little flippantly with what, somehow, feels like a largely light-hearted backing track. The same writing team come together once more on 'Gates of Tomorrow', the intro of which references The Who and launches into a typically rollocking, rock 'n' roll-based slab of Maiden, which meanders a little round its allusions to the future, where relying on your own wits may still not be enough. In truth, it's one of the weaker points of what is generally a very good Maiden album indeed. Bruce's vocals, for once, are fighting with a thick, multi-tracked assault of rhythm guitars with little countermelody to bounce off, although its five minutes fly by solidly enough. This is followed by – shock – a Nicko McBrain track. The drummer's first ever on a Maiden album (he'd brought the bassline and drum tracks to the table), 'New Frontier' was written in collaboration with Adrian Smith and marks a return to melodic darkness for singer Bruce, who revels in the retelling of Mary Shelley's *Frankenstein* for an era of cloning.

Dickinson, Smith and Harris contribute. two more tracks as a writing team, the first the desperate, synth-soaked 'Face in the Sand' which imagines everyone waiting for death to fall from the sky, or to watch it on the television. It is very tempting to peg this as being about the atmosphere of paranoia and bemusement at the terrorist attack on America on 9 September 2001 – Bruce had been in New York at the time, and experienced the horror first-hand before managing to catch a flight back the day after. On this track, Nicko's double-bass drums beat insistently like an accelerated, relentless heartbeat, pausing not for a second until four minutes in, thus lending the track a hypnotic quality. The other track penned by that trio is the album's tour de force: the acoustic magnificence of 'Journeyman' – a remarkable track distinguished by its complexity and maturity. The beautiful arrangement features an incredible, controlled vocal performance from Bruce that perfectly delivers as resonant and powerful – and honest – piece of writing as perhaps ever has been on a Maiden album. Conflict, misunderstanding, sleep, dreams, wakefulness, fitfulness, hope, desolation and finally a clenched-fist affirmation of self; all are here in a track of magisterial, piquant acceptance of humanity. It's an astonishingly grounding, and in many ways exceptionally upbeat, way to complete a long and often complicated album. That this is the same set of musicians who made *Number of the Beast* is, in one sense, difficult to comprehend. And yet, at the same time, *Dance of Death* is a beautiful counterpoint to the ... *Beast* LP conceptually, musically and historically. *Brave New World* showed that Maiden could still make a very good album, but *Dance of Death* showed that the band, and their singer, had much left to explore yet.

The group toured throughout the world over the period of 2003 and 2004. By now, the shows were back to the enormous events of previous years, although this would be the last year that Maiden would embark on such relatively punishing schedules. By now, they all had families and the group – who had put it beyond all doubt on *Dance of Death* that they had nothing whatsoever left to prove – had surely earned the right to spend a little more time with their nearest and dearest. As was becoming the norm, there was to be a live album and DVD associated with the tour, in line with Bruce's idea of the *Alive* albums of the mid-1990s – both designed to stifle bootleggers and offer a real memento of the excellent tours on which Maiden continued to pull up trees left, right and centre. On the European leg, some fans were able to experience an unique moment, by buying special tickets to be flown to and from the gigs by Bruce himself. Bruce Air was born – a taxi service of some quality, and how many other heavy metal legends could offer such a service?

Outside Maiden, Bruce contributed his vocals to the mighty Sack Trick on their Kiss covers album, *Sheep in Kiss Make Up*, lending his vocals to 'Shout it Out Loud'. Somehow seven years had passed, however, since *The Chemical Wedding* tore a hole in the heavy metal scene; returning to Maiden had been a jolt and a half to the system, getting his new job as a commercial pilot a demanding profession, but the fires still burned inside creatively. Bruce then spent October recording for a television series – a look at aviation for the Discovery Channel that was to be somewhat inevitably entitled *Flying Heavy Metal*, and which had morphed from the initial idea of a reality show about airline pilots in training. Over the best part of two weeks, Bruce interviewed engineers, designers and individuals involved in all aspects of the process, something he enjoyed immensely. He spent time at the Boeing factory in Renton, USA, enthusing to *Heraldnet* that he could, 'quite happily spend ages poking around and watching. As a pilot, we never see these planes stripped down like this.' The series was first aired on Discovery in the spring of 2005, and was regularly repeated. Bruce's enthusiasm and knowledge of the subject, plus his ready wit, make him a natural, and engaging, host. His fixation on heavy engineering then led him to a guest appearance on Discovery Home & Leisure's *Trainspotting* show on Friday, 22 October 2004; he was a guest of presenter Mark Collins, and Bruce was delighted to spend the day at Bluebell Railway on a steam train driving day. Strange to think now, but driving a train used to be every small boy's dream job.

All great fun, but quite frankly it was time Bruce really let rip again with some solo material, and so he turned his hand back to getting the licks licked. Bruce and Roy had been writing demos – on and off – since 2001, but work began in earnest around November 2003, with both of them firing ideas backwards and forwards to refine the collection of new songs. Initially, this included 'Believil', 'Tyranny of Souls' and 'Eternal' – 'Broken' and 'Silver Wings' having been nicked for Bruce's 2001 *Best of...* release already. The intent was to keep the project manageable alongside all of Bruce's other activities, so the (roughly) twenty demos and sketches were refined down to a slick ten that the pair would be working on for the new album. Once the songs were decided, recording sessions began with Bruce asking Roy Z to lay down the drum tracks with the very talented Dave Moreno in Castle Oaks, Calabasa and Signature Sound in San Diego. Most of the rest of the album that eventually took the title *Tyranny of Souls* was in fact recorded in Roy Z's living room!

Roy aside, and with Adrian Smith back of course in the Maiden camp, the *Tyranny of Souls* line-up was an entirely new band. Bass duties are handled by Z and also Ray 'Geezer' Burke – a moustachioed stylist whose influences and fluidity range from Jack Bruce to Geezer Butler, and a mysterious keyboard player known only as Mistheria. The keyboard parts on *Tyranny*… came together in a very technologically up-to-date manner, with ideas and audio being fired backward and forward over the internet before Bruce would pick the tracks he liked for the album.

It was even more remarkable given Bruce had recorded a large amount of the vocals in rather a lot of pain, having fallen into the drum kit after one particular Iron Maiden gig where he slipped on some wet steps. 'Navigate the Seas of the Sun' is one of Bruce's trademark acoustic-based esoteric epics, this time a Bowie-esque effort that looks to the stars for answers, and for possibilities therein, and stands strong against anything he had ever previously written. All in all, *Tyranny of Souls* is a more-than-worthy addition to his canon; very different from Maiden, it is nonetheless a slab of excellent heavy metal. *Kerrang!* rated it as, 'the glorious sound of a heavy metal master in full flight' on its release on 23 May, 2005. By which time, of course, the Iron Maiden machine was kicking firmly into action once more.

CHAPTER 24

CONFLICT

The major retrospective of the early part of Maiden's career, *The History of Iron Maiden – Part 1: The Early Days* had been a massive success among the fans after its release in November 2004. As 2005 dawned, the band announced their intent to take to the road for the *Eddie Rips Up... Europe* leg of their world tour, which would then join the travelling metal festival Ozzfest, in North America, for most of the rest of the summer before returning to Europe (and missing the last seven dates of the Ozzfest tour) for the late summer festivals. Further, the set-list would concentrate largely on earlier material, in line with the focus of the DVD, intended to be the first in a set of six or so such releases that would tell a comprehensive official history of the group.

When Ozzfest came around, Maiden were sharing the main stage with such luminaries as Mudvayne, Shadows Fall and headliners, Black Sabbath. It was some reunion for Bruce and Ozzy, who during the 1980s had been, on and off, drinking buddies – there's a story that on one occasion in 1983, they ordered fifty beers from their hotel bar before stumbling out on the streets to find and then hopefully steal a taxi, which they singularly failed to do. Sabbath had been one of the bands that Bruce had idolised over the years – they were one of the reasons he and Steve Harris had both been motivated to get into music in the first place. All of which made what happened next even more bizarre.

As has been well-reported in the press, there had been, shall we say, differences of opinion between the Maiden singer and Sharon Osbourne over comments that Bruce had been making onstage during several of the Ozzfest shows. He'd referred to Ozzy's memory not quite being what it used to be, and that Oz needed lyric sheets written onstage to remember his tracks, and also raged against the reality TV show *The Osbournes*, which was aired with spectacular success that year. Things came to a head at the show at San Bernadino, on 20 August 2005 – Maiden's last appearance on the tour. The band's set was interrupted several times by someone taking over the PA to shout 'Ozzy, Ozzy'; Maiden were pelted with eggs, and the stage was invaded twice by a guy dressed in a US flag during 'The Trooper'. The constant interruptions to Maiden's set looked rather like an orchestrated campaign to make the band look ridiculous. They, of course, not only completed the set, but ended up with the crowd chanting their name at the tops of their voices, despite the problems that had been put in their way. As Bruce said, draped in the Union Flag, while all around him was falling apart, 'These Colours Don't Run'. And they did not.

In the aftermath of the incident, both Sharon Osbourne and Rod Smallwood had their own take on matters, the two managers releasing statements to the press. Smallwood had clashed, of course, with Sharon's father, the legendary Don Arden, over the notorious sleeve for 'Women in Uniform', and was simply not a man to be messed with. Sharon released a statement on 20 August on *Ozzfest. com* that began by saying Maiden had been chosen to play by the Ozzfest committee because they'd not toured America for a while, but noted that from the outset, 'Bruce Dickinson started berating Ozzy and belittling the Ozzfest audience. He stated he, "didn't need a reality show to give him credibility", "we're not just some fucking reunion band" and continuously complained about the sound system, saying that when he comes back to America he'll have a better one.' The statement went on to state that because Bruce hadn't toured the States for a long time [Bruce had in fact toured the US with his solo band as well as Maiden], that he didn't grasp how things had changed over the past ten years, and that Bruce felt he had to belittle other artists. Osbourne then made it absolutely clear that it was the singer with whom she had a beef, rather than the rest of the band and crew, who she said were 'great' and 'professional'.

'How sad it was, after ten years, that this little man tried to ruin it for everyone,' she wrote. 'The bands of Ozzfest don't even look at Ozzfest as touring, but as its heavy metal summer camp. Bruce is in fact a jealous prick and very envious. None of his tirades were directed at Sabbath, only Ozzy… It also offended me every night how he took out the English flag in America. There are American boys going to war alongside the English boys every day. How dare he forget the American troops on their home turf?' She concluded that Bruce had no respect for his audience.

In response, Maiden kept their counsel for a few days, aside from apologising that their involvement with Ozzfest had ended on quite such a bizarre note, before Rod Smallwood's release to the press revealed the Maiden camp's take on events. He began by stating that Maiden were preparing for their headlining dates at the Reading and Leeds festivals, 'and don't wish to waste time giving Sharon Osbourne's statement the dignity of a reply. Considering the disgraceful nature of the events that occurred, they feel it's a pretty dismal effort at self-justification and they don't think Metal fans are at all gullible and that they will easily see through it. They want no more to do with this sorry incident and are very much looking forward to headlining Reading and Leeds Festivals this weekend.'

Smallwood, however, had his own personal feelings about matters, musing that after three decades of being in the rock business, he had never seen anything quite so 'disgusting and unprofessional as what went on that night. I was standing on our sound desk out front as usual, but ran to the stage as soon as the hail of missiles began and from then on watched from the front of the stage right next to Bruce's walkway. The scale, viciousness and concentration of the throwing made it obvious that this was a premeditated and coordinated attack. Assaulting musicians while performing by throwing bottle tops, lighters and eggs at them from just a few yards away is vile, dangerous, criminal and cowardly. It is incredible that Ozzfest security apparently did nothing about it – aren't they there to protect the bands too?' He concluded by saying how proud he was of Maiden, and the singer, for standing their ground for the sake of the fans, and felt that, 'the imperturbable attitude and ability of the band shone through and in the end made this a truly remarkable rock and roll event, even if for all the wrong reasons. We will have no more to say on this matter except that I do think the band deserve an apology from a number of people, and you know who you are.'

It rumbled on and on. Sharon Osbourne came back in 'an open letter' to Rod Smallwood's statement, reported widely by the press including *Metal Underground*: 'It's shameful that Dickinson felt he had the right to air his issues publicly onstage every night as a way to boost his own ego. Dickinson never once came up to Ozzy and me to voice any concerns. He certainly had the opportunity to do so every night. If he wasn't able to show us that courtesy then why should I give him the respect to air my grievances with him in private? Ozzy's only interaction with Dickinson was on the first night of the tour. Ozzy, being the true gentleman that he is, passed Bruce in the hall and said, "Good luck and have a great show." Unfortunately Dickinson felt the need to turn his back to Ozzy and walked away. Frankly, Dickinson got what he deserved. We had to listen to his bullshit for five straight weeks. He only had to suffer a couple of eggs on the head.'

Sharon Osbourne went on to conclude that perhaps 'Dickinson doesn't have the manners to realize that when you are invited into someone's home, are seated at their dinner table, are eating their food and drinking their wine, you shouldn't talk disrespectfully about them [i.e. Ozzy, Black Sabbath and Ozzfest], otherwise you just might get your ass handed to you. Every action has a reaction. Was Dickinson so naïve to think that I was going to let him get away with talking shit about my family night after night? I don't think he realises who he's dealing with. I will not endure behaviour like this from anyone.' And after speculating that this had created the most press interest in the band for twenty years, she signed it 'The Real Iron Maiden'.

BRUCE DICKINSON

Bruce's only response was in an interview with *The Sun* newspaper, during which he made it clear that he believed it had been an orchestrated attack, reiterating his pride that Maiden had been so stolid, and commented that 'Everyone knows it's Sharon Osbourne. It's certainly not Ozzy or Sabbath – they have too much class to condone stunts like that. She hates me for making remarks about reality TV. I hate reality TV. People should get off their arses and do stuff and not be so voyeuristic.' He ended by stating that it was lucky that the audience had been happy with Maiden's set despite it all, otherwise there could well have been a rather serious situation develop as a consequence. No matter, Bruce and Maiden came out of it with dignity enhanced rather than damaged, and anyone who was lucky enough to catch the band at those Reading and Leeds performances would have seen an act even more fired-up than usual.

On 2 September, Maiden played another Clive Aid set, this time at Hammersmith Odeon, raising profile and cash once more for their erstwhile drummer, with tickets sold mostly to fan club members with a small amount set aside for the general public. The remainder of 2005 saw Bruce and the band have some time off before intending to hit 2006 running by writing and recording sessions for another new album. Bruce spent most of the rest of his time in the sky, concentrating on his day job, although he did manage to find some time to contribute to another interesting musical project, which also involved Chris Dale, Roy Z and the legendary Brazilian metal artist, Renato Tribuzy. The pair had met some four years earlier, but it took some time for them to pin down a recording session. Bruce lent his singing to the very metallic 'Beast in the Light', one of the many highlights on an excellent album that also features Michael Kiske of Helloween, Mat Sinner of Sinner and Andreas Kisser of the legendary Sepultura. Bruce performed two concerts with Renato and his band at São Paulo and Belo Horizonte on 12 and 13 November 2005. It had been another year of creativity, triumph, lots of flying and general mischief for Bruce, proving that things were never likely to truly settle down for the mercurial vocalist.

CHAPTER 25

A MATTER OF LIFE AND DEATH

Iron Maiden's fourteenth studio album, *A Matter of Life and Death*, was written in early 2006 and the band set to recording sessions during spring that year. Bruce told *Music Mirror* that the process had been a relatively quick one. '[I]t was three weeks to write it, three weeks to rehearse it, and three weeks to record it. The very shortest time was, actually, *Number of the Beast*, but we rehearsed this faster than any other album. I mean, we spent fifteen days rehearsing it, we spent fifteen days recording it, and then we spent an additional fifteen to twenty days doing some overdubs and mixing. But to learn this album in fifteen days and then go straight into the studio and play it live is incredible.'

He also expressed his belief that he had progressed personally as a vocalist during his time away from Maiden. 'I really expanded my range, not just vocally, but in terms of songwriting, and I brought that back, I think, into Maiden, and each album, I think, we've been moving towards really interesting territory. And I'm so pleased with this one. *Brave New World* was good as far as it went. It didn't step into any really, really new territory. And then [...] we tried a few things on *Dance of Death*. Some of them worked, some of them didn't work quite so good, but you know what? It gave us the confidence to do this album, and this album, I think, is really special.' He also said that there was likely to be another solo record from him at some stage.

In another interview at around the same time, with *Dose.ca*, Bruce said that Maiden's longevity was a band that came from the street and did not conform to the expected route to fame. Indeed, the group was far from mainstream pop or even mainstream metal. He once more blasted the TV reality shows that were all the rage at the time. 'I just think reality TV showcases all the lowest forms of human nature. In effect, it's a freak show. Creativity is bound up in being eccentric, being different, not just giving the people what they want. What you need to do is to elevate things, to take things beyond the norm. Reality TV shows don't encourage that whatsoever. They dumb everything down to horrible, uniform level of acceptable talent. The only people with less talent than the worst performers are actually the judges. The sight of all the judges back-slapping themselves like a pack of smug hyenas does nothing for me whatsoever. I know people like it, but so what? I'm sure people would like watching snuff movies, too, but that doesn't make it right.'

With tour dates being arranged at a rate of knots, the Maiden machine was lurching into familiar action once more. By mid-May, 2006, the band was ready to master the new long player. The remarkable thing about the band's third record as a six-piece is the ease with which they scale musical, lyrical, production and mood heights turn after turn. It is sprawling and challenging but also a listener-friendly piece of work, one that could only have been written and recorded by a set of musicians who had lived, as they say, in interesting times. Listening to *A Matter of Life and Death* is like listening to Iron Maiden's life stories, their hopes, dreams and musical influences. In a sense, it goes even further than its predecessor, *Dance of Death*, in laying bare the personalities of its creators. In that all art has an essentially naked, autobiographical element if it is truly successful, *A Matter of Life and Death* stands up as a documentation of the band's development over the years.

Although it is not a concept album in the sense that *Seventh Son...* is – or come to that, *The Chemical Wedding* – the themes running through the LP are those of war, conflict, the place of the ordinary soldier in a greater and more overpowering system, and the common man seeking to reconcile the often dichotomic demands of duty and moral consistency. There's paranoia, sleeplessness and resolution, fire-eyed defiance and retribution. Although the tracks are not overtly political, the album nevertheless presents the listener with demanding questions. And although these are stories, tales and epic imaginative filmic scenarios, the common ideas running through the album demand an interaction with the fan that is frequently missing in the bellicose cacophony of the heavy metal genre. Like the previous Maiden LP – and elements of *Tyranny of Souls* – it serves to put the band's previous work in a new context. Listening, for example to 'These Colours Don't Run' back to back with 'The Trooper' – or even 'Tailgunner' – swipes away the linearity of time and reveals the tracks to be part of a greater whole that is bound not by chronology but by wider, more universal themes. Some thirty years – give or take – since Bruce first began writing songs in earnest, there is a sense that, not only is there still fuel in the tank, but he – and Maiden – are entering an adventurous and vibrant period of their careers.

Bruce told *Kerrang!* of his excitement about the new record. '*Brave New World* and *Dance of Death* were both good records. But they weren't anywhere near as good as this one! This one is *Dance of Death* without the effort. This whole album feels effortless. It's like driving a big, gas-guzzling motor car. You just put your foot down and there's limitless power under the bonnet.'

The band, and producer Kevin Shirley, were rightly enthused about the quality of the work they had produced. Said Bruce to *Metal Underground*, 'There is such a wide scope of musicianship on this album, and in parts [it is] truly epic. I thought with the likes of "Paschendale" from the last studio album that we could only hope to surpass that but having now heard the album back as well as sitting with a few select people and hearing their reactions as well, I truly believe we have managed it. Every one of us has put everything into this record and it's really paid off. However, we've had such fun making it that it's almost difficult to believe what we've managed to achieve in the time it took.' Old 'Arry 'Arris made reference to the fact that it was the most natural-feeling writing and recording process of their entire career, praising the power of the record, while expressing his excitement about playing the new tracks in the live arena. The album – which was largely recorded live, and features very little in the way of additional sonic manipulation – was not mastered, on the insistence of Steve Harris. Kevin Shirley, writing on his own *Cavemanproductions.com*, explained that it 'means that you will get to hear the new album exactly as it sounded in the studio, no added EQ, compression, analogue widening, etc, and I must say, I am pretty happy with the end result. I think some tracks could use a smidge more top end, and others a bump of bottom — but I know 'Arry well enough now to know how wary of outsiders he is, and I fully expected he may have done that, so I made sure I was happy with the results when I printed the mixes in the studio.' Which says much about Steve's traditionalist approach; despite the increasing complexity of the material, there is still a strong streak in the bass player – and driving force of the band – that seeks to retain the unpolished aggression inherent in the music he loves so much. There are very, very few albums these days that are unmastered: to most bands it is an aspect of the process that is as familiar as setting up a SM57 and setting it live with its own designated tape machine to record their farts all day.

Bruce's first writing credit on the new record is the near seven-minute beast, 'These Colours Don't Run' – a phrase with many connotations, but in this context a discussion of the role of ordinary soldiers in conflict. Bruce explained to *Revolver Magazine* that it was about what, 'motivates soldiers and what they fight for. Some of them have a big flag tattooed on their ass and genuinely believe all the patriotic stuff, and they'll get their heads blown off for Uncle Sam. But I think most of them fight because if they didn't, their buddies would get killed.' The team of Smith/Harris/Dickinson also collaborated on the mighty 'Brighter Than a Thousand Suns', which, echoing the singer's historical leanings, and – again, coming full circle – compares the Cold War to the very hot war *du jour*, the arguably more horrific, less tangible and inhuman aspects of post-9/11 war on terror. 'I spent most of my adolescence under the shadow of the atomic bomb,' he said. 'I was brought up in a generation that was led to believe that a klaxon siren would go off, and you'd just have four minutes to kiss your ass goodbye. This generation has a different paranoia. Today, it's all about terrorism. We just thought we were going to get wiped off the face of the earth. So the song looks at how you reconcile building something as destructive as the bomb with sleeping at night.' Given Harris's well-documented insomnia and/or nightmares, it is a powerful metaphor.

Together, the three constructed another one of Bruce's soldier epics – 'The Longest Day', which draws on the D-Day landings and the extreme circumstances and acts that the soldiers (many of them only around eighteen years old) were put through. In a sense, its lyrics – referring to both God and Valhalla – present an interesting collision of mythology, reality and desperation. 'Lord of Light' is, essentially, the trio's extended discussion of the Cathars' concept of there being a benign spirit and an Old Testament-type, vengeful Lord; except this time, and in a move that would no doubt cause outcry in the moral majority, it seeks to present an alternative perspective. That the Lord of Light – or, to put it another way, Lucifer, the 'Bringer of Light' – has basically had some bad press. The singer collaborated also with his bassist on 'Out of the Shadows' – at five-and-a-half minutes, one of the shorter tracks on A Matter of Life and Death, which speaks loudly of rebirth, karma and the central idea that what doesn't kill us will make us only stronger. And, again, should you choose to, there is obvious resonance there in terms of the pair's sometime fractious relationship.

Maiden could do no wrong in the eyes of the press. On the

album's release, *Kerrang!* said it was, 'another Maiden classic'; *Metal Hammer* gave it full marks and felt that the band had 'utterly surpassed themselves' and *Classic Rock* enthused that Maiden were all-time greats, both living up to their reputation, as well as having released what that magazine thought was 'possibly the album of the year'. Not bad for a bunch of old grunts in or approaching their fifties. For Bruce's part, when asked about the plans the band had for the next decade, he referred to the fact that he now considered his airline work his bread and butter, having spent eight hundred hours in the air (the maximum is nine hundred) over the previous twelve months. 'I'm one of these guys who always has the glass half full,' he told *Toronto Star*. 'I'm looking ahead going, "Okay, I'm almost fifty. What am I going to be doing when I get to sixty?" Well, I might be running around with Iron Maiden. But probably not. So what am I going to be doing? Shit, I'll be flying airliners – that's cool!'

The extensive tour took in much of the world as usual, the band playing to huge crowds night after night alongside support acts Lauren Harris (daughter of Steve) and metal upstarts Trivium, who had just released their third album, which in another of those satisfyingly circular moments, is called *The Crusade*. Tom Parker was one of the PA engineers for the shows. He gave me an insight into the Maiden camp on the album tour. 'Their travelling and stuff isn't done together at all,' says the audio technician, giving an invaluable insight into the slickness and tightness of the Maiden touring machine – as well as the intense, professional trust the band and their crew have between each other. 'Everyone turns up about an hour before the actual show, maybe two hours. It's Steve that turns up before everybody else, unless something's gone wrong the night before and then they'll come and iron it out, but they [rarely] do their own soundcheck; it's always the roadies that'll do that. Now and again, like when it's coming to the end of a tour, they'll come and chat with the crew and everything, but it's only the actual guitar techs for each member that'll really have a chat. They're quite anonymous otherwise. 'Cause they all travel separately, they drive to all the venues, or fly to them, especially in Bruce's case.'

Parker feels that Maiden's continued longevity is down to the fact that the band have been able to not only keep their own fan base intact, but to add to it with every passing generation of music and metal fans. 'The things that surprised me the most,' he muses, 'are the actual facts that they could sell out a sixteen-thousand-capacity arena every night, and also the *diversity* of the crowd was absolutely ridiculous – from the age of eight to eighty-eight. Seeing as though they are the forefathers of British heavy metal, I think that every single band that's been in that genre has been influenced by them in some way, it's fair to say, really.' Not least Trivium, whose driving force and singer Matt Heafy was widely quoted as saying what a massive part Maiden's music has had in their own nascent career; and although Trivium's most obvious reference point is Metallica, that band were firmly inspired by the New Wave of British Heavy Metal themselves. There were other more 'revealing' insights from Parker, too: 'One thing Bruce isn't scared to do is be naked, he'll just stand there and talk to anyone or anybody who comes in after a shower and everything.'

The year 2006 was, then, one in which Bruce's band retained their dignity under pressure, while wowing audiences across the globe. The singer had also appeared alongside many other metal legends in the documentary *Metal: A Headbanger's Journey*, presented a satellite television investigation into the phenomenon of spontaneous human combustion (a show cunningly entitled *Inside Spontaneous Human Combustion With Bruce Dickinson*), joined many others to pay tribute to DJ Tommy Vance, who had recently passed away (as legend has it, Vance was the only person to advise Bruce *not* to take the job as singer in Iron Maiden) and was even banned from watching the gigs of his son Austin's rock band (perhaps even the vocalist in the greatest heavy metal act of all-time comes under the heading of 'embarrassing dad' sometimes).

Incredibly, he even undertook a mercy mission to Cyprus on 20 July 2006, airlifting two hundred Brits fleeing war-torn Lebanon and bringing them safely back to the United Kingdom. (On 12 February 2007, Bruce would fly the Glasgow Rangers football team to their UEFA Cup game against Hapoel Tel Aviv.) The group then took their huge production – almost 20 tons of backline equipment – to India. The Bangalore gig was one of the biggest that country had ever seen, with 30,000 people in attendance. Bruce was suitably up for the cup: 'To say we're all really looking forward to going to Bangalore is something of an understatement. It's very special to us to be able play to new fans in countries we've never been to before, and we hear the Indian fans are very loud and into their metal. The whole trip will be an exciting time for us and we intend to enjoy every moment there,' *Blabbermouth* reported.

June saw Maiden once more headlining Donington Park for *Download*, the rock festival that replaced *Monsters of Rock*. It was their fourth headlining slot and they went down exceptionally well. The band pulled up to 80,000 people and Bruce spoke directly to the crowd before the lads launched into 'Children of the Damned'. 'It is twenty-five years since we released 'Number of the Beast' and this song is very special to me because it is one of the first we rehearsed when I first joined the band. It is a song that brings a tear to the eye.' The gig was also filmed with an eye on an upcoming DVD. On 24 June, the group were at Brixton Academy for another Clive Aid gig. A writer from *Metal Rules* was there. 'Bruce, for me still one of the best frontmen in the world, was everywhere on the two-tiered Maiden set. Never a still moment with the little buzzy fella. Bouncing around on stage one second, climbing up the set another, teasing poor Nicko, shining spotlights and chucking water into the crowd, jumping star kicks, the lot. And his voice, well, all I can say is that it's still there, even the screams. All in all, vintage Iron Maiden.'

The first single to come from *A Matter of Life and Death* was the epic 'The Reincarnation of Benjamin Breeg', an intense, hefty and atmospheric track described by *Kerrang!* as 'an intricate seven-minute epic that starts with a creepy, ominous intro before erupting into a crushing, almost Led Zeppelin-esque riff and a powerful, emotive chorus.' It was released as a seven-inch picture disc, with B-sides 'Run to the Hills' and 'The Trooper' from a previous Radio 1 Legends session. There was also a two-track CD that had a different B-side – the same radio session's run-through of 'Hallowed Be Thy Name.'

Maiden decamped to the United States for eight dates, then three in Canada, beginning in Hartford, Connecticut. Bruce was voluble about the prospect in a widespread press release. 'This is the first time we've started a tour in the States for many, many years,' he said. It's going to be great to get out there so the fans can get to hear the new material and see the new show first for a change. We're all incredibly pleased with the album, and the tremendous response of those people who have had the chance to hear it so far. Their reaction has been phenomenal and we expect to play a lot of it on tour.' He went on: 'We will be bringing the full show to America, which we are currently putting the final touches to, and we fully intend to make it as spectacular and memorable as we can. And of course, our mate Eddie has already booked a place on the plane with us.' As for the album, it had been hugely successful following its release on 28 August 2006, soaring to No.1 in Poland, Sweden, Germany and Finland. It hit No.9 in the *Billboard 200* Stateside, and No.4 in the United Kingdom's Official Album Chart.

The second single to be taken from the album was 'Different World', the video of which was a splendid animation directed by Howard Greenhalgh, who had previously been known for Soundgarden's 'Black Hole Sun' video. Maiden's newest hit MTV2 from 16 October onwards, with the single having various B-sides in different formats including live versions of 'Iron Maiden' or 'Fear of the Dark'; for the United States contingent, a CD single included 'The Trooper' and 'Hallowed Be Thy Name' from the BBC radio sessions. Bruce's singing was in a relatively low register, something of a tribute to Phil Lynott of Thin Lizzy. It was also the first song the band had played on the current tour. Bringing the metal to yet another new generation, the track also appeared on a skateboard game, *Tony Hawk's Downhill Jam*. There was also a non-animated video, which showed the guys in the recording studio. 'Different World' reached No.3 in the UK and topped the Finnish singles chart. Business-wise, Rod Smallwood and Andy Taylor left the company they founded, Sanctuary, but would continue to manage Maiden.

The latter stages of the *Life and Death* world tour were dubbed *A Matter of the Beast*, which nodded to the fact that it was some twenty-five years since the band's breakthrough album, the mighty *Number of the Beast*. So much had happened for Bruce and the boys individually and collectively during that period, and yet when the band kicked into the song itself onstage it was blasted away as if it was merely yesterday. The concept of acknowledging their musical past was one to which the band would return imminently, while also giving Bruce the opportunity to bring two of his major obsessions – flying and music – into closer quarters than ever before.

CHAPTER 26

BACK IN TIME, SOARING TO THE FUTURE

Iron Maiden may have had a massively successful new album out, but it was also important to recognise the sheer weight of that immense back catalogue. Thus, 2008 began with a bang and the *Somewhere Back in Time* world tour, which brought 1980s classics from the *Powerslave, Somewhere in Time* and *Seventh Son of a Seventh Son* LPs back into the live arena. There was also another DVD in the on-going *History of Iron Maiden* series and the year-long tour spawned *Somewhere Back in Time*, another greatest hits compilation.

The tour was also unique in that the band, crew and gear would be travelling in their own customised Boeing 757 aircraft, *Ed Force One*. The call sign for the plane was *666* – perhaps unwisely, given what had happened with Blaze Bayley's spooky encounters with that number. Tempting fate? The aircraft, leased from Astraeus Airlines, was flown by none other than Bruce himself. He told *The Sun* that it was quite an experience. 'We've been around the world many times and done some pretty momentous things but this is a first, not just for us but for any band on the planet,' he admitted. 'When we came up with the idea of getting one big plane with all the band, crew and equipment on we didn't realise how complex it was. But here we finally are on our 757, which we've christened *Ed Force One*, with yours truly wearing his captain's uniform, ready to fly us off around the globe.' Enthusiastically, he continued: 'We're doing fifty thousand miles in forty-nine days and bringing Maiden mania to India, Australia, Japan, Mexico, all round South America and finally the US and Canada. That's twenty-one concerts, nineteen cities, ten countries and four hundred thousand fans. And we're bringing a monster of a show with us —pyramids, cyborgs, special effects and a set list to blow every Maiden fan's mind.'

In a press release of the time, Bruce explained further. 'Looking at the list of places we would like to play we have always had problems joining up the dots. With sea containers in various places it slows down the whole touring process, which is fine if you want a holiday but not if you want to play. It's great to see places but we don't want to sit around for a week waiting for gear to get from, say, Australia to South America, so this way we can get to more fans in more places en route in the same time period.'

Saving time would enable Bruce to concentrate on other projects, such as his long-mooted film on occultist Aleister Crowley. Bruce and Julian Doyle spoke to an interviewer while at the Cannes festival about the subject matter of the *Chemical Wedding* movie. 'When I started reading his stuff I was interested in what the film has as a base – the chemical wedding,' Doyle said. 'Chemical being science and wedding being spiritual... a wedding of science and music. Crowley brought yoga to England, lived in China, lived in Mexico, understood the ancient religions of those countries but was also fascinated by quantum physics. He wrote a lot about how quantum physics is the most interesting side of mysticism, and this was way back… Not only that, but he is an extremely gross character.'

Bruce jumped in, 'Tantric sex […] at its heart is an offshoot of yoga and it's the idea that the ancients had, that there was something very special about bodily fluids… you put these two things together and you got a spiritual creature, so surely there is an essence inside all of us. They also had spiritual centres that corresponded to chakras of yoga and things like that. Tantric sex, at its highest level, aims to achieve, through controlled sex and controlling orgasms and everything like that, union with God.' The obvious question follow-up was whether the Maiden man had ever tried it himself; he replied, simply, that he didn't have the patience. He also noted that Simon Callow had been perfect for the part, as he had planned a Crowley movie himself in the past and so knew a great deal about the character already. Flippant to the last, Bruce also said that Crowley had three days (in the movie) to come back from the dead – a key theme of the film - so he was, 'Just like Jesus, but better.'

Music-wise, there was also the small matter of the release of a DVD version of the 1985 classic live album *Live After Death*. The DVD also contained an hour-long documentary and live footage shot during that year's tour of Eastern Bloc countries – at a time in which the Berlin Wall still existed, of course – and at the 1985 *Rock in Rio* gig, where Maiden supported Queen in front of 300,000 fans. There was also a quickie fifteen-minute look at the band's 1983 show in San Antonio, Texas, promo clips and miles more. Another top Maiden package for the fans to slaver over.

Bruce's plan to blow people's minds began in Mumbai, India. The band has been credited as kick-starting the market for metal and rock in that country. *The Guardian* explained in 2014 that, 'Before Maiden, India figured nowhere on the tour circuit for any international metal band – the country had nothing to show in terms of record sales or album numbers, then the only indicator for a band's fan base in a country. Although promoters had been trying to bring down international metal acts for years before Maiden, the bands were understandably leery of taking a chance on a country they knew nothing about. Maiden's very well documented 2007 show [...] opened the floodgates for international bands and India was suddenly a viable metal destination.' The metal scene in India had been bubbling under for years, but Bruce and company had pushed the genre into the mainstream with all the critical mass of their stature.

Back in the UK briefly, Bruce then managed to head back to Wiltshire, UK, to take part in a mini-display of vintage aeroplanes at the Kemble Air Day. He told *This is Wiltshire* about his enthusiasm for all things aviation-related. 'It's a great airfield and event to support, and it has a nice theme this year [celebrating the one-hundredth birthday of jet-engine inventor Frank Whittle.] It's a great story and I don't think people are aware just how switched on the British aviation industry was in the fifties, sixties and seventies. The Red Arrows were based in Kemble for twenty years and Kemble itself has a huge association with the jet engine, so it's great to reflect that in the display. Kemble is a great airfield, because it is one that is still enthusiastic about aviation. It seems to be a place that is very well embedded in the community.'

The tour rolled on, with audiences absolutely up for it– some slightly too much. At the gig in Bogotá, Colombia, more than a hundred people without tickets tried to get in. Riot police were called in and fired tear gas at rock-chucking hooligans. The *BBC* reported that 'Local authorities said they would debate whether Bogotá should host any more heavy metal concerts in future.' As reported by *Ultimate Guitar*, Rod Smallwood wrote on the Maiden website that the news was 'wildly exaggerated', but added that a small minority were not helping the cause. 'They do Iron Maiden, Metal and the real Colombian fans a disservice and sadly just provide a reason for the military to feel they need to be there,' he commented. 'Our fans are there for the MUSIC. We definitely intend to return to Colombia and trust the authorities will not be swayed to banning Maiden and Metal because of a minority of trouble makers spoiling it for the huge majority of true Iron Maiden fans.'

It was typical of Maiden not even to be remotely fazed by a power failure at the gig in New York's Madison Square Garden. A football was produced from the side of the stage and consequently Team Maiden proceeded to have a quick kickabout instead, while the technical team worked on fixing the issue. Steve Harris's soccer-ball chops were well known: he'd even spent time on the books of his beloved West Ham United before becoming one of the biggest rock stars on the planet. Still, music came first and foremost, and when the power came back on Maiden hammered straight into 'Heaven Can Wait', which seemed more than appropriate.

Bruce's schedule continued unabated, with the release on 4

May 2008 – at the *Sci-Fi London* film festival – of *Chemical Wedding*, the movie that he'd worked on with Julian Doyle as director and co-writer. On the soundtrack, songs by Maiden and Bruce as a solo artist were interspersed with classical tunes by Mozart and Handel and even something by George Formby. The singer also played different cameo roles on the movie, although the main role was taken by respected actor Simon Callow. The plot concerns a professor at Cambridge who experiences a virtual-reality glitch and becomes stuck in a possession by Aleister Crowley – the 'Beast' himself – because the VR software has been reprogrammed by a Crowley acolyte. Although the movie had originally been optioned by Terry Jones, in the end David Pupkewitz and Malcolm Kohli of Focus Films took the production on, alongside Bill and Ben Productions, Duellist Film Production, MotionFX and E-Motion. It was later released as *Crowley* on DVD in the United States and Canada.

The Observer didn't quite know what to make of the whole thing. '*Chemical Wedding* is one of the most bizarre movies to come out of a British studio in recent years,' commented Philip French. 'The plot is labyrinthine [...] Stylistically, it resembles a demented version of those Hammer Studios occult horror flicks, based on black magic novels by Dennis Wheatley, a writer much influenced, in his fiction at least, by Crowley's personality and works. There are references to Einstein, L Ron Hubbard, Stephen Hawking, black holes, alchemy, quantum physics, along with much copulation, masturbation, urination, decapitation and mortification.' French concluded that, at times, the movie was funny without being intended to be, but admitted that although the acting – Callow aside – wasn't up to much, it was, 'never boring'.

In truth, *Chemical Wedding* was probably always intended for a more niche audience, and it found one in *Horrornews*, who absolutely loved the movie. 'The film is directed by Julian Doyle, editor of Terry Gilliam's *Brazil*, and is quite an undertaking in itself. Though you might be better off in the first viewing to leave the subtitles on to get all the information as it passes back and forth on screen. The journey also takes on the issues of time travel, multi universes and the astral plane. So if you end the film scratching your head, remember that time is a element of quantum physics [...] which can be displaced.' In short, the reviewer summed up the movie as: 'Deeply sustaining, and historically engaging! Brilliantly intelligent horror that comes from a darker place close to home and place in science that is just around the corner.'

Bruce told an interviewer for *Toulecinema* that work on the film had been on-going for four or five even before his solo album – which bore an almost identical title, of course. 'When we first started having an idea about doing a film about Aleister Crowley [...] the working title for the script was *Number of the Beast*,' he revealed. 'And we changed that because a friend of Julian's had written a novel called *The Chemical Wedding* [...] the chemical part is actually referring to the alchemy. The Al-chemical Wedding.' Bruce added that he was interested in Crowley's failures and flaws as much as anything. 'What made Crowley *not* one of the great religious leaders of the twentieth century? What made him the wickedest man in the world? He was a supreme narcissist and he never knew when to shut up.' He also noted that Crowley had put it out there that there were many ways to meditate including short cuts through drugs. 'He turned magic from being something that you sat around and talked about, as a philosophical concept... [to]

something scientific […] He was to magic what Bruce Lee was to the martial arts.'

In *Chemical Wedding*, the main character only thinks he is Crowley – rather than actually being Crowley himself – which enabled the story to pick and choose the main events from the life of the 'Beast' for dramatic effect. The singer also pointed out that 'occult' only meant 'hidden' teachings. 'Sometimes they are hidden because people need to discover them, and seek them out, before they become real,' he said. 'That's something that would be quite familiar to every sportsman. You can read about how to be a great tennis champion, a magician, or a witch, but the secret hidden knowledge is not reading about it. It's doing it, and experiencing it.

'So when you are a tennis champion,' Bruce continued, warming to his theme, 'when you have understood the meaning of combat against another guy, and you feel it as part of your soul and your being, you are different. You have secret knowledge. You have hidden knowledge. And the occult knowledge is the same.' In other words, he concluded, the knowledge was only secret because it was hidden within themselves. The project was another externalisation of Bruce's continuing search for answers – or at the very least, some interesting questions to occupy his ever-curious mind.

Back in Maiden-ville, meanwhile, the tour continued throughout the year, culminating its South America leg in February and March 2009. There was also the small matter of the summer release of the documentary *Iron Maiden: Flight 666*, which had debuted in some cinemas on 21 April. The movie follows the band on that famous aircraft and significantly spends a lot of time concentrating on the fan base that has sustained the Maiden camp for so many years.

That relationship is so strong that it is near enough unbearable. Of course, the film shot at the gigs was superb, showing exactly why the lads have been so successful for so long.

The documentary was directed by Sam Dunn and Scot McFadyen, and was released on Blu-ray and DVD on 25 May. The *Toronto Star* summed it up niftily. 'The boisterous rock documentary [...] explodes from the screen with such roaring, surround-sound presence during its performance segments that one might as well be pressed up against the security fencing in the front row, throwing two-fingered metal salutes to the sky, at an actual Maiden show.'

Things were as busy as ever for Iron Maiden. Even while on tour, Bruce and the gents were looking toward a possible new album. To that end, the band decamped to Paris for three weeks during November 2009 in order to get some serious writing done, before taking some time off over Christmas. Sessions for the album were scheduled again at the band's favoured Compass Point Studios in the Bahamas, with Kevin Shirley once more at the helm.

CHAPTER 27

THE FINAL FRONTIER

The album was to be called *The Final Frontier*. Not only was it a return to their stamping ground of the fertile 1983–86 period, but the band also recorded live as a unit in the studio before adding overdubs. The pace was incredible: they were laying down a track a day. For a band as massive as Iron Maiden, with all their attendant resources, that represents exceptional work rate – particularly as the gap between *A Matter of Life and Death* and *The Final Frontier* had been the longest ever between Maiden albums. That said, the intervening projects such as *Flight 666* (which went platinum) had filled the gap quite nicely.

Blabbermouth reported Bruce's delight at returning to Nassau. 'The studio had the same vibe and it was EXACTLY as it had been in 1983, NOTHING had changed! Even down to the broken shutter in the corner... same carpet... everything... It was really quite spooky. But we felt very relaxed in such a familiar and well-trodden environment and I think this shows in the playing and the atmosphere of the album.'

It all begins in some style with the spacey, heavy-as-hell 'Satellite 15... The Final Frontier', which stretches out its classic metal riffery for nearly nine minutes. Epic is hardly the word; chugging guitars, insistent drums and lyrics looking back at a life lived to the full make it an enormous opener to an album. Instantly, the listener is plunged into a humungous universe replete with sampled, looped bass, hugely dramatic vocals and a prowling, portentous metal opera. Bruce's signature vocal is framed exceptionally by a band not just at the top of their own game, but seriously challenging themselves to push back boundaries left, right and centre. The introduction gives way after four full minutes to a more traditional Iron Maiden sound.

Second up is 'El Dorado,' which, at just under seven minutes, is practically punk-esque in its brevity, when compared to the opener. It's Bruce's first writing contribution to the LP, alongside Adrian Smith and Steve Harris this time. And what a track it is, from the huge statement of intent of the intro chords, which settle down into one of 'Arry's familiar galloping basslines and an AC/DC-esque rolling riff. Bruce's voice is dripping with gleeful evil as he tells of the titular apocryphal city of gold; it's a real attack on those seeking to sell anything to anyone, to cheat them and to manipulate people out of lust for money. There's room for some stunning, *Powerslave*-esque soloing, as Maiden stretch their wings and fly close enough to the sun to revel in its blazing heat – though not so close as to suffer the fate of Icarus. Third track, 'Mother of Mercy,' is a Smith/Harris ditty concerning death, religion, soldiers and war. Heavy stuff, but then this is a band that has rarely shied away from tackling life's big questions. It's one of Maiden's prog growers, this one, soaked in FX. An acoustic guitar underpins matters before a huge, machine-gun-like riff pulls the song into another rampant, but tuneful, pre-chorus and chorus. Again, Bruce's vocals are supreme, whether he's reaching for the high notes of his register or using his gravel-growl. He's a student of style, a singer who has the ability to tailor his delivery to the specific requirements of the material at hand.

Next up is another Smith/Harris/Dickinson co-write, 'Coming Home', the subject of which is simply summed up by the title. A descending riff opens out into a keyboard chord and chorus-soaked guitars in a very reflective moment. Four songs in and we've already been taken up, down, sideways, into space and back to earth; we've been navel-gazing and enjoyed spectacular musical moments.

Janick, Steve and Bruce team up for the excellent 'The Alchemist,' which could happily have sat on *Piece of Mind* or *Powerslave*. Arguably, it provides the most 'classic Maiden' moment and the twin-harmony guitars make a very pleasing comeback atop a track that has half an echo of a suspicion of a hint of 'Number of the Beast' about it in places! This relatively short song is followed by another mighty track, Harris and Smith's 'Isle of Avalon', which deals with subjects as diverse as environmental catastrophe, paganism, Mother Earth, mysticism and rebirth in its full nine minutes and six seconds of it.

Bruce, Adrian and Steve team up again for 'Starblind', another mystical rumination on the oneness of things – whichever god you happen to believe in. It's a passable ditty, but by the exceedingly high standards of the rest of the album so far, it's not quite up there as one of the record's best. No matter: there's another nine-minute symphony to come, the Gers/Harris-penned 'The Talisman', which takes the metaphor of an ocean voyage to illustrate the often rocky seas of a life. The start of the track is a distant cousin to 'Hallowed Be Thy Name', at least in delivery – part neo-folk, part acoustic rock and more in the vein of Wishbone Ash than Judas Priest. As a result, when the track proper kicks in, the riffs feel absolutely gigantic.

'The Man Who Would Be King,' a Murray and Harris composition, again begins with a restrained atmosphere ripe for storytelling. Destiny cannot be outrun, and the song's main character is looking for answers, trying to make peace with a deity, in the aftermath of having killed another man. The track features a splendid middle eight in which the guitarists are given loads of space to explore. The album is rounded off by one of Steve Harris's sprawling epics, 'When the Wind Blows' – all eleven minutes of it. It's remarkable to think that this is the same group – more or less – that once had punk urchin Paul Di'Anno up front. Nonetheless, it's immediately clear that this is an Iron Maiden song. Who else could really pull off a poetic end-of-days essay and still keep it firmly within the realms of the genre?

The album was released on 13 August in the UK, debuting at No.1 there and in more than twenty-five other countries. On the *Billboard 200* it came in at No.4. One unusual aspect of *The Final Frontier* was that it had not gone through the usual mastering process (which 'evens out' the volume throughout most records and brings most frequencies to an ear-friendly level), because Steve wanted to keep the power of the performances intact.

Lyrically, Bruce plays with some of his favourite themes across the set. Brigitte Schön, author of *Insights*, which discusses the singer's solo lyrics, analyses his contributions. 'Bruce contributed the lyrics to four songs and I think you can find three of his key themes in them,' she says, in an interview for this book. 'First, there is the blame of ruthless businessmen ("El Dorado"). Every now and then, Bruce pours out his disdain for those kinds of people who deceive and abuse others to make money. You can find this subject also in "Be Quick or Be Dead" (from *Fear of the Dark*) or "Shoot All the Clowns" (from *Balls to Picasso*). One of his all-time favourite subjects, apparently, is aviation. In "Coming Home", Bruce expresses his feelings of being a pilot and on tour with Maiden.

'Finally,' she continues, 'there is a subject involving two songs which seems to be quite close to Bruce's heart. It revolves around enlightenment and deeper understanding. "The Alchemist" takes up again the matter of alchemy; Bruce already made a whole album about it: *The Chemical Wedding*. The philosophical aim of the alchemists was to achieve enlightenment by purifying their souls. It's a wide and quite complicated field. Furthermore, Bruce seems to reflect on gaining insight by using the imagery of exploring the universe, as in "Starblind".'

The reviews were all pretty positive. *Rock Sound* alluded to the fact that *The Final Frontier* as a title had brought rumours that it would, indeed, be the band's final album. Not so. Indeed, the album title was more of a reference to *Star Trek* than anything else, Bruce being a major sci-fi fan and admirer of his fellow captain, Jean-Luc Picard. 'Iron Maiden have always gone large with their ideas,' the mag wrote, 'but since Bruce Dickinson and Adrian Smith returned to the fold in [1999], the band have sauced their patented gallop with a generous dollop of musical adventurism.

It's as if every track has to carry the same weight of narrative as legendary, career-high watermark 'Rime of the Ancient Mariner'. The magazine did bemoan the fact that there was no obvious 'hit' on the album as a single, such as 'Flight of Icarus', or 'The Trooper', while also noting that Bruce's vocals – particularly on 'El Dorado' – had been taken by some as evidence that his power was failing him. In fact, if any decline had been evident (and that's debatable) it had been coming gradually over the decades. And in any case, *Rock Sound* acknowledged, 'his style has always sailed close to the wind of full-capacity'.

The Guardian commented that the album's industrial metal opener was the first of many surprises on an album that featured, 'the lush prog of the sublime "Starblind" [and] the genuinely affecting "ballad" "Coming Home".' That said, the sheer length of some of the songs made it, 'less an exercise in experimentation than old-fashioned endurance, and the hushed-intro-bombastic-chorus dynamic begins to grate a little'. The reviewer, Jamie Thomson, concluded by suggested that some editing and even more experimentation would have made the album 'something special'.

The *BBC* simply called *The Final Frontier* 'A remarkable achievement from the metal titans,' commenting that there was always huge anticipation for any new Maiden album and that 'there are almost as many visions of a perfect Iron Maiden album as there are Maiden fans'. The overwhelmingly positive review concluded that the second half of the album was immense, with plenty of tempo and tonal changes, twists and turns that delivered the statement 'this is Iron Maiden truly living their purpose. No compromises, just complexities and challenges and more moments of brilliance than perhaps even they thought they still had left in them.'

Bruce hadn't had the best of starts to 2010, however, with news that his long-running *Friday Rock Show* on 6 Music was to be dropped. *Music Week* quoted a spokeswoman for the BBC station: '6 Music is currently reviewing the way it reflects the rock and heavy metal genres across the network and has decided to decommission the *Friday Night Rock Show*. The network, however, remains committed to reflecting both genres throughout the schedule as part of its core music offering. We would very much like to thank Bruce Dickinson for the hard work and commitment he has shown to 6 Music over the past eight years.' Some of Bruce's interviewees during that period included Metallica, Slash and deliciously, Blaze Bayley.

With his last show, broadcast on 28 May, Bruce got the last word by playing 'Take This Job and Shove it,' a song made famous by Johnny Paycheck and memorably covered later by Dead Kennedys. The rest of the programme was taken up by tributes to Ronnie James Dio, who had sadly passed away. Bruce's slot on 6 Music was taken by Tom Ravenscroft – son of pioneering DJ John Peel. The whole station had been threatened with closure, so cuts were inevitable. Still, losing someone of Bruce's knowledge and calibre wasn't the smartest decision the corporation had ever made.

In the immediate aftermath of the news breaking, *Planet Rock* looked toward Bruce as a potential signing. Owner Malcolm Bluemel told *The Guardian* that some discussions had taken place. 'Bruce is interested in doing a show for Planet Rock and I am interested in having him. Whether we can put a deal together remains to be seen,' he said. In the event, nothing came of it. In

2014, a deal would be reached whereby *TeamRock Radio* would rebroadcast fifty-two of Bruce's shows.

There was some good news that spring, though, with a special documentary airing on BBC Radio 4 entitled *Big in Bangalore*. The two-part series involved presenter Rajan Datar tracking Maiden to India to investigate whether the increasingly powerful BRIC countries – Brazil, Russia, India and China – offered more opportunities for Western acts. The programme featuring the band was broadcast on 8 May.

'El Dorado' was made available for download on 8 June, the day before the latest tour began. Bruce wasn't too enamoured by the quality of the MP3 audio, though, telling *Rock Radio* that, 'The problem is that when you listen to it on tiny little headphones, propelled by a battery, on a device made by Steve Jobs and Google, it sounds like shit. But the song itself doesn't sound like shit when you listen to it in the studio or when you buy the CD – it sounds fucking awesome. So we're going to play it for you and it's going to sound great.'

Bruce was never one to mince his words and such was the case at Maiden's 1 August headline slot at the Sonisphere Festival in 2010. While onstage, Bruce took the opportunity to exhort metal to take over the world, telling the huge crowd that, 'Today is like a special day, a celebration of everyone that likes heavy metal. If we left it up to the media and the BBC, no one would know about this music. If heavy metal bands ruled the world we'd be a lot better off. There would be more a lot more drinking and a lot more shagging and nursery rhymes would sound like this.'

In another interview, he talked about Eddie and possibilities of movies to come. *Noisecreep* reported him as saying that the band didn't want to exploit Eddie. 'He's enigmatic. He's the ultimate monster anti-hero who you love; he'd be the coolest guy to have on the school bus with you, but you wouldn't really go to dinner with him. He does bad things, but only to people that deserve it. But he is an enigma and you lose the enigma at your peril, really. You lose that enigmatic thing about him. You lose the mystery.' Eddie – or at least his spaceship – also appeared in a special online video game in which cargo containing the band's gear on the way to an intergalactic gig is collected, baddies are shot and lots of hours of work time is lost as a result.

The live dates were as well received as ever and Bruce was in typically strident form, particularly when talking about ticket prices. In the States and Canada, the most expensive tickets cost $90, with most well below that. This was in marked contrast to other acts, whose shows often featured tickets up to $250 or more. Talking to *Rock Radio*, the singer emphasised that 'No, we don't do $250. But that's bullshit anyway. What is it with these quote-unquote "heritage" acts. That's the name they've branded themselves with.' 'Basically,' he seethed, 'you're going and seeing a bunch of bands that have been around for a while doing the same old shit. They just come out of the woodwork after ten years and go [...] "You're going to pay through the nose for seeing the same old shit so we're gonna rape you for two hundred bucks a ticket.'

Clearly, he was riled, continuing 'What that says to me is, "We won't be doing this again any time soon" or "If you're crazy enough to pay this money and sell out, well maybe we'll come round next year and see if it works again." An Iron Maiden show should not be like going to see the Eagles, with $50 hot dogs and dickie bows. It should be dirty and smelly and sweaty. 'I'm fifty-one,' Bruce concluded, 'but if I had an audience of people my age, I think I'd kill myself. At least I wouldn't be there next time.'

It was a typically forthright statement of intent that fully summed up the ethos of the band itself, not least on their challenging new album. Speaking to the *Telegraph*, the frontman insisted that the band was not interested in being famous for the sake of it. 'We don't want to be recognised really, except for what we do. The celebrity thing, I mean, Lindsay Lohan – what's she for? I look at that and throw my hands up in despair. Maybe we're some kind of antidote to that.' He went on to talk about stagecraft rather than gimmicks being the order of the day and that each new generation who discovered Maiden did so through a new album, before working back through the mighty Irons catalogue.

The live dates weren't without problems, though. On 11 March 2011, a massive earthquake and tsunami had struck Japan. Bruce and the band were in the air at the time, coming from South Korea, and were diverted to Nagoya from their original landing at Tokyo. Two gigs were cancelled due to the devastating quake. Bruce explained to *Vorterix.com* what had happened. 'Honestly, it was really no big drama, because they shut the airport ten minutes before we were gonna land,' he revealed. 'There was a lot of quite frightened-sounding people on the radio, because they are used to earthquakes in Japan. So when they come on and they say, "There's been a massive earthquake", you think, "Wow, this is really big." So we made the decision to divert to our diversion airport, which was about a half an hour away in Nagoya. And we landed in Nagoya, where the weather was lovely and there was no earthquake. Our biggest problem was finding accommodation, because everybody else was diverting there. But we got that sorted out. And, actually, we really didn't have any idea how serious it was until we saw the news in Japan that day.'

The group decided to head straight to Mexico after the gigs were pulled. Japan is still rebuilding from that horrendous day. Another gig had to be cancelled in Brazil: during the first song at the Rio bash on 27 March, a barrier gave way under pressure from the crowd. Bruce tried to calm the situation, asking people to take a step backwards en masse before informing the crowd that the band would take a ten-minute break so the fence could be repaired. Sadly, that proved impossible, so Maiden had to restage the show the next day. The audience wasn't happy but Bruce had to tell them, 'We were told that there is no way to way to get the fence repaired tonight. I know it sucks. But please do not break anything when you leave. Those of you who cannot make tomorrow's concert, we will post on our official web site information on how you can get a refund. I'm really upset. But I can assure you that tomorrow night we will have the best fence in the world.'

Meanwhile, Bruce's son Austin was busy keeping up the family tradition as his metalcore band Rise To Remain released their debut single, 'Nothing Left', on EMI on 10 June. The band had already been praised by *Kerrang!* and *Metal Hammer* as a promising new act and signed to the major label in March that year. Austin told *RockAAA* that his old man had always been there for advice. 'He has told me not to fuck up enough times,' the younger Dickinson revealed. 'He also tells me all the usual father stuff and he is supportive, which is all I can ask. I don't think either of us could stand it if either of us stepped into each other's musical endeavours. Dad wasn't in Maiden for the majority of my childhood,' Austin continued, 'so I didn't have a concept of what he did, although I do now, of course. He was a lot more creative than active, and he wasn't touring constantly. I did tour the world when I was very young, only around one or two years old, so I can't remember that. So I didn't really grow up around music in that way, although it has always been a big part of my life.'

Meanwhile, Pops had got himself into a spot of hot water in *Metal Hammer* that month when he, tongue somewhat in cheek, said Maiden were greater than Metallica. 'You've just got to have a sense of fearlessness,' remarked Bruce. 'I got into trouble for saying that we're better than Metallica… and, it's true! They might be bigger than us and they might sell more tickets than us and they might get more gold-plated middle-class bourgeoisie turning up to their shows but they're not Maiden.

'I did say it's a bit of a wind-up,' he confessed. 'I thought, if I'm going to turn into an asshole, I might as well, you know, go for it!' Ever the role model. In fact, Lars Ulrich of Metallica took it all in good heart when later asked about it by *The Guardian*: 'I will never argue with that,' he said. 'I will always support Bruce Dickinson in whatever nonsense he says. That's part of the fun. So go Iron Maiden! It's fine.' Bruce also continued on his crusade against talent shows, turning down a chance to become one of the judges on *The Voice*. 'That show sounds so crap and demeaning to everyone involved, I took great delight in turning the BBC down. *The X Factor* is appalling enough, it's no better than *Opportunity Knocks* [a talent show that ran on UK TV in the 1970s and 1980s].'

The tour wound its way around the States and on into Europe, with the final show of the first leg taking place on 21 March 2010 at Valencia's Auditorio Marina Sur – in a rather lovely part of Spain, where the horchata is poured liberally and the paella is the best on the planet. Bruce Air — a special trip for fans, piloted by the man himself — flew specially for the gig. In the aftermath, Bruce told *The Sun* about how things were in the Maiden camp. 'At the start of every tour we think this will be the last one,' he reflected. 'By the end we're disappointed and we think, "Is this it?" So we'll carry on as long as we're having fun. We'll be back to tour this album, and after that we should be looking at [...] an unashamed tour with all the greatest hits.' The setlist for the *...Frontier* tour had been heavy on tracks from the three post-reunion albums with a smattering of classics, so this would mark a change in focus for the act.

With the band off the road, Bruce returned to his day job as a pilot, which now involved flying routes to Iceland and Orlando. In October, he got the plum job of flying none other than Liverpool Football Club to an Europa League away game against AC Napoli. Liverpool weren't doing too well at the time and Bruce, although more of a rugby fan, offered his support via the *Liverpool Echo*. 'I would like to see Liverpool winning again,' he stated. 'They have had a hard time recently but they are such an institution and mean so much to so many people. It would be nice to see them with their tails up.' He also revealed that he felt he was living the dream. 'When I was five, I had Airfix kits like everyone other boy, but I was always too busy doing music. Once I did find the time to fly I was completely hooked. I am not sure how I became a captain of an aeroplane.' The reporter asked if singing or flying was his preference and Bruce hedged his bets. 'I don't know — that is one of those questions, like which one of your kids would you throw out of a hot-air balloon,' he replied, somewhat gnomically. 'Iron Maiden fans would lynch me if I stopped singing,' he added.

He also revealed that he had piloted the actual FA Cup on one journey, although an unfortunate incident had befallen it. 'I will not say which team it was but they snapped the base off by accident,' he teased.

The tour resumed in Moscow on 11 February 2011, would continue to span the world under the title *Around The World in 66 Days*. Ed Force One would be in action again, with the dates heading to new climes including Singapore, Indonesia and South Korea, which very much pleased all concerned. Bruce told *Blabbermouth* that the set list would include more classics for those new places. 'Of course we will play more songs from the new album and some other recent material, but we will include a healthy dose of older fan favourites as we will be playing to so many new faces who we know will want to hear those songs live for the first time. We will cram into the plane as much of the production we used this year as is physically possible, including of course Eddie, and intend to replicate the spectacular light show in as many places as we are able. All in all it promises to be a fantastic trip for everyone.'

Maiden received a further boost on 13 February, when they finally got their just deserts, winning a Grammy Award for Best Metal Performance with 'El Dorado'. The singer, though, wasn't having any of it, as he told *Vorterix.com*. 'I think it's 'cos we're still alive,' he sneered. 'If they were going to give us a Grammy they should have given us one about 1986, but they gave it to Jethro Tull, and it took another twenty years... The mainstream media don't understand metal. Unless you are a fan, unless you really understand the music, it's difficult to give it the coverage it deserves.' Maiden had previously been nominated in the same category for 1994's 'Fear of the Dark,' and 'The Wicker Man' in 2001.

It seemed everyone wanted a piece of the band – even Lady Gaga hung out with the lads at a gig in Tampa. The pop provocateur told *Rolling Stone* that she and her long-time friend Lady Starlight originally had a private box but during 'Number of the Beast' they went to rock out with the rest of the fans. Of course, she was recognised, but the response was a welcoming one. 'I mean, Iron Maiden is all about, "We don't care who our fans are. We love everybody."... I guess what I'm trying to say is the devotion of the fans moving in unison, pumping their fists, watching the show, when I see that, I see the paradigm for my future and the relationship I want to have with my fans [...] when we got into the crowd, there was no pretension. I'm a pop singer I didn't know what it would be like in a crowd of a Maiden [fans],' she admitted. 'Everybody was hugging me, high-fiving, fistpumps in the air "Oh, it's so cool you're at Maiden." Jumping and dancing... I mean, it was like absolute [sic] no judgment, no prejudice, freedom and love for music. It doesn't matter who you are; you don't need to know anything about music to love it. And it was just so it was just awesome... Maiden changed my life.'

Bruce began flying planes for Iceland Express that summer and managed to appear in a video too. Nothing to do with the band, Crowley or anything like that: it was a safety video for the Civil Aviation Authority with the catchy title 'Safety in the Balance'. The twenty-minute film introduces him as Captain Bruce Dickinson, and – bedecked in a yellow hi-vis overjacket – he enlightens the audience about weight, balance, load factors and all manner of fascinating things for the aviation–obsessed.

As 2011 continued, there was news that Maiden would release another compilation, this time concentrating on the years 1990–2010, to be entitled *From Fear to Eternity*. It came out on 6 June 2011 but did not feature Blaze; the only signs of his involvement were a couple of tracks from his era re-imagined as live performances: 'Man on the Edge' and 'The Clansman' were both included, with Bruce singing. Technically, perhaps, that ought to be Doctor Paul Bruce Dickinson, as the singer received an honorary doctorate of music from his history alma mater, Queen Mary University, on 19 July. Boffins from the institute were proud to bestow the honour. 'I know that Iron Maiden appreciate honours from their fans and as a fan it is my privilege to present the award,' said Professor David Baker. 'Bruce excels in so many ways and if we can aspire to a fraction of the achievements that have been made by him, then the world will be a better place.' His colleague, Professor Peter McOwan, was also delighted. 'Scientists and engineers the world over owe Bruce a debt of gratitude,' declared the clever chap. 'Heavy Metal music seems to have played a big part in making many of us who we are today. Bruce's time with Iron Maiden, his intelligent lyrics and brilliant theatricals were a positive part of our youth, and his amazing accomplishments in entrepreneurship, aviation and entertainment make him a genuine British polymath to be proud of.'

Bruce's charity work was also part of the rationale behind the award. Over the years, he has happily offered his time to many charities, including Rock Aid Armenia, Red Nose Day, War Child, Sunflower Jam, Sport Relief, Nordoff Robbins, Flying Scholarships for Disabled People (he is vice patron), Team Rossi, the Vulcan Restoration Trust, Scope, Survival International and oodles more.

Indeed, on 22 October 2011, he opened the mini-music festival Oxjam Chiswick, cutting the red tape at midday as more than sixty bands took to the stages for Oxfam.

There was also time for Bruce's foreword to the photo-documentary book *On Board Flight 666* to land in bookshops as an excellent 2011 began to wind up. There was one special gig left to do, however, with a performance alongside Ian Anderson of Jethro Tull and The Moody Blues' Justin Hayward in the stunning surroundings of Canterbury Cathedral, on 10 December. Bruce joined in for his own 'Jerusalem', Maiden's 'Revelations,' and the Tull's 'Locomotive Breath at the 10 December *Canterbury Rocks at Christmas* shindig. The gig raised money for upkeep of that magnificent edifice (that's the cathedral, not Anderson).

'If our generation and the future generations don't [take care of] it, then it will be lost,' Anderson was reported as saying by *Blabbermouth*. 'There is a real parallel regarding the preservation of our great buildings, and the greater sense of conserving our world. We need a huge change of thinking about the stewardship of our planet and all it contains, both natural and man-made. Canterbury Cathedral is a place for life today. But it is also a place for the future and, whether you are a Christian or not, it is a place which should remain forever close to our hearts.'

CHAPTER 28

SKY-HIGH AMBITION

With Maiden taking a little time off to pursue personal projects, 2012 brought the opportunity for Bruce to develop his offstage endeavours. Chief among those was the aviation string to his bulging bow; he'd been made marketing director and senior pilot for Astraeus in 2011, but the company ran into financial difficulties when business proved less than brisk. Bruce heard that the company was being put into administration when he was flying back from Jeddah International in Saudi Arabia with 250 people returning from holiday to Manchester.

In November 2011, Hugh Parry, chief executive of the company, told the *Daily Mail* what had happened. 'We battled hard to save Astraeus, but lower-than-expected levels of business during the summer of 2011, a lack of contracts for winter 2011–2012, and some extremely bad luck with a number of technical issues mean that we have no option but to cease all operations and put Astraeus

Airlines in the hands of the administrators,' he admitted. 'Every effort has been made to ensure that any passengers affected already have or will be able to complete their journey. It is small comfort to those affected and impacted, I realise, but Astraeus comprised a fantastic team who did a fantastic job – quite possibly the best team in their aviation business sector.'

Bruce's love for aviation had been noted by many media outlets outside the metal and rock press. In August 2011, he told *Lonely Planet* why he took to the air. 'I wanted to try to get my hands on something a little bigger than my little twin-engine, piston-engine airplane, and sadly, I can't afford to get my own airport and jumbo like John Travolta, so I thought I'm going to have to get a job,' he stated. 'I thought I'd get some sort of job flying cargo, I never expected flying on an airline. But ten years ago, I did. And been flying long enough, they gave me my fourth stripe, and I'm sitting here as a captain.' He went on to remark that there was so much to do on the plane that there was no place for daydreaming, but that he often felt that being in charge of a hundred-ton aeroplane was a real privilege. 'I never get tired of pinching myself and going, "That's pretty cool."' He also noted that one of the awesome things about his job was flying over the world as day and night broke below the plane. 'You're actually flying along the line where the sun's rising and setting. And you can go, "Down there they're still in night, down there it's daylight." Day/night: it's such a primordial thing. To be above it all is quite mind-boggling.' He explained also that his favourite ways to travel were the slower ones, because it gave the luxury of time to find things to do. Of course, one thing he had done on previous train journeys was write books, so the evidence is there in black and white – with garish cartoon covers and lots of shagging.

Trying to keep Astraeus in the air was the order of the day and to that end Bruce and business partners were doing their best either to save the stricken company or to start a new one that would provide jobs for his former colleagues. *Blabbermouth* reported Bruce's plans and quoted him as saying, 'Frankly, now Astraeus has been relieved of the business model imposed upon it by Icelandic owners, who, to be honest, perhaps did not fully appreciate the way the key commercial aviation markets operated, I see the potential for a viable operation should acquisition of the company prove achievable. There is no reason why the original business model, which established Astraeus as possibly the best and most successful organisation in its sector, cannot be resurrected to the benefit of former employees and airline partners and clients alike.' He added that a number of potential investors had contacted him already and that he had received many messages that had encouraged him. He promised he would be back behind the controls of a plane in the near future, this time possibly also being in control of the company that operated it.

Bruce also revealed he was involved in a project in South Wales that could provide up to 1,500 jobs and that he was also quite far down the line in creating a flight training company, Real World Aviation, which would produce the next breed of qualified commercial pilots. Fans now also had the opportunity to experience a simulation of Flight 666 in a special flight simulator at Heathrow Airport. Members of the fan club got the chance to sit with Bruce in the high-tech machine.

The singer now began to conquer the seas, having temporarily been forced out of the sky. He had been invited onto HMS *Victorious*, a nuclear submarine, by the captain at Faslane naval base and reportedly spent three nights on board, finding out exactly what the workers had to go through to keep the sub going. One of the crew was commented that 'He was extremely down to earth and hung around with everybody asking questions and chatting about his life... Everyone was happy to have him on board with us. Lots of people were stunned by it but some didn't know who he was.'

Maiden revealed that there would be a series of gigs in the summer, to be called *The Maiden England World Tour*. This would revisit the *Seventh Son of a Seventh Son* days, with particular emphasis on the 1988 video of the same name. 'We have great fun playing the history of Maiden tours because it gives us an opportunity between new albums to go out and play songs from our earlier catalogue,' Bruce said in a press release. 'It's always fantastic seeing the crowd reaction from a new generation of fans who have never experienced some of these tracks performed live before, and of course we know our longstanding fans will enjoy seeing the original *Seventh Son Tour* revisited — with many other surprises! Our intention is to play about two thirds of the original track list of *Maiden England*, including some songs we have not played live in a very, very long time, plus other favourites we just know the fans are going to want to hear!' Alice Cooper would support up to 21 July, after which upcoming New Yorkers Coheed and Cambria would back Maiden. The band released *En Vivo!* on 23 March 2012 as a double DVD, Blu-ray or double CD. It was recorded to a hugely high specification during the *Final Frontier* tour and also included *Behind the Beast*, which gave fans an insight into the logistics of delivering one of Maiden's shows. The Santiago concert that was featured showed modern Maiden at their brilliant best and was another treat for fans awaiting new product from their heroes.

Rumour had it that the group was also wanting to concentrate on snappier singles: Adrian Smith told *VH1's That Metal Show* that he admired Jimi Hendrix, Free and Thin Lizzy's penchant for the shorter form and noted that perhaps it was time for Maiden to do the same. He also made reference to Bruce's flying chops: 'Anything he does, he gets right into it and he does it really well. And he does it for a living, it's not like he does it as a hobby,' he said. 'I've seen him check out flight plans, literally just before a gig. It's like, 'We've got to go on stage in a minute!' But he can switch on and off. He's very professional. It's amazing.' Bruce showed that professionalism onstage with a guest appearance singing with the Buddy Rich Orchestra on 2 April. The event was the 25th Anniversary Memorial Concert and Bruce would have been over the moon to do so, particularly as the drummer was none other than Deep Purple's Ian Paice, who provided the backbeat for many of his most treasured albums including the wonderful *In Rock*. Paice and Dickinson would again team up later that year for a special gig at the Royal Albert Hall in London. *Sunflower Jam* had been set up in 2006 by Ian's wife Jacky, to support cancer victims. Performers at the 2012 gig also included Brian May of Queen, Mark King, bassist of Level 42, the amazing John Paul Jones of Led Zep plus contemporary acts Alfie Boe and Kerry Elllis. Bruce said it was a great meeting of different musicians for a great cause.

Bruce's airline maintenance business came online in May. Cardiff Aviation Ltd was the company to which he'd previously referred, and the business leased the portentously named Twin Peaks Hangar at St Athan in the Vale of Glamorgan. The business was set up to maintain airliners, large aircraft, provide training and approve certifications in several different countries. Bruce told reporters that he was looking forward to the project. 'We're coming into this enterprise with the knowledge that we'll also be bringing business to South Wales,' he said. 'South Wales has long had an association with the aircraft industry and I am delighted that I am able to have a small part in the continuation of that tradition.' He also told *Travel Trade Gazette* that he was frustrated at the United Kingdom's failure to sort out its airport capacity problem. 'Aviation is a massive driver of so much in the UK, especially in terms of employment. We need to develop our regional capacity – it's crazy that people have to drive from Cardiff to Heathrow to get a flight to the US. They should be able to fly direct,' he commented.

Bruce also commented that plans to build a new airport in the Thames could be boosted by generating its own energy by tidal flow. It would cost the same, he reckoned, as the government's plans to build the new HS2 rail link, which would merely save minutes on journeys. Bruce also reckoned that travel agents needed to update themselves, particularly the high street outlets that looked 'like DHSS offices'. He felt that they had to be on call twenty-four hours a day, because talking to a human being was such an important part of the process.

More aviation-related adventures took place when Bruce collaborated with Buffalo Airways and Joe McBryan, who starred in History Television's *Ice Pilots NWT*. Bruce flew a DC-3 from World War II in the episode, and a local journalist from the *Edmonton Journal* was there to cover it on Twitter. 'Spectacular forests and lakes up here! About to land with my Spro–pilot,' the awesomely named Fish Griwkowsky tweeted. 'I don't believe I ever sat in the pilot's seat of a DC3 over Yellowknife beside the lead singer of Iron Maiden before. […] Bruce gave me two barf bags for our next leg from Hay River to Yellowknife. My record was 7 bags.'

Things were a lot more civilised when Bruce donned a suit to speak, first at the Forum IAB conference in Warsaw on 23 May – the topic being the lengthy *Customer Value Management: Do You Really Respect Your Customer? The Importance of Creativity in Planning Marketing Budget* and then at the PLASA technology association's European AGM on 29 May. The day before, an interview with the singer aired on the BBC's *Hard Talk* business and news show. Presenter Sarah Montague asked him about business regulations in the UK and whether restrictions being lifted would help matters. 'Of course it would,' Bruce replied. 'I think this is a time when people really need to think outside the box and for governments to take really courageous actions.' He continued, 'My tax bill makes my eyes water [but] if I knew where that money was going I wouldn't be whinging about it. But actually rather than giving that money to the government, I'd [say] "OK, you want to tax me and give me a huge bill, fantastic. I'll spend that money, not on me, but on doing stuff that will create jobs."

'Why can't I do that?' he mused. 'If you could do that for people a lot more people would start businesses […] If you're going to lose money anyway and you've always wanted to start a corner shop or something, let the government give you money to do that rather than putting it into the black hole that is the government coffers. There is still so much waste.' Bruce also revealed that he had a penchant for Radio 4 documentaries and tried to avoid listening to music unless he really wanted to. He admitted that sometimes he'd ask his kids what they were listening to, too.

Montague also observed that Maiden's approach had more or less stayed the same for three decades and wondered whether they felt the urge to update or change their image to 'a mature' one. An incredulous Bruce replied, 'A mature image? Why? Inside this fifty-three-year old exterior is a seventeen-year old. Probably a mental age younger, I don't know. But that's the core of why you do this thing. When you're a kid, and you experience something, whatever it is that makes you feel, "Wow, walking on air" […] you have to ring-fence those and guard them against what I would describe as the cynicism of the world. Because the world eats into people and destroys those hopes and those dreams.' Clearly, Montague had touched a nerve with her question. Bruce continued: 'The things that people call childish, those are the things that motivate us and keeps our creativity precious. That is what is inside people and they lose it at their peril. I have seen people that have lost it, and it's really sad.'

In July that year, Bruce unleashed his wrath a punter in the crowd at Maiden's concert in Indianapolis's Klipsch Music Center. The band was about to launch into 'Wasted Years' when the singer spotted a dude fiddling with his mobile phone. Bruce addressed him personally: 'Oh, for fuck's sake, the guy with the bald head in the white shirt, you've been texting for the last three fucking songs! You're a wanker!' Wasted years indeed, and someone wasting the opportunity to experience the moment.

His son Austin's band Rise To Remain had gone through a couple of line-up changes by this point, but were together enough to pay tribute to Metallica on a special twenty-first-anniversary tribute CD, issued on the front of *Kerrang!* to celebrate the *Black Album*. Their contribution was a cover of the all-time classic beloved of guitar-shop noodlers – 'Enter Sandman'. The younger Dickinson's pipes are one hell of a lot gruffer than his dad's; he is part Hetfield, part Matt Heafy of Trivium. The song is well-served by the young band, who imbue it with power and an up-to-date sound. It's an intriguing insight into how metal traverses generations and shows why Metallica have lasted so long and continue to pick up fans.

The same can, of course, be said for Iron Maiden, and they had heroes of their own to credit. A tribute to the fortieth anniversary of Deep Purple's *Machine Head* album came out on 25 September, entitled *Re-Machined* and featured such diverse acts as Carlos Santana, Flaming Lips and Maiden. The band contributed a version of 'Space Truckin''. Bruce explained that it was fortunate that the group had some unreleased material to draw on. 'Initially we didn't think we'd be able to contribute anything due to our touring commitments,' he admitted in a press release. 'Then we remembered "Space Truckin'"', which we'd recorded as a single B-side during our *A Matter of Life and Death* album session, but never used. However now, thanks to Kevin Shirley's remixing skills, we're able to include it on *Re-Machined*.'

The touring continued, but Bruce was always on the lookout for opportunities to feed his addiction to the other kind of heavy metal. While in Seattle, he managed to zip into the Boeing training facility to get into a 747-8 simulator. He admitted he was a lucky chap to have two awesome careers and said that it was as essential as breathing. At root though he was also drawn to the industry by the individuals involved. 'It's all about people, actually,' he said in a video for Boeing. "'Cause the airplanes are wonderful, but they're built by people, designed by people, flown by people, operated by people, so actually, it's the people, I think, that really get me very excited.'

As part of his efforts to maintain his fitness for stage work after the tour, Bruce competed in a fell race in Grasmere that August, coming 161st out of 181 participants. He ran the race alongside Tasha Murray – daughter of Dave – as they were in the area for the wedding of manager Andy Taylor's daughter, Louise. Tim Farron, the MP for the area, told *The Westmorland Gazette*, 'There were no airs and graces about him and he said that Grasmere was one of his favourite places. He was shaking people's hands.'

In October, Bruce opened Oxjam once more and gave an interview on *Your Business Channel* about Cardiff Aviation. 'In order to trigger the amount of funding that we will be getting from Finance Wales, we have to commit to, I think, it's half a million that we have to demonstrate. We don't have to spend half a million straight away. But I think we're going to end up probably spending around four hundred thousand pounds before Christmas, because we're now in the expensive start-up phase where we're really hiring people. We're buying tools,' he explained, in reference to the mind-boggling sums on the table.

He added that although the money was going to be spent, there was also a joint venture with a Birmingham engineering firm that would help the bottom line as well as discussions going on for a paint hangar that would also enable them to respray planes as large as an Airbus 330. Business, he pointed out, was just about enabling people to do things. 'Businesses need to recognise this fundamental fact. Too often businesses are blinkered into getting the job done. If the job is no longer enabling any one to do anything, then what is the point? When you cut human beings down to size, we're really quite simple creatures: food, shelter, warmth, light, heat and you build it up from there really until you finally [get to] Gucci shoes or whatever it is, or whatever your consumer desires are. But all those desire are ultimately, they're about gratification.' He proclaimed that people would always want to travel, and furthermore to get from A to B as quickly as possible rather than wasting time on the process. Humans were always central to the process, he emphasised.

Bruce was becoming more and more popular for his conference talks. In November, at the Entrepreneurs Wales 2012 conference in Cardiff City Hall, he spoke about start-ups. 'The key thing is to figure out how to make yourself invaluable – to be the ultimate virus – to get into the system, a corporate, or somebody's head and become indispensable,' he insisted. 'They can't do it without you because you have invented some widget or some software or because you are who you are.' By now, his philosophy of business was clearly well-honed. 'Everything about being an entrepreneur is about the customer,' he continued. 'If I turn the word "fan" into "customer" that's not a bad customer satisfaction rating, is it?

'Are all your customers fans of what you do?' he asked his audience, provocatively. 'Apple have got fans – people who believe their little devices are a pathway to a better tomorrow. To turn your customers into fans you really have to target them and know exactly who they are and what you are going to deliver for them that is different to everybody else.'

Bruce also spoke at the 2012 Móvil Forum Conference in Barcelona on 22 November, covering everything from business start-ups, creativity and entrepreneurship to the similarities between music and business. In an interview with *Con Tu Negocio* he summed it up: 'The only thing you have in the music world that you can sell is your integrity. And in the business world that would be called your brand.' Warming to his theme, he explained, 'You get different levels of integrity in the music industry. On one hand there's *The X Factor*, which has no integrity at all and is the medieval equivalent of the stocks, where people turn up and they throw rotten fruit at them, and the guys that get the least amount of rotten fruit thrown at them get to advance to the next stage – and then there's a prize at the end.' Needless to say, Bruce's priorities lay elsewhere. 'Whereas at the other end of things,' he continued, 'you get the Iron Maiden situation, where we have created our own niche, our own identity, and we resist the rest of the world trying to change it. Because we exist and we do not adapt artistically to any other regime except our own.'

For that to happen, of course, the band needed strong management, a good lawyer and other buffers between them and any interested parties looking to spin money from the band by making – for example – an Iron Maiden perfume. The band would never do things that were not appropriate to the project, Bruce insisted, and didn't want to be famous for the sake of being famous. For some people, their image is their life, he emphasised, and for such people it was artistry that was important. 'That's how I'm able to talk about business, be an airline pilot and things like that,' he explained, 'because actually it doesn't conflict with what happens in Iron Maiden. Because it's not related. It's actually entirely separate.'

Bruce said that he applied that concept to where he wanted to be in business and life, too. 'I feel more comfortable turning things down, because they are not right, than just than going, "Oh yeah, yeah, yeah. Any publicity is good publicity." Nonsense. It's not true.'

CHAPTER 29

BUSINESS
AND BOOZE

One reference point for a band's popularity is when they cross over into the educational sphere. That happened to Maiden in early 2013, when one Martin Jacobsen of West Texas A&M University ran a course called 'Introduction to Literature: Heavy Metal as a Literary Genre'. The linguistics educator had identified the genre as having some very well-read lyricists and of course Maiden have written countless songs based on poems, epics and tales over the years. Moreover, the professor said, the literary references meant that the writers were themselves to be considered as exploring the literary realm. 'You constantly see these nods to the intellectual tradition that these writers, these lyricists come from,' he told *Amarillo.com*. 'It's connected itself and grounded itself in literary tradition,' he noted. 'Therefore it's reasonable to conclude that it is a form of literature as well as a form of music. In much the same way, you might say country music is a species of folklore.'

An example for the students to discuss was none other than 'Out of the Silent Planet,' which was one of Bruce's co-writes – alongside Janick and Steve – on *Brave New World*. The song's influences are from the movie *Forbidden Planet* and a 1938 sci-fi novel by C S Lewis. 'The students were mad for it,' revealed the lecturer. 'They just thought it was crazy and they loved it.' He admitted that it had been something of a spontaneous idea on his part: 'I threw it out there just as an offhand comment one day – "What we ought to do is have a class in heavy metal" – and there was universal agreement from the students in the class, like, "Yes, we should actually do that."' Seems Bruce was right when he called for heavy metal to take over the world, after all.

Bruce gave a lengthy interview to the *Wall Street Journal* which was published on 3 January 2013. Therein, he revealed that he wasn't interested in being a tax exile because he enjoyed living in the UK. This was despite the fact he was eligible for the top tax rate, which at that time was a hefty fifty per cent of all earnings. He felt that there was a simple answer to the question of revenues: 'You simply say everybody has to pay it – if you're born in this country, you pay twenty per cent. End of story, no tax exiles, you want to live in Monaco, fine – twenty per cent.' He said that would take all the costs and waste from the system that were built up by chasing tax avoiders and the like.

It was a far cry from one of his first ventures in business, he revealed: realising there was a pencil shortage at school, he started renting them out. Obviously, once in possession of a pencil, though, his classmates simply pocketed them, pulling the rug truly out from under his feet. He was to share that story many times in his increasing number of bookings as a speaker, in such far-flung places as Harstad, in Norway, and Hull. He was also planning a one-man spoken-word show, which would take place in Oslo on 2 November that year. It would tell the stories behind *Flight 666*, particularly from his experiences piloting the plane on tour.

Flying, of course requires the utmost sobriety, but while off duty Bruce had always been a fan of the odd tipple – and specifically, real ale. It was therefore no surprise when Bruce and Maiden hooked up with Robinsons Brewery to announce the imminent arrival of a premium British beer: Trooper Ale. Bruce visited the brewery in Stockport to help develop the flavour of what was to be a golden ale with a hint, perhaps, of lemon. Bruce told *Classic Rock* that he was 'a lifelong fan of traditional English ale; I thought I'd died and gone to heaven when we were asked to create our own beer. I have to say that I was very nervous,' he admitted. 'Robinsons are the only people I have had to audition for in thirty years. Their magic has been to create the alchemical wedding of flavour and texture that is Trooper. I love it.' The brewery said it was a great partnership, as Maiden genuinely did love a pint of proper beer, as did their fans.

The first bottles were available in May 2013. Bruce later spoke with *CNN* about the process. 'The original idea was that they'd just slap a label on it,' he revealed. 'We can't do that, we've got a reputation to keep up. Anyway, I like beer – why don't we really, properly create our own brew?' It was a fine balancing act, he felt: 'I wanted a beer that post above its weight in terms of flavour, but which didn't knock you on your ass in terms of alcohol content. Real beer is not an industrial process, it's more than that because it is genuinely an art. The bitterness content of the hop changes every season, so how do you make a beer that tastes the same when the ingredients change every year?' He added that it was vital that the beer was a truly great one because – being so brand aware – he knew that if it was horrible it would reflect badly on Iron Maiden.

Luckily for all concerned, it is a very fine ale. By May 2013 had sold over a million pints – the equivalent of around 20,000 being quaffed daily. That figure reached 3.5 million by November, and it was even featured in the House of Commons' Strangers Bar as a guest ale! The beer ran into a spot of bother in Sweden – rules and regulations banned the skull and crossbones logo on the label, so a different label was used. Bruce told *Off Licence News* that the band's tastes were hardly the rock 'n' roll cliché that many people assumed. 'Fuck off! I am fifty-five. There's no way I could go out and jump around if I was whacked out on hallucinogenics, and I wouldn't enjoy that. The nice thing about doing it straight is you can enjoy it.' He added that if the band ever found cheap generic lager in their dressing room. they'd not stand for it and blasted chancellor George Osborne for shaving off a penny from the price of beer as a publicity stunt. Bruce also confessed that he hated music in pubs. 'There's nothing worse. Having people's music inflicted upon you – it's like someone shouting in your ear,' he fumed.

Bruce also dipped his toes back into the fencing arena during April, with a challenge bout against Norwegian Olympic silver-medal winner Bartosz Piasecki in Oslo. The challenge took place just before the Norwegian fencing championship and Bruce did pretty well against a master swordsman, although Piasecki eventually brushed him aside. Talking to *Aftenposten*, Piasecki praised the Maiden man's performance, though. 'He's kick-ass,' declared the Olympian. 'He is short but incredibly fast, that's his weapon. He looked like Rocky when he arrived in a brown robe with his fencing kit in a shoulder bag.' Bruce, meanwhile, said that he'd given up competing officially at the age of twenty-three but continued to practise the art because he enjoyed it and it kept him in good shape. He noted similarities between the sport and his own onstage charging about, and mused whether his stage style was influenced by fencing.

There had been some tragic news in March, with the passing of former drummer Clive Burr, whom Bruce had worked with both in Samson and Maiden. The sticksman passed away in his sleep. Bruce offered his condolences in a statement from the band: 'I first met Clive when he was leaving Samson and joining Iron Maiden. He was a great guy and a man who really lived his life to the full. Even during the darkest days of his MS, Clive never lost his sense of humour or irreverence. This is a terribly sad day and all our thoughts are with Mimi and the family.' Tributes poured in from many huge names in the business including Slayer, Saxon, Anthrax, Megadeth, Judas Priest, Paul Di'Anno and more. Burr was just fifty-six. The funeral was held at the City of London Crematorium on 25 March.

In an interview with *Talaforum* in April, Bruce seemed to indicate that a new album was in the planning, hinting that it might hit the streets in 2014. In the same interview, he said that he had once been down to his final ten quid and was technically homeless. It was summer, he recalled, and he was wandering around with a suitcase looking for somewhere to lay his head. After assessing his options he went to a rock show, intending to spend his last cash on some beers at the venue: Dingwalls. As luck had it, he knew the sound engineer and ended up staying on his couch before meeting more friends as time rolled on. He said that his decision had had huge repercussions – because it had led indirectly to him singing in Maiden – and used it as an example of how taking risks and responsibilities for decisions could pay off.

Ever the socially responsible chap, Bruce his down time from the ongoing *Maiden England* tour on more charity work. The *Leicester Mercury* noted that the vocalist had met three graduates from the Flying Scholarships for Disabled People scheme at Castle Donington's Priest House Hotel – rather an apt location. 'It's not just about teaching people with disabilities to fly, it's much more than that,' he insisted. 'It's about creating friendships, and there's a whole community around it and support system that comes with people encouraging each other. It's something I'm very proud to be involved in.'

Rumours abounded in September that Iron Maiden would host their own festival. These were largely down to a massively successful performance at the San Bernardino gig on 13 September. It was Nicko who told reporters that anything was fair game, and certainly the San Bernardino line-up had been an amazing one, also featuring Megadeth, Anthrax, Testament, Overkill and Warbringer. Dave Murray also nodded toward there being a new album in a Chilean radio interview that October, but explained that – with the group having been on the road a lot in 2013 – there was time off to recuperate built into the schedule. Something was bound to happen in due course, he added.

Rumours being what they are, at one point Bruce had to release a statement to confirm that his company was definitely not manufacturing drones for the United States military. The non-existent contract was supposedly worth $500 million, but the story was based on an online blog, the writer of which had referred to an announcement on a South African conference speaker's website (since taken down.) Bruce's people immediately sent a response to *NME* with a firm denial of any such involvement. 'This is a totally inaccurate and malicious piece of writing that seems to have stemmed from an unfortunate mistake in terminology on a South African website that the writer of said blog has since used as a starting point and catalyst to go off on a flight of sheer fantasy,' it stated. 'Both Bruce Dickinson and Iron Maiden's manager Rod Smallwood were early investors in, and remain great supporters of, Hybrid Air Vehicles (HAV), a company that has nothing whatsoever to do with drones, "lighter than air" or otherwise!'

The statement went on: 'The future implementation of HAVs is a likely global trend which has massive positive implications in many areas of life and both Bruce and Rod are proud to be involved with a British company at the cutting edge of this technology. As with many far-sighted technological advances, early adopters and financial supporters tend to be military-based as they have the resources to invest and develop, be that everything from space-travel to medicine. Possible military use of HAVs in future could be for heavy-lifting, transportation or high altitude detection of IEDs (Improvised Explosive Devices), or similar, thus saving lives, both military and civilian.'

'Rather than being involved in attacks in the Third World, as this writer had claimed in such an erroneously dramatic and defamatory manner,' the statement concluded, 'HAVs are designed to offer much needed assistance to civilians, businesses and governments that would be unavailable otherwise, due to the unique nature of these incredible vehicles.'

One thing that Cardiff Aviation had genuinely invested in was European Skybus flight training, based in Bournemouth. Bruce's business partner, Mario Fulgoni, insisted in a press release that it was 'an exciting addition' to the portfolio. 'For the time being, the flight training centre will remain located at Bournemouth International Airport on the south coast of the United Kingdom, but we are likely to incorporate it into our base at St Athan, South Wales in due course.' That November, Bruce joined Aeris Aviation, who were the European distributor for Eclipse aircraft, as non-executive chairman. It was dubbed as the most economical and eco-sensitive business jet. He said in a press release that 'Now that the jet is back in production, the market for it to reach its full potential is enormous. There are no other twin engine jets that can come close to the Eclipse in terms of cost and economy and, with a range in excess of 1000nm, it is ideal for Europe. It is great to fly and I am excited by the future for this remarkable aircraft.'

Bruce spoke to the *Campus Forum* in Colombia on 11 October. Linguist, researcher, educator and major Maiden fan Michelle Ferreira Sanches was there. 'His lecture in Colombia really seemed much more like an informal conversation,' she said in an interview for this book. 'No visual displays, no data show, just Bruce speaking about some of his first attempts to establish a successful business. There were great lessons there […] but there were jokes too. One of them happened when a guy from the staff offered him a bottle of water, and he refused, saying, "Water? Oh no! you know what they say about water? Fish fuck in it!". There was also a bodyguard on stage with him in Colombia, following him during his lecture, which I found a bit odd.' During the lecture, Bruce revealed that his first business idea came to him as a five-year old. 'I had a little fireman's hat and I had a little cape like Superman, and I had a ladder from my bunk bed,' he said. 'And I would walk around my neighbourhood, waiting for houses to catch fire. And the idea was that I would run up, go rescue somebody and then I would charge them some money. Well, it didn't work. What a disappointment. First of all, I failed to do my market research. How many houses just catch fire spontaneously in the neighbourhood? Not too many.'

He also told the story of how he'd met someone who could potentially change the world of aviation. That man's name was Roger Munk and he had built giant airships. Bruce had seen Munk's work with lighter-than-air technology on television previously and remarked that the old technology – which once saw giant zeppelins floating in the skies worldwide – had failed because there were some problems technologically. Munk, however, had worked on some new ways to make it work and invited Bruce to go and visit him.

'[As] a little school boy, I built a big model of a zeppelin when I was a kid and it fired my imagination because I always wanted to be an astronaut, and I read Jules Verne's *Twenty Thousand Leagues Under the Sea* and it really inspired me,' Bruce recalled. Later, as a successful rock star, 'I went up to see [Munk's] facility. It was a shed in the field and in it there were lots of English guys with beards, smoking pipes [...] and I said, "Well, what do you need?". "Well, we're a bit short of money and we keep going almost bankrupt." I said, "How often does that happen?" He said, "About every week." I went, "Oh, okay: explain it." So he explained his concept and, like a great genius usually is, it was very simple and very clear. Because people who know what they're talking about can make very complex things very understandable [...] I invested some money.'

Well, Bruce does love his aircraft. But then, 'My manager at Iron Maiden, to my great surprise, also invested some money, and the next thing that happened […] is that we've got a five-hundred-million-dollar contract to build one […] So we built a hybrid airship, which cost a hundred and six million dollars; it flew for the first time last August and then the US government ran out of money.

'So now,' he continued, 'we've got a vehicle which is one hundred and ten metres long, four engines […] twenty-one days' flying endurance time, [that] can potentially lift vertical take-off and landing, a payload of fifty thousand kilos, that is the payload of a jumbo jet, but it burns less than twenty per cent of the fuel. So not only is it eighty per cent more efficient than the most efficient airplane even dreamt of in the future, but it takes off and lands and leaves no traces. It doesn't use an runway, anything flat will do: a field, a desert, an ocean… for humanitarian relief, for a remote area's supply […] This thing is a game changer.'

Because the United States government had run out of money, the ownership reverted to the British investors and the vehicle was to be transported back to the UK, where further technological tweaks were made to it. From heavy metal to lighter-than-air, potentially world-changing stuff in one conversation. That's pretty awesome, whichever way you'd care to look at it.

For Bruce, 2013 had been a great year, both on- and offstage. But the following year was to prove not just challenging but harrowing for the singer, those close to him and millions of fans across the earth.

CHAPTER 30

CAN HEAVEN WAIT?

While on the road, Bruce had been rather unguarded in a few press interviews. Once again, Metallica were somewhat in the firing line, as the singer commented that the Glastonbury festival – at which the American metallers would be playing – was 'middle class' and 'bourgeois'. According to the *Daily Star*, he'd said that 'Personally I have no interest in going to Glastonbury. In the days when Glasto was an alternative festival it was quite interesting. Now it's the most bourgeois thing on the planet. Anywhere Gwyneth Paltrow goes and you can live in an air-conditioned yurt is not for me.' He had another dig at BBC for covering Glastonbury with 'thousands' of reporters, but added, 'They can't be arsed to turn up to Sonisphere or Download with a camper van and a hand-held [camera]. […]We'll leave the middle classes to do Glastonbury – and the great unwashed will decamp to Knebworth, drink a lot of beer and have fun.'

CAN HEAVEN WAIT!

Later in June, he was interviewed by fellow musician Frank Turner for an article that appeared in *The Guardian*. Therein, he mused on the often culturally dismissed genre of metal. 'The closest the "art establishment" ever came to embracing metal was punk,' Bruce offered. 'The reason they embraced punk was because it was rubbish and the reason they embraced rubbish was because they could control it. They could say, "Oh yeah, we're punk so we can sneer at everybody. We can't play our fucking instruments, but that means we can make out that this whole thing is some enormous performance art." Half the kids that were in punk bands were laughing at the art establishment, going: "What a fucking bunch of tosspots. Thanks very much, give us the money and we'll fuck off and stick it up our nose and shag birds." But what they'd really love to be doing is being in a heavy metal band surrounded by porn stars.' Many punks responded to that accusation, not least Dead Kennedys who wrote on Facebook, 'I don't think he has ever heard East Bay Ray play guitar.' Rat Scabies, of The Damned, also had a view to share: 'Bruce Dickinson can think what he likes – but I defy Iron Maiden to play "Smash it Up" as it was written.' Which would be really, really interesting. Paul Di'Anno, of course, would be more than happy to do just that, given his own love for punk rock.

Bruce hurled out more zingers in the same interview. He also had a pop at rock stars who used Autocues to help them remember the words. One example he gave was apparently Judas Priest: he said he'd actually seen them with the words to the chorus of 'Breaking the Law' on autocue. For the record, the chorus is the title repeated eight times. On Californian radio station *107.7 The Bone*, Rob Halford responded that it was all in good heart. 'What we British say is it was just a storm in a teacup,' he insisted. 'I love Bruce. I love Bruce. He's a great friend of mine. And he's very outspoken. [He's a] great frontman, a great singer from a great band. And, you know, these things are said in many ways, and I'm sure he didn't mean it in any other way than Bruce sometimes goes off in one of his rants.' Less controversially, Bruce had also mentioned in the interview that he'd noticed that his voice had changed over the years, his tone altering along with his body shape.

In the live arena, on 4 April 2014 Bruce joined Ian Paice again, plus Nicky Moody (Whitesnake), Rick Wakeman and Glenn Hughes at London's Royal Albert Hall, to celebrate the life and music of the late Deep Purple keyboard player Jon Lord, who had passed away from cancer on 16 July 2012. Bruce sang 'You Keep on Moving' and 'Burn' at the gig. A DVD, Blu-ray and CD was released of the event later that year, raising money for The Sunflower Jam.

The three-year long *Maiden England* tour finally came to an end in extremely spectacular style at Sonisphere festival on 5 July. Bruce had flown a 1917 Fokker DR1 triplane already that day and brought in the rest of the memorial flying team, the Great War Display team, to stage a mock-dogfight close to the arena. There were eight planes involved in all and the crowds, as they say, went wild. It was to commemorate the hundredth anniversary of World War I. The show took place at 6pm and involved nine planes in all, including British planes the Sopwith Triplane, BE2c and SE5a and a German Junkers CL1. Bruce's plane was the same model that was flown by pilot Manfred von Richthofen – the man with the nickname of "The Red Baron". 'What some of these fighter pilots achieved back then was nothing short of miraculous given the

CAN HEAVEN WAIT!

conditions they were working under and the seriousness of what was at stake,' Bruce was reported as saying by *Blabbermouth*. 'We hope to stage a memorable display which is equally entertaining and poignant, celebrating not only the bravery and heroics of all the pilots involved but remembering the sacrifices made on both sides.' And, of course, a brilliant gig an hour or two later.

Bruce continued to put the pedal to the metal during August, announcing the winner of the Campaign For Real Ale's award for the Champion Beer of Britain at the Great British Beer Festival and telling reporters that there was a plan for Cardiff Aviation to build up a fleet of aircraft. He then took his Fokker DR1 back to the skies at the Duxford Air Show on 2 September with the rest of the team. Excitingly, the Maiden mob, spent September to December of 2014 writing and recording with Kevin Shirley in Guillaume Tell Studios, Paris, where they had recorded *Brave New World* back in 2000. Things seemed rosy in Maiden world, at least from a musical point of view. But there was a major shock in store that transcended music entirely.

It was December 2014. Chris Dale and Alex Elena were joined by Trevor Gibson and Major Martin Morris in Sarajevo. It was an emotional meeting, which was based on an article about the Bruce Dickinson solo gig there so many years previously. Bassist Chris wrote extensively about that experience for his *Metal Talk* column, as he explains. 'I wrote the articles because I'd never told anyone the full story. Anytime I'd meet someone and they'd ask me about it, I could only really give a ten-minute reply, which didn't tell the half of it. So I started writing all of it. It was good from my point of view to get it off my chest too,' he admitted. 'It started out as one article but ended up as three. I knew it'd get read by some

Maiden fans around the world but it didn't really occur to me what the reaction would be from Bosnian fans who remembered the gig themselves. I started getting quite a few emails from them, thanking me for it and being very complimentary. Of course from our point of view, the Sarajevo gig was one weekend of our lives getting a glimpse into what hell is probably like. From the view of Bosnian fans at the gig, it was one evening of light and hope in the middle of their four-year hell. Quite different perspectives.

'Two different Bosnians came to me with the idea of making a documentary after reading the articles,' he continued. 'One was Jasenko Pašić, a Sarajevan actor and stage producer. The other was Tatjana Bonny, a London-based Bosnian also involved in documentary production. Between them, they organised a local director, film, crew and producer and the whole team. Jasenko and the film crew interviewed some Bosnian fans that had been at the gig and started putting together a very serious documentary. Me and Alex Elena were very much involved from the beginning and many aspects of it. Alex does a lot of photography these days and also produces album for artists, so his angle was very valuable visually and sound-wise. I was very concerned that the right people would be involved and that the film should tell the story as it was, without glamorising it in any way.

'Funnily enough,' he added, 'Trevor Gibson – the security guy who'd looked after us in Sarajevo – read my article by chance and got in touch. Through him, we contacted Major Martin Morris the British army officer, who'd booked the original show. Me, Alex, Trevor and Martin went out to Bosnia to be filmed for the documentary in December 2014. It was on the one hand great to see Sarajevo being a youthful, thriving, vibrant city these days –

which it clearly wasn't the last time we'd been there. On the other hand it was very emotional seeing the scars of war and all the memories came flooding back.'

Dale explained that Bruce was due to join them for the documentary. 'Bruce was supposed to join us for the filming but at the last minute, he sent an email saying he had a check-up at the doctors and couldn't make it. I knew that was something serious. Bruce is a reliable guy. He doesn't cancel appointments or flights for no reason.'

But there was a very good – or very bad – reason indeed for the cancellation. A statement released by the Iron Maiden camp was released in early February explaining what had been going on. 'Just before Christmas, Maiden vocalist Bruce Dickinson visited his doctor for a routine check-up. This led to tests and biopsies which revealed a small cancerous tumour at the back of his tongue. A seven-week course of chemotherapy and radiology treatment was completed yesterday. As the tumour was caught in the early stages, the prognosis thankfully is extremely good. Bruce's medical team fully expect him to make a complete recovery with the all clear envisaged by late May. It will then take a further few months for Bruce to get back to full fitness. In the meantime, we would ask for your patience, understanding and respect for Bruce and his family's privacy until we update everyone by the end of May. Bruce is doing very well considering the circumstances and the whole team are very positive.'

'I was pretty shocked,' admitted Chris Dale. 'He's one of the healthiest people I know, he doesn't smoke, drinks in moderation, has lots of exercise and eats very healthily. I guess it just shows cancer can hit anyone at any time.' Needless to say, messages of support came in from thousands of concerned friends, colleagues and musicians and millions of fans held their breath and crossed their fingers.

Bruce continued to work despite the often gruelling radiology and chemotherapy treatments, even growing his infamous moustache back on a visit to the Hybrid Air Vehicles company behind the enormous Airlander dirigible in March. As his recuperation continued, the album was kept on ice until he was fit and ready to go again. Wonderfully, Bruce was given the all-clear in May 2015, after a MRI scan. Despite this, in order to make sure he was completely fit and ready to run around like the usual crazy metal monkey, live dates were to be held off until 2016.

In July, Bruce told the *BBC* about the time he found out about his two tumours. 'One was three-and-a-half centimetres – the size of a golf ball – and the other was two-and-a-half centimetres and getting a bit bigger. The only symptom was I had a lump in my neck […] I went to the doc and they went, "Ooh, that's a bit weird" […] [They] had a poke around and went, "You have head and neck cancer."' He said that he was still healing, because the radiation from the treatment had cooked the inside of his head. That said, he was realistic about it: 'I can sing, I can talk. I haven't gone out and done the equivalent of trying to run a hundred metres in the same way that I used to sing before, because, let it all calm down. I only finished coming out of treatment two months ago, for God's sake. And the doctor said, "It'll take a year for you to be better." Well, we've beaten that by about six months so far, you know? But I'm not going to try to push things to prove a point.'

Later he spoke with *Metal Hammer* on the subject. 'You end up with the metabolism of a hummingbird during this treatment because you're being cooked from the inside out,' he admitted. 'But your body's also trying to heal itself rapidly, and it goes into overdrive. I think that's one reason why you lose weight. It's simply because your system is banging away and then eventually it all dropped back down to normal. It's fascinating. Basically, I am my own science project.'

He later spoke with *Sirius XM* about the type of cancer that he had been stricken with. 'I never smoked,' Dickinson explained. 'It's a virus. HPV – Human papillomavirus. They all are. I'm almost willing to bet any time you hear of someone getting tonsil cancer, throat cancer, lymph cancer whatever it is, if they're not heavy smokers and not massive heavy drinkers, it's a five hundred per cent increase in this type of cancer in men over forty.' He also referred to a famous actor, Michael Douglas, who famously announced that he had contracted HPV in 2013 through cunnilingus. 'And everybody makes the jokes about Michael Douglas, 'cause he was having oral sex,' Bruce continued in the interview with Eddie Trunk, 'and it's just, like, OK, we need to get over that one, guys, because this is kind of serious. There's hundreds of thousands of people at risk for this. And guys should know if you get a lump here and you're over forty don't just assume antibiotics will get rid of it out. Probably go and get it checked out.' He clarified things further in a subsequent interview with *The Daily Mirror.* 'Eighty per cent of people in the UK have been exposed to HPV,' he told *3AM.* 'You can acquire it in all sorts of ways, you may have been in high school kissing someone, it can be transmitted from mother to baby. I said to my wife I was going to say what it was. I could possibly do a bit of good. The fear was that I'd get those headlines.

'They have been potentially embarrassing, but actually not,

because what is needed is for someone to stand up and say, look this HPV cancer is an epidemic among men. It will outstrip cervical cancer in women by 2020. I'm a rock star, so let's take the piss – but actually this is serious. People are trivialising what is a really serious public-health issue.'

As Chris Dale says, 'He's a tough one. Being physically fit and having a strong mental attitude probably helps a lot, but probably mainly he had a great medical team and luckily he'd spotted the symptoms himself early enough.'

Cancer conquered, Bruce set about announcing the launch of a new airline, VVB. It would provide ACMI: Aircraft, Crew, Maintenance and Insurance. 'In the last two years, we've grown relentlessly, thanks to our unique entrepreneurial style of MRO and training,' he said. 'We're now looking to bring that approach to the airline market with VVB. This is a huge opportunity to create new jobs and further increase our already impressive roster of services.' Cardiff Aviation had also signed a memorandum of understanding to create a new national airline for Djibouti, Africa, as well as developing a 360-degree approach to establishing airlines for other people, in which CA would do everything. The aviation pioneer described it as a 'one-stop 'airline in a box'.

In August, Aeris and Bruce opened a shop in famous department store Harrods at which a limited-edition Harrods Eclipse 550 jet would be on sale. The price? About three million US dollars, but as a sweetener you'd get a 50k store card as a thank you. His old Fokker probably could have done with an upgrade: it ran low on fuel on a flight in early August, necessitating a quick detour to RAF Halton. That base's squadron leader, Gary Coleman (not that one) told the *Bucks Herald* that it was a good lesson for aspiring pilots.

'We applaud Bruce Dickinson's decision to divert to RAF Halton rather than press to his destination with potentially low fuel. To see such a well-regarded pilot, and world-renowned rock singer, make this decision is great for our student pilots to see. It makes them realise that anyone can find themselves low on fuel due to unforeseen circumstances and that the right decision is to divert.'

Back on land, though, there was the small matter of the delayed release of Iron Maiden's sixteenth studio album to take care of. It would be pioneering on many counts, not least that it was to be the group's first-ever double album. Clocking in at ninety-two minutes for the eleven tracks, it looked set to be another epic release in the band's career. Release date was set for 4 September 2015 on Parlophone in the UK and Sanctuary Copyrights/BMG in the States. And it would have one of the longest tracks Iron Maiden had ever recorded – clocking in at eighteen minutes and penned by Captain Doctor Paul Bruce Dickinson.

CHAPTER 31

THE BOOK
OF SOULS

Iron Maiden's sixteenth studio album, *The Book of Souls*, will be seen in future years as the record that took a metal band with a love for wide-screen and progressive rock into the territory of composers. The rhythms, themes, riffs, melodies and variations deliver moments of high drama interspersed with the delicate touch of musicians with a lifetime of refining their craft behind them. It may not boast the immediacy of an 'Aces High' or a 'Number of the Beast', or the poppiness of a 'Heaven Can Wait', but the facts are that this band has been there, done that, sold millions of T-shirts and developed way beyond a three-minute single.

First track, 'If Eternity Should Fail,' opens with a doomy synth chord, atop which a lone flute introduces Bruce's vocals, heavily soaked in reverb and echo, as he sings of a soul, humanity and what lies beyond. The massive, chugging song is credited to Bruce Dickinson alone and settles down into a typical Maiden slow-burner. His vocals are central and the song is built around the tale he so skilfully weaves over eight-and-a-half magnificent minutes. Given his recent bout with mortality, the lyrics about God, Lucifer and eternal darkness take on an even more resonant aspect. The band, intriguingly, is playing with a drop D – the usual lowest note possible on a guitar or bass is the E, so the string is detuned by two semitones. This adds a dark tone to matters. Bruce originally mooted it for a possible solo record, even demoing it with Roy Z out in LA, but Maiden definitely give it the oomph nobody else could. After six minutes or so, the song moves into another gear and the guitarists intertwine melodies and countermelodies in a distinctly Eastern key. Steve Harris plays a blinder here, keeping things locked down with Nicko and moving melodically with the guitars when the song demands it. The final two minutes are back to the main theme, with Bruce in awesome voice. The acoustic coda with the spoken-word verse is frankly terrifying, too.

'Speed of Light' follows, released on 14 August as the first single from the album. This one was written by Bruce and Adrian Smith and has a great video to accompany it, directed and produced by Llexi Leon, famous for *Eternal Descent* – which is both a band and a comic book. The Brewery added special effects. The short film starts with a hand pressing a button; this is quickly revealed to be Eddie, who – *Tron*-like – gets stuck inside a video game machine, pixelating and roaring into cyberspace. In essence, the video tracks the development of video games over the last thirty years or so, beginning with Eddie in a very low-resolution ladders-type game, saving the gal from the enemy and gaining one of the four hearts he needs to successfully complete his task. Next up for the unmistakable mascot – who gains more and more of his body back as he moves through space – is a Zombie-like shoot 'em up, reminiscent of old-school games such as *Robocop*. The *Powerslave* graphic makes an appearance in the backdrop here.

Eddie moves through another wormhole, having nicked a heart to open the portal. His next destination is a battle with the devil, à la *Mortal Combat*. It's the devil from *The Number of the Beast* who seems to defeat the mascot before Eddie rises from the grave to turn the tables, smacking Beelzebub around the noggin with the 'The Devil Wins' graphic. This leaves our hero free to fight skeletons and a *T. rex*, this time in a *Tomb Raider*-like game. Eddie has collected three hearts out of four by now and realises the final one is his own. He tears it out and completes the game. His high score? Why, 666,666, of course. He finally 'wakes up' from inside the game and is back in a video game arcade, somewhat bemused by his experience. It is a brilliant video, which has humour, skill, self-awareness and a cracking song to accompany it. There would later be a special game available on the band's website. Bruce is playing again with the cosmos, mortality and taking a one-way ticket to the edge.

Steve Harris and Adrian Smith team up to pen 'The Great Unknown', a discussion of what drives humans – specifically, men – to be violent. This has brought the world right down to a terrible place and Bruce delivers the words gravely in the first section before opening his lungs out when the riffs of the main song kick in. These are big topics that Maiden are dealing with and the songs are suitably big to accommodate them – albeit that at six-and-a-half minutes it's a mere stripling compared to the thirteen minutes that follow. 'The Red and the Black', one of Harris's self-searching moments, is introduced (and completed) by the bassist playing chords and runs up and down on his instrument, before a galloping, near-folky riff is underpinned by an ace drum pattern from Nicko. He provides interesting hi-hat work before moving around the kit, subtly using cymbals to bring a shimmering feel. Bruce's vocals are heavily-FX-oriented here, to brilliantly unsettling effect. There's also some whoa-oahs to sing along with, which is always a bonus.

The Smith/Harris axis then contributes 'When The River Runs Deep', an energetic and tuneful balls-out rocker with a surprise in store as the tempo is halved during the chorus to really emphasise it. The final track on the first disc is 'The Book of Souls' itself, written by Harris with Janick Gers. This one is ten-and-a-half minutes' worth of Mayan references, sky gods, arcane knowledge and sacred mysteries. The artwork for the album is similarly themed, of course. There's a feel here that echoes some of the sonic palette of *Powerslave*,

The second record of the double LP begins with another Smith/Dickinson song, 'Death or Glory'. Both this and 'Speed of Light' are relatively short, much in line with the guitarist's previous proclamations that snappy songs were to be – at least in part – the order of the day. They were also mostly written before recording began, in contrast to the rest of the tracks, which were only created in skeleton form before being refined in the studio. The track's a straight-down-the-line war-themed tale that mentions a triplane the colour of blood. That's clearly a reference to Baron von Richtofen once more, whose Fokker was that colour and the same model as the one Bruce later owned. Janick and Steve's second song on the album is 'Shadows of the Valley', which almost quotes the opening of 'Wasted Years' before the song takes on its own immense form. Ravens, death, sins and shadows are the order of the day on this one. Adrian and Steve's 'Tears of a Clown' follows. It's dedicated to Robin Williams, a much-loved comedian who tragically took his own life in August 2014 following a long and largely unreported struggle with depression. Bruce was reported by *NME* as saying, 'I ask myself how could he be so depressed when he always seemed to be so happy.' Dave Murray's only writing credit on the album is up next, a collaboration with Steve called 'The Man of Sorrows', a dark and lonely discussion of death. In fact, Steve had experienced two tragic deaths during the album process. The song is weary, despairing and very evocative.

The double album comes to an extraordinary end with Bruce's enormous and ambitious 'Empire of the Clouds', which he largely composed on a Steinway grand piano. The lyrics trace the fate of the ill-starred R101, an airship that crashed on its first outing with the loss of forty-eight lives. The age of the huge airships came to an end during the 1930s, following other disastrous crashes – the fact that the balloons were filled with hydrogen, a highly flammable and lighter-than-air gas, was partly to blame. Given Bruce's involvement with the new breed of giant airships, the subject matter was obviously very close to his heart. Originally, Bruce had intended the song to be about World War I, but that idea morphed into 'Death or Glory', so he checked his surroundings at home, as he told *Radio.com*. 'I've got artefacts from airships sitting around. I went to some auctions and bought some stuff. I've got the pocket watch from one of the survivors from the R101, I've got a tankard from the R101, I've got various bits and bobs of other airships. I went, "Why don't I tell the story?"' He'd also read a massive crash report about R101, called *To Ride The Storm*, which inspired the track.

Having come up with a few verses and musical motifs, Bruce began to work on the intro – and had a brainwave. 'I suddenly realized that that then enabled me to do like a little overture piece at the beginning, which I would state most of the little melodies that were going to come later and put them as one separate little piece on its own, and then we put some cellos and some bits over it and some other little countermelodies,' he explained. 'Opening, setting the scene instrumentally. And then we just tell the story through the various transitions that dramatise it, that build up the ash of leaves, the masks, the people are clapping and cheering, we've got that scene in there. It's very cinematic.' It's also one of the best things he's ever written.

Maiden released a twelve-inch picture disc of the track on 16 April, Record Store Day, when many acts release special editions or unique tracks on vinyl. Bruce told an Australian site, *News.com.au* that he'd bought the original keyboard on which the piece was written at a charity dinner hosted by Jamie Oliver, in a charity auction. It was even signed by Jamie Cullum, the tiny jazzer. He summed up the album with one typically insightful snippet. 'Maiden, on its best day, has always been an acoustic theatre of the mind, provoking pictures and images. With the yelled stuff, you don't have much time to conjure that because it's full on but when there is more space, as there is on a lot of this album, you can go on your imaginings.'

Brigitte Schön notes that Bruce's lyrics on *The Book of Souls* follow some themes that he has often played with in his career. 'You find once more the subject of aviation on *The Book of Souls* […] What I like more than the obvious is Bruce's skill to convey the thoughts and emotions of the characters in his lyrics. When

The Red Baron as a character expresses – during his aerial combat – [that] there is no difference between death and glory, then you catch the absurdity of the whole game. I think on "If Eternity Should Fail" Bruce criticises again misunderstood religion like he already did in many a song on his solo albums (above all on *Accident of Birth* and *The Chemical Wedding*). You are to question your faith and not to believe blindly the things you got taught. Another favourite subject of Bruce seems to be science fiction as in "Speed of Light". Interestingly enough, I am sure he takes this issue to express deeper truths, his ideas of life and death and why we are here.

'Bruce uses the subjects close to his heart like aviation, deeper understanding and science fiction,' she concludes. 'The messages of Bruce's songs on the last two albums are sometimes similar. But I don't see a real thread between them. In general, the main topics of Bruce's songwriting are found here. One important subject does hardly appear, though: individual freedom.'

The Book of Souls was released in various formats on 4 September 2015, including a triple-gatefold vinyl package that is quite simply a thing of beauty. The record shot to No.1 in twenty-four countries and hit No.4 on the *Billboard 200*. Reviews were largely positive about the release. 'While it's certainly outsized (and does crawl part way through disc two), the rock outfit's sixteenth studio album is surprisingly engaging overall,' *Billboard* wrote. *Classic Rock* acknowledged the impact of Bruce and Adrian since they'd come back into the fold. 'Since the return of Bruce Dickinson and Adrian Smith for 2000's *Brave New World*, Maiden have not only cemented their status as metal's most revered band but, audaciously, built upon it, becoming ever more dominant and in-demand as a result.' *The Guardian* praised the band's development over the years, saying that the past decade's albums had been challenging, at a time when other acts would be tempted to stay within expected boundaries. 'For the most part, *The Book of Souls* is marked by a impressive rawness that scratches against the album's more grandiloquent moments,' it noted. *NME* chipped in with something of a beauty: 'The devil might reckon he has all the best tunes, but it's a hollow claim when Iron Maiden are in town.' And *Rolling Stone* was on the ball, too: 'What's most impressive is how vocalist Bruce Dickinson, who recently survived a tongue-cancer scare, still sounds like a cross between an air-raid siren and Maria Callas. And tracks like the eighteen-minute closer, "Empire of the Clouds", ensure that these guys will never be short on ambition.'

Ambition was the byword for the tour, too. Ed Force One was back in action, but this time it would be an enormous Boeing 747-400, about twice the size of the 757 that Bruce had previously flown the band around in. He was quoted by *Blabbermouth* thus: 'When the opportunity arose from my friends at Air Atlanta Icelandic to lease a 747 for *The Book of Souls World Tour*, of course, we jumped at the chance. Who wouldn't?

'The greatest benefit of travelling in a 747,' he explained, 'is that because of its colossal size and freight capacity, we can carry our stage production and all our stage equipment and desks in the cargo hold without having to make any of the immense structural modifications needed to do this on the previous 757, the extent of which fans will have noted on the *Flight 666* DVD.

'Although in reality we cannot carry much more gear, the savings in complexity, time and cost make using the 747 even more practical,' he argued. 'All we will need to do is "paint" it and move a few seats around, with the added advantage that there is much more room for band and crew.' Bruce did however need to upgrade his skills, undergoing further training in order to be able to actually fly the bigger beast. Luckily, there was a rather excellent 747 simulator down at Cardiff Aviation that would enable him to do so. In the meantime, he flew 150 fans to Paris in a 737-400 for a special listening session at the Guillaume Tell Studios. In a Q&A session, one fan asked if *The Book of Souls* was going to be Maiden's swansong. 'I really hope that this is not the last album. I've had way too much fun making this one,' Bruce replied. 'I'm gonna have way too much fun and enjoy the next tour for a variety of reasons. I'm happily chatting to you and running around and leaping around or flying airplanes. And the next stop is gonna be a tour and some singing.' *Metal XS* videoed the chat.

Despite being able to fly one of the most intricate, complex and expensive pieces of technology on the planet, Bruce revealed that in other ways he wasn't that bothered. He told *Grantland*, 'I understand that in this day and age everybody has to have a big social media presence, and you have to look after your social media, and blah blah blah – okay, that's great. We've got a great team and they just look after the social media. I just completely ignore it. It's as if I live in another world, devoid of Twitter, devoid of Facebook, devoid of all the bullshit that gets talked about by all of these people. I just live in my own little head world. That's what makes the records. So I have no idea what's going on on Twitter, and I couldn't care less.' He added that he didn't even know how to log on to Twitter, and that his mobile phone was so old it was held together by tape and couldn't even take photos.

He also told the interviewer that he had little truck with some aspects of the mainstream. '[One of the] trendy things that bands do now to maintain their "pop culture" is sit there obsessing and tweeting away drivel to the unwashed masses. It's just crap. It's self-indulgent, narcissistic bollocks. I have no interest in that whatsoever. If I want to be self-indulgent and narcissistic, I'll put it on a record. Don't sit there tweeting, I don't even know how many words you're not allowed to say in Twitter before you run out of intelligence.' Strident stuff, as ever.

Bruce also revealed that he was working toward another solo album and that he had already demoed six songs. But he wasn't going to push matters, as he explained to *Hard Force*. 'One idea I had was maybe in November or December [2015] or something, maybe to go out and start doing some writing and a little bit of demoing, just to try my voice out – under no stress, no jeopardy; just as an experiment to see what it sounded like. But we'll see. I mean, there's no way, even if I had a solo album finished and ready to go, it's not gonna come out next year, and it's probably not gonna come out the year after. So it's not to stress about it.'

He also paid tribute to Lady Gaga, one of the band's unlikeliest fans, but one who had apparently stayed up till 5 a.m. in order to snag one of the first copies of *The Book of Souls* when it came on sale. He told *Corus Radio* of his admiration for the New York artist. 'I think she's great, and I agree with her: she's not the next Madonna; she's way better than that […] 'Cause, first of all, she can sing – she's got a belter of a voice – [and] she's a really good instrumentalist. And, I mean, she's got a great sense of drama. And anybody that could turn up to an awards ceremony dressed as a bacon sandwich gets my vote.'

With the album finally out, Bruce turned his attention back

to the aviation business and at the Farnborough International
Airshow he chatted about his company. Summing up his first
years with Cardiff Aviation, he said that it was an exciting time.
'We've gotten two-and-a-half years from zero, and after two-and-
a-half years with nothing, with not a single penny of government
money of any description, going into this business, we've got a
full-service MRO with all Boeing and all Airbus narrow-body
approvals, with Part 21 design and manufacturing waiting in the
wings,' he enthused. 'We've got an airline up and running, which
should be profitable within the first six weeks. We've got a training
company that's gonna start turning out type ratings and cadets,
and is already doing training for major airlines. And, on the side,
I'm a shareholder in Hybid Air Vehicles and I'm waiting to see
this astonishing airplane back in the skies. So that's enough for
me to lie awake at night and pinch myself and go, "How'd we do
all this?"' In December too, Bruce finally managed to get over to
Sarajevo to shoot some footage for the forthcoming documentary
Scream For Me Sarajevo.

The Book of Souls World Tour began on 24 February 2016 and
was set to once more span the globe with a full show, including
Maiden's first ever gigs in China, with concerts scheduled for 24
April in Beijing and Shanghai two days later. The tour proper began
in Fort Lauderdale, where *Loudwire* commented on Bruce's energy
levels. 'Dickinson would sprint from one end of the scaffolding to
the other while singing his highest notes, never taking breaks to
catch his breath,' wrote the reviewer, who noted that the singer's
'golden pipes' were still intact.

The gigs continued to great effect, but Ed Force One was in
the wars after an incident on 12 March at Santiago's Comodoro

Arturo Merino Benitez International Airport. A steering pin failed and the aircraft careered into the ground tug. Two people were taken to hospital, and two engines were badly damaged. There was no disruption to the tour, however, and the Chilean staff made a full recovery. The plane was duly repaired and flew to Brasilia. Ed Force One, however, wouldn't be allowed to land in Dortmund ahead of the Rock Im Reviewer festival on 27 May because it was simply too heavy for that airport. No problem, Bruce and the band would simply land at Dusseldorf and take the old-fashioned tour bus to the gig instead.

Maiden's only UK appearance on this part of the tour was to be a headlining slot at Donington Park on Sunday, 12 June 2016. Other headliners for the three-day bash were Rammstein and Black Sabbath. It is a sign of the bands' relative stature that one-time contemporaries Saxon were way down on the Third Stage. For Bruce Dickinson, and his band, there was only one place to operate and that was at the very top. The musician, the polymath, the phenomenon himself knew no other way. To celebrate this, the third limited-edition beer, Trooper Red 'N' Black – a darker porter – joined the stable of the original Trooper and the subsequent Trooper 666, a stronger beer (at 6.6 per cent, naturally), to help quench thirsts around the globe.

The name of Captain Doctor Paul Bruce 'Bruce' Dickinson is intrinsically linked with that of Iron Maiden. Their successes, their greatest moments, are also his. The band that was never part of the mainstream and always ploughed their own furrow has the alchemist himself as the singer. Without him, Maiden would still truck onward, but with him they truly fly. Expect a knighthood one day for the vocalist – but, ironically, it may not necessarily be awarded for his musical adventures. It is entirely possible, in fact, that the Airlander 10 in which he has invested so heavily will be the project with which he makes the biggest impact on the world. Three hundred and two feet in length, it is the biggest aircraft the world has ever seen. It can fly without refuelling for days; it can lift up twenty tons of cargo. Bruce enthusiastically told *The New Yorker* about its capabilities. 'You want to put a hospital into Africa? You put the whole hospital in the inside of this – whoosh. Start the generator. "Here's your hospital, buddy!" Job done. You know?

'You can just plunk the vehicle straight down on the farm, load it with fifty tons of green beans [presumably without Bruce's 'special seasoning'] or whatever, and twenty-four hours later you land right next door to the processing plant. It's a global conveyor belt. And water! With these vehicles, you could drop off a twenty-ton slab of water that is clean, drinkable, to an African village. It's astonishing what you can do that you just can't do with anything else. Shit, you can do that with it? Wow, you can do that with it? Seriously fantastic!'

It is a quote that sums him up: full of enthusiasm, drive, vision, talent and a never-ending curiosity. Bruce Dickinson is a man ready and willing to change the world. He's already changed the lives of millions of music fans for the better, and he's nowhere near finishing yet. His Maiden Voyage, it seems, has only just begun.